Rangers Hall of Fame

Rangers Hall of Fame

An indispensable book showcasing Rangers' greatest ever players

LINDSAY HERRON

 hachette
SCOTLAND

First published in 2009 by
HACHETTE SCOTLAND, an imprint of
HACHETTE UK

1

Cataloguing in Publication Data is available from the British Library

ISBN 978 0 7553 1916 9

Designed and typeset by Avon DataSet Ltd,
Bidford-on-Avon, Warwickshire

Printed and bound in Great Britain by
Clays Ltd, St Ives plc

Hachette Scotland's policy is to use papers that are natural, renewable and
recyclable products and made from wood grown in sustainable forests. The logging and
manufacturing processes are expected to conform to the environmental regulations of
the country of origin.

HACHETTE SCOTLAND
An Hachette UK Company
338 Euston Road
London NW1 3BH

www.hachettescotland.co.uk
www.hachette.co.uk

Contents

Foreword
by Sandy Jardine

WHEN YOU join a club like Rangers as a player you are privileged because you become part of the rich history and the great traditions of a unique institution. The club has always been about setting standards and maintaining them. Today, this is best illustrated by a visit to the club's home at Ibrox. The stadium has a wonderful traditional exterior, which leads through to a modern and vibrant amphitheatre in which to watch the most popular sport on earth. Some of us have been fortunate enough to travel around the world and visit some superb venues and marvel at state-of-the-art stadiums. However, few of these can compare to Ibrox, which remains steeped in history but with the most modern facilities on offer. For supporters, players and club officials alike, a visit to Rangers is a marvellous experience even for the big clubs like AC Milan and Barcelona. They all leave with the same impression: that Rangers is 'a real football club'.

This has always been a successful club; the teams have always been full of great players and always played in front of great crowds. Of course, as a player it takes a while to understand what being a Rangers player means, but when you do, it never really leaves you. So, when a player walks through the front door at Ibrox and sees his name on the Hall of Fame board in a list of the greatest players who have played for the club, then he is entitled to feel that he has achieved greatness in his chosen field. To be included in the same company as Moses McNeil, Alan Morton, Davie Meiklejohn and John Greig, for example, is the ultimate honour for anyone who has ever worn the Light Blue shirt.

Taken as a whole, the players in the Rangers Hall of Fame represent the club's legacy to its supporters. After all, it is these players who laid the foundations of the club and have made it what it is today. The purpose of the Hall of Fame is to recognise and reward those players for their efforts.

The idea of honouring the club's best players had been discussed for many years, but began to take shape at the Greatest Ever Rangers event in 1999. It came out of a conversation that night between TV broadcaster Dougie Donnelly, club historian David Mason, vice-chairman Donald Findlay and me about how best to honour the players who had made the club what it is today. We all agreed that a Hall of Fame would be just the thing. Unable to contain himself and wanting to take advantage of his audience, Donald Findlay announced the setting up of the Rangers Hall of Fame that night. He indicated that Bob McPhail, Jock Shaw and Willie Woodburn – who were all in attendance – would be the first three inductees and, of course, there was rapturous approval.

A committee was immediately set up to formulate plans for the project because we wanted to make sure that we went about it in the right way. Our first task was to delve into the club's early history to find players from that era who were deserving of inclusion. Of course, few people had actually seen these players in action, so we had to go by what has been written about them to be able to assess their achievements. After exhaustive but rewarding research we selected 15 players from the early years for inclusion.

The next step was to get the supporters involved and we offered them groups of players from specific eras and asked them to vote based on a set of strict criteria (see page 6). Supporters took the whole thing very seriously, sparking great debate and voting for their favourites in huge numbers. We added ten new players each year for the next three years because we wanted the project to take shape as soon as possible. Gradually, however, we reduced the number of inductees because we wanted to make sure we maintained the integrity of the list of players, whose names now feature on a board that hangs above the marble staircase in the Ibrox foyer. Because of the care that we have taken, we can be sure that every name on the list deserves to be there.

I have been very fortunate that in my career I won a lot of major medals and received a lot of honours, and, although I cannot speak for everyone, for me the biggest honour of all is to be included in the Hall of Fame.

One unexpected by-product of this project is that in the course of my research into this great club's history I have managed to collate a considerable collection of books for the club archive, which now stands at over 200 volumes. As a result of reading them I can certainly recommend this book to Rangers supporters as it is the most comprehensive and detailed account of the greatest players that have ever played for this famous football club.

Sandy Jardine

Introduction

MORE THAN 800 players have pulled a Light Blue jersey over their heads since Rangers' inception in 1872, and each of them has made his own contribution to one of the great Scottish institutions. There are, however, a number of players from this group who stand head and shoulders above the rest; men who have shaped the destiny of the club and brought glory and fame to Ibrox through their efforts.

These are the men of the Hall of Fame; the men who have made Rangers one of the most successful football clubs in the world. From Moses McNeil, the young man who got together with his brother Peter and friends Peter Campbell and William McBeath, to form the great club, through to the nine-in-a-row heroes – the men of the Hall of Fame represent everything that is great about Rangers.

Some gave fantastic service, some were great captains and others were simply exceptional players. However, they all made a huge impact on Rangers Football Club and that's why they are included in the Hall of Fame. There are now 74 great men in this unique group with more to be added in the spring of 2010.

In this book we try to give a flavour of what each of them

contributed to Rangers during their time at Ibrox. In some instances it is almost impossible to explain the impact they had on the club – men like Bob McPhail, Ian McColl, Willie Waddell, George Young, John Greig and Ally McCoist, who all left lasting legacies. But their stories, and others, cover the key periods in the club's history and there are representatives from each of the famous teams over the decades. There are wildly contrasting figures from the incomparable Davie Meiklejohn, who led with honour and authority through the 1920s and 1930s, to the maverick genius of Paul Gascoigne.

The club inaugurated the Hall of Fame in 1999 when three players were nominated at the Greatest Ever Rangers dinner; and a year later 15 pre-war players were inducted by the committee. In 2001 supporters got the first chance to have their say – voting in ten post-war players for the next three years – before the number of inductees each year was cut in order to maintain the integrity of the unique group.

Club legends Sandy Jardine and John Greig along with historian David Mason and chairman Sir David Murray set up the Hall of Fame to honour the exploits of Rangers' heroes using five criteria:

1 Service to the club
2 Number of games
3 Honours won with Rangers
4 International caps won while at Rangers
5 Exceptional abilities

Every living recipient of this honour has made it clear that it is something they cherish – in most cases more than anything else.

The dinners held to celebrate the stars of the past – now biennial events – are something to behold as they bring together so many great Rangers at one time. Men who used to worship great players of the past now share the same stage with them; Willie Thornton was Billy Simpson's hero, Alex MacDonald looked up to Jimmy Millar and Ian Durrant used to sneak in to Ibrox to watch Derek Johnstone.

The Hall of Fame board that hangs above the famous marble staircase in the Ibrox entrance foyer is a litany of greatness. It is a constant reminder of the special qualities that are required to play for Rangers and to be included on it is undoubtedly a massive incentive for any player with ambition to give his best for the club.

Ally McCoist succinctly summed it up when he said, 'Honouring and celebrating the history of Rangers is something that is right and should be done. However, I also have no doubt that everyone on the Hall of Fame board hopes that there are even greater successes for Rangers in the future.'

Chapter 1
The Gallant Pioneers
– 1872–1920

Moses McNeil
Tom Vallance
John McPherson
Nicol Smith
Alex Smith
Jimmy Gordon

THE FOUNDATIONS for the remarkable story of Rangers Football Club were laid in the west end of Glasgow in 1872 when football was still in its infancy and it was just a raw version of the game millions enjoy today.

Formalised the following year, Rangers then joined the Scottish Football Association and their first competitive matches were in the Scottish Cup led by co-founder Moses McNeil and the club's first great captain Tom Vallance. The

Scottish Football League was then formed in 1890. John McPherson was a key protagonist in the team at that stage and Rangers went on to share the first title with Dumbarton that season.

Their first Scottish Cup triumph came in 1894 and the seeds were sown for decades of incredible success. Nicol Smith was in that Cup-winning team and namesake Alex arrived that year, bringing spectacular wing play that was to be a feature for 21 years. He was a huge figure in the remarkable run of four successive League titles at the turn of the century.

By this point the famous rivalry with Celtic was well underway and Rangers dominated the honours during this period.

Jimmy Gordon, who saw active service in World War One, relished games against the Glasgow rivals in this period and was largely responsible for the Rangers successes up until his departure in 1920.

Moses McNeil (1872–1882)

BORN: 29 October 1855, Rhu nr Helensburgh

APPEARANCES: 34
GOALS: 9

HONOURS WON WITH RANGERS
CAPS: 2 (Scotland)

RANGERS FOOTBALL Club is a name that resonates around the world with a remarkable history of success, innovation, great players and glory. The club can rightly be classed as one of the most important anywhere given the achievements of the great teams throughout the decades and the impact it has on hundreds of thousands of people every day. It is incredible, therefore, that this institution of Scottish life began in the mind of a 16-year-old student who, like many in the Victorian era, had become excited by the new sport of Association Football.

Moses McNeil, his brother Peter and their friends William McBeath and Peter Campbell were walking in a park, now no longer in existence, in the Kelvinbridge area of Glasgow in the spring of 1872 when Moses suggested starting a football team. He had become excited by the game, pioneered in Scotland by Queen's Park, and was eager to be a part of it all. He had seen the name 'Rangers' in an English rugby football annual and suggested he and his friends adopt it. In a carefree moment, the

11

teenager with the biblical name had given birth to a club which would have an impact of biblical proportions on so many in the years to come.

Football was rough and ready to say the least in those early days and clubs played 'friendly' matches that regularly featured fist fights and other such rough house activity. There were no goal nets, those watching regularly impinged on to the playing area and tactics were as rudimentary as those used by primary school kids kicking a tennis ball about a playground.

The details are not completely clear, but it is thought that Rangers played their first ever match in May 1872 at Flesher's Haugh on Glasgow Green where they played out a goalless draw with a team called Callendar. Moses was in that first line-up along with Peter and two other brothers, William and Harry, the latter already a successful player with Queen's Park who was 'borrowed' for the occasion. In that first match Moses, his brothers and friends simply played in their street clothes. However, in their second game against Clyde – not the Clyde FC we know today – Rangers wore their famous light blue for the first time and won the match 11–0.

The first two years of Rangers' existence are lacking in documented detail but it is generally accepted they played a team called the Rovers on at least three occasions and beat them each time, but lost 1–0 to sides known as Havelock and Star of Leven, both long gone.

Perhaps indicative of the pioneering age, Rangers had failed to join the fledgling Scottish Football Association, formed in 1867, in time to play in the 1873/74 Scottish Cup. So it was the following season that they played their first competitive match in the same competition. On 12 October 1874 Rangers took on Oxford at the Queen's Park recreation ground and beat them 2–0. Moses, a small but powerful winger who liked to tackle back, scored the second goal in that historic match with David Gibb scoring the first. Sadly, they were knocked out in the next round by Dumbarton, a team with whom they were to have a great rivalry in the future.

Rangers, who had to compete with other teams to play on the public park at Glasgow Green, moved to their first 'home' at Burnbank near Kelvinbridge in 1875. But they were on the move again within a year, this time to Kinning Park on the south side of the River Clyde, taking over from Clydesdale Football and Cricket Club who moved to Titwood where they still play cricket to this day.

By this point Moses and Peter Campbell had become the first Rangers players to gain representative honours when they played for Glasgow in a 2–0 win against Sheffield at Bramall Lane. Then on 25 March 1876 Moses became Rangers' first international player when he lined up beside his brother Harry in the Scotland team that beat Wales 4–0 in front of 17,000 fans at Hamilton Crescent in Glasgow. He played for a second time in 1880 when Scotland defeated England 5–4 at the first Hampden Park.

McNeil was also a key protagonist for Rangers on the club's march to its first ever Scottish Cup final in 1877. En route they knocked out Queen's Park Juniors, Towerhill, Maunchline and Lennox and faced Vale of Leven in a highly controversial final that took three matches to decide.

The first game on 17 March at Hamilton Crescent ended in a 1–1 draw. They replayed the game on 7 April and produced the same scoreline. It was agreed that 30 minutes of extra time would be played – thought to be the first time this had happened in world football – and Rangers scored what they thought was a legitimate goal. They claimed the ball had crossed the line, hit a spectator – there were no nets in those days – and bounced back into the hands of the Vale keeper. But the referee, James Kerr of Hamilton, disagreed and when spectators spilled on to the field during the incident, he terminated the match.

Rangers led 2–1 in the third match on 13 April – this time played at Hampden – with Moses scoring the second goal, but the experienced Vale of Leven proved to be too strong and they scored twice more to deny Rangers their first major honour.

McNeil was also heavily involved when Rangers played in England for the first time on 16 February 1878 when he scored twice in a 4–2 win over Nottingham Forest and then played in the 2–1 win over The Wednesday, as they were known then, in Sheffield two days later.

There was more controversy in 1879 when Rangers reached the Scottish Cup final for the second time. Again it was Vale of Leven who were their opponents. With Moses at the heart of the action, Rangers were leading 1–0 thanks to a Willie Struthers goal when they thought they had scored a second goal through a Willie Dunlop header, but it was ruled offside. To make matters worse Vale of Leven equalised near the end.

Rangers lodged a protest on the grounds that their second goal should have stood but the SFA ordered a replay. In protest Rangers refused to turn up. The players were actually at the Ayr Races when the match was due to kick off and Vale of Leven were awarded the trophy – the third time they had won it in three years.

Revenge, however, was sweet. A month later Moses was in the Rangers team that won their first ever trophy – the Glasgow Merchants' Charity Cup – when Vale were defeated 2–1 in the final at Hampden. It was to be his only honour and he retired from playing in 1882 to pursue his profession as a commercial traveller.

His last appearance for Rangers was in a goalless draw with

South Western on 5 April 1882 – almost ten years to the day that he had brought Rangers to life. The young man from Rhu had little idea at the time, but he had set the wheels in motion for one of the greatest stories in world football. He no doubt looked on with pride as Rangers became the best team in the country in the 1920s and 1930s.

McNeil died of heart disease at the age of 82 in 1938 and he is buried in Cardross cemetery, a matter of miles along the coast from his birthplace in Rhu. His place in Rangers' history is, of course, assured forever.

Tom Vallance (1873–1883)

Born: 27 May 1856, Renton, nr Dumbarton

Appearances: 37

Goals: 0

Honours Won with Rangers

Caps: 7 (Scotland)

ANY TEAM in any sport requires a leader, organiser and inspiration and Tom Vallance possessed all of these qualities when he joined the fledging Rangers. In the next few years he went on to become the club's first great captain, his leadership skills also earning him the post of president of the club for six years after his playing days were over.

A keen sportsman as a youth, and at 6ft 2in extraordinarily tall for the time, he used his physique to good use as an athlete and an amateur rower, particularly after moving from Renton to Shandon on Gare Loch. During the 1870s he moved to Glasgow to work as a civil engineer, and then became a mechanical engineer working in a number of the Clyde shipyards. He started playing football with some fellow rowers on Glasgow Green in order to keep fit and was soon recruited by Moses McNeil's fledgling club. He was in the team that played its first competitive match on 12 October 1874 when they beat Oxford in the Scottish Cup and became a key figure in the early days.

A strong player with good judgement, neat and tidy in the tackle, Vallance played at right back and did not miss a match for his first two seasons. He was rewarded with the captaincy in 1876, leading the club to its first two Scottish Cup finals. He won six international caps between 1877 and 1881, representing Scotland against England and Wales. According to Rangers' historian John Allan, Vallance was, 'Tall and spare, he administered many a shock to opponents who had not previously made his acquaintance, for he was big-boned and could take or give a charge with any man.'

In 1882 Vallance retired from football and decided to take up the post of engineer on a tea estate in Assam, India. At a farewell party staged at the Bridge Street Station Hotel he was presented with a gift of 50 sovereigns, and a large crowd of well-wishers turned out at Glasgow Central Station to watch him leave on the first leg of his journey to London.

Ill health forced him to return from India, however, and soon he was back in Rangers colours although his first-team appearances were rare and he took to playing for the club's 'Ancients' team in charity and challenge matches. In 1883 he was elected president of the club and continued in the post for six years.

After his return from Assam, Vallance turned his back on engineering. He worked for a few years as a travelling salesman for a wine and spirit merchant and then for a brewer. During the early 1890s he opened a licensed restaurant, The Club, at Paisley Road Toll. Its success encouraged him to acquire other licensed premises in Glasgow's city centre, and he became a leading figure in the trade, serving as President of the Restaurateurs and Hotelkeepers Association in 1906.

Vallance was not only a distinguished footballer but also a fine athlete, and the Scottish record holder in the long jump. He was also an artist of note, exhibiting paintings at the Royal Scottish Academy in 1899 and 1914 and also at the Royal Glasgow Institute of the Fine Arts.

John McPherson (1890–1902)

BORN: 19 June 1868, Kilmarnock

APPEARANCES: 218

GOALS: 121

HONOURS WON WITH RANGERS

League titles (5) – 1890/91,
1898/99, 1899/1900, 1900/01,
1901/02

Scottish Cups (3) – 1893/94,
1896/97, 1897/98

CAPS: 5 (of 9 for Scotland)

THERE HAVE been some hugely talented players who have pulled on the Light Blue over the decades but it is fair to say that John 'Kitey' McPherson was the club's first superstar. The recruitment of the Ayrshireman coincided with the formation of the Scottish Football League in 1890 and he became a huge figure in what was a highly successful era for Rangers.

Indeed, his career had the kind of start that dreams are made of. He scored on his Rangers debut – a 5–2 win over Hearts – scored four times in his second game, a 6–2 thumping of Renton, and then hit five goals in an 8–2 demolition of St Mirren.

It was an unbelievable start, but it was no flash in the pan. McPherson was a pivotal player during 12 years on the field and subsequently a skilled administrator of the club. He actually played in every position for Rangers, including goalkeeper, but it was as an inside forward that he shone brightest. A powerful dribbler, he had the ability to beat players and the vision to make passes for others to score as well as possessing a powerful shot himself.

He was part of the first championship-winning team when Rangers and Dumbarton shared the inaugural Scottish League title in 1890/91. The two sides had finished level on points and the authorities ordered a play-off, which finished 2–2, so the teams were declared joint champions. How the clubs' fortunes quickly differed. Dumbarton won the title again the following season but have never been champions of Scotland since.

McPherson was captain by the time Rangers achieved one of their main ambitions: to win the Scottish Cup. They had not been in the final for 15 years when they faced Celtic at Hampden in front of 17,000 in 1894 and, fittingly, McPherson scored the third goal in a 3–1 victory over the team that was fast becoming Rangers' main rival.

John had scored in every round en route to the final as Rangers finally claimed the prize seen as the blue riband of the Scottish game. McPherson was on the scoresheet again when Rangers won the trophy for a second time in 1897, this time thrashing Dumbarton 5–1, and a year later the old trophy was retained when Kilmarnock were beaten 2–0.

Season 1898/99 was astonishing even in the annals of Rangers' history and McPherson was a key man in a League campaign that has never been equalled anywhere in the world. Rangers won all of their 18 League matches, scoring 79 goals and conceding just 18. It was the perfect campaign and McPherson played in 15 of the games, scoring seven times. It was the start of a wonderful stranglehold on the Scottish title and the team that did it is undoubtedly on a par with the great sides that dominated the 1920s and 30s, the late 1940s, the early 1960s and the 1990s.

With McPherson at the hub of it all, Rangers retained the

title in 1899/1900 by seven points from Celtic. He only missed two matches the following season and scored seven times as the title remained at Ibrox for a third successive year. And then Rangers made it four in a row in 1901/02, McPherson's final season in the first team.

Incredibly, his final League appearance was as goalkeeper – regular keeper Mathew Dickie was injured – in a 3–2 win over St Mirren on 18 January 1902, a match Rangers had to win to hold off Celtic and take the title.

McPherson had been a massive player in a fantastic era for Rangers. In 1907 he became a director of the club and served until his death in 1926. He collapsed and died while watching the Clyde Sports at Shawfield; one contemporary described him as 'the finest player in the first 50 years of the club's history'.

Nicol Smith (1893–1905)

BORN: 23 December 1873, Darvel, Ayrshire

APPEARANCES: 205

GOALS: 5

HONOURS WON WITH RANGERS

League titles (4) – 1898/99, 1899/1900, 1900/01, 1901/02

Scottish Cups (3) – 1893/94, 1896/97, 1897/98

CAPS: 12 (Scotland)

THE WORD tragic barely begins to describe the story of Ayrshireman Nicol Smith who was undoubtedly one of the best players anywhere in the world at the turn of the 19th century. He was only 31 when he died of a gastric infection in 1905, his death coming just a matter of weeks after he had lost his wife to the same ailment. His teammates were shattered. The effect on them was considerable and his loss coincided with the break-up of the first great Rangers team.

Smith was already a junior internationalist when Rangers signed him in 1893 having played for his local team Darvel among others and it didn't take him long to establish his place in the first team at right back. A powerfully built player, Smith was wholly committed and always put the team's cause ahead of his own personal safety. Strong defensively with a tremendous ability to anticipate what an opponent might do, he also contributed to the team in an attacking sense as his ability to pick out front players was considerable.

In his first season impressive displays helped the Light Blues to several landmark victories – the 5–0 League thrashing of Celtic on 2 September 1893 which remains Rangers' best over their old rivals (apart from an 'unofficial' wartime 8–1 rout on 1 January 1943). Although not renowed for his goals, he also helped Rangers get to the Scottish Cup final of 1894 by scoring the opening goal in the 3–1 semi-final victory over Queen's Park, cup holders and kings of the Scottish game at the time. He capped a great first season as he helped the club secure its long-awaited first ever Scottish Cup triumph when they defeated Celtic 3–1 in the final that year.

Over the years Smith struck up a tremendous partnership with left back Jock Drummond – the defensive wall on which so many Celtic attacks fell during that final at Hampden. Although it took a while for Rangers to build on their cup success, the two men were still there as the club racked up four successive League championships between 1899 and 1902. Undoubtedly their greatest triumph was the 1898/99 campaign when they won all 18 matches – a record that still stands unequalled – conceding just 18 goals in the process. But Smith can also lay claim to a New Year's Day goal against Celtic, scoring the first in a vital 4–2 win in 1902, which set Rangers on the way to their fourth successive crown.

Smith was a major international player as well, playing in a side that often also included his teammate Drummond. He captained his country twice and was involved in some terrific and unusual victories like the 4–1 win over England in 1900 and the 9–1 and 11–0 victories over Northern Ireland in 1899 and 1901.

Of course, medicine was not as advanced then as it is now and fate was to deal a cruel blow when in late 1904 Smith was struck down by a bout of enteric fever. He died in January the following year of an illness that has since become easily treatable.

Alex Smith (1894–1915)

BORN: 7 November 1876, Darvel, Ayrshire

APPEARANCES: 481
GOALS: 152

HONOURS WON WITH RANGERS
League titles (7) – 1898/99, 1899/1900, 1900/01, 1901/02, 1910/11, 1911/12, 1912/13
Scottish Cups (3) – 1896/97, 1897/98, 1902/03
CAPS: 20 (Scotland)

RANGERS CAN boast a long tradition of men who have dazzled opponents and supporters alike with their trickery, speed and skill on the left wing. Alex Smith was the original wing king in the Light Blue, electrifying Rangers fans for all of 21 years with his terrific ability on the ball and a fabulous return of goals with a ratio of nearly one in every three games.

He only got his chance at Rangers when a fellow Darvel villager Nicol Smith, who was no relation, convinced the club to give the 18-year-old a trial in a friendly game towards the end of the 1893/94 season. Alex was outstanding in a 3–1 win against FA Cup holders Notts County at Ibrox and went on to enjoy one of the longest and most productive careers of any Rangers player.

At just under 5ft 8in and weighing around 11 stone, the Darvel lad had a typical winger's build and he was also blessed with great pace and stamina. His reputation was that of an unselfish player who loved to create for others and his low, swerving crosses were said to be a nightmare for opposing goalkeepers. It is a sign of his huge contribution and consistency that he appeared in 69 of the 74 matches during Rangers four-in-a-row championship run between 1898/99 and 1901/02. He regularly set up chances for Robert Hamilton, known to all as 'RC', who was top scorer in each of those glorious campaigns, though he shared the accolade with Smith in 1901/02.

The Ayrshireman was equally productive in the Scottish Cup at that time, scoring in the 5–1 crushing of Dumbarton in 1897. The following year he scored in the final again when he and Hamilton got the goals in a 2–0 win over Kilmarnock. Remarkably, of the 22 men on the field that day on 26 March 1898, 16 were from Ayrshire. Killie had nine local men and Rangers featured seven from the area.

Smith was on the winning side again in 1903 when Hearts were defeated in a second replay 2–0 after a 1–1 draw and a goalless second match. It was the fourth time that Rangers had lifted the cup in nine years. Incredibly, it would be 25 years before they lifted the old trophy again.

For the next few years Rangers lived in the shadow of their Glasgow rivals as Celtic won six successive League titles. But Smith was still a key man in the new Rangers team that ended that run and started one of their own. They scored a record points total of 52 in 1910/11, from what was now an 18-team division, and Smith played in 29 of the 34 matches. There was the added bonus that season of beating Celtic in both the Glasgow Cup and Glasgow Charity Cup finals.

Rangers retained the title the following season and again Smith was at the hub of it all, creating the chances mostly finished by Willie Reid who scored 33 goals during the League campaign. They made it a hat-trick in 1912/13 with an even better points tally of 53, although in a benefit match for Smith in January 1913, which drew a crowd of 35,000, Rangers were beaten 5–1 by an International Select XI.

Scotland also made good use of the winger's services and he took part in 20 internationals in total, a record at that time for a Rangers player, including the famous 4–1 home victory over England in 1900.

His last match was in October 1914 and he retired at the end of that season, returning to his native Darvel to work in a lace-making business in which he was a partner.

He died in November 1954.

Jimmy Gordon (1907–1920)
BORN: 23 July 1888, Saltcoats, Ayrshire

APPEARANCES: 334
GOALS: 65

HONOURS WON WITH RANGERS
League titles (5) – 1910/11, 1911/12, 1912/13, 1917/18, 1919/20
CAPS: 10 (Scotland)

FIRES RAGED on the track around the pitch at Hampden Park, barriers were broken and outnumbered policemen were brutally attacked by a baying mob as Jimmy Gordon ran for cover in one of the most shameful incidents in Scottish football. The talented midfielder, as he would be termed now, was just 20 years old and had scored against Celtic in a replay of the Scottish Cup final in 1909 which finished 1–1.

It had been suggested in one newspaper that in the event of a draw extra time would be played rather than a second replay and the 60,000 crowd were expecting more action. When they did not get it, they reacted violently, charging on to the field and attacking the vastly under-strength police force. Fires were set as anything combustible was burned and the rioters even severed the hoses of the fire brigade, who arrived to put out the flames. The mayhem lasted for four hours but it has to be made clear that this was not rival fans clashing. The supporters were united against the authorities, their actions undoubtedly fuelled by whisky.

The two clubs agreed that the tie should be abandoned and encouraged the SFA to withhold the trophy that season. Both halves of the Old Firm were fined £150 each.

Having endured all of that, Gordon was no doubt toughened for the horrors of the First World War as he was one of a number of Rangers players who saw active service. He served with the Highland Light Infantry, who were based at Maryhill Barracks in Glasgow in 1916, although details of his exact involvement in the conflict are sketchy.

Gordon had been signed by manager William Wilton in the summer of 1907 from junior side Renfrew Victoria. He played 22 games in his first season, scoring just once in a 2–0 win over Clyde on 14 March 1908.

Most comfortable at right half, Gordon's great natural ability allowed him to figure at left back, centre forward and both wing berths too. It took him four years to win his first major honours as a Rangers player as Celtic had a stranglehold at the time, winning six League titles in a row. But Rangers were about to turn things around.

The 1910/11 campaign was a huge one. In those days the Glasgow Cup was a major event and 65,000 watched Rangers – including Gordon – beat Celtic 3–1 as the Light Blues won the trophy for the first time in nine years. They also won the Glasgow Merchants' Charity Cup, beating Celtic 2–1. But then, as now, the League title was the main thing and Rangers pipped Aberdeen by four points with Gordon at the hub of things in the middle of the pitch and Willie Reid scoring goals for fun, ending the campaign with 38 goals from 34 games.

Rangers retained the championship the following season, finishing six points clear of Celtic, although Gordon missed the title-clinching win at Raith as he was playing for Scotland against England at Hampden Park on the same day. They achieved the hat-trick in 1912/13, winning ten of their last 12 games to finish four points clear of their Glasgow rivals.

It was a further five years before Gordon tasted championship success again by which time players like Sandy Archibald and Tommy Muirhead had come into the team. Gordon scored 11 goals in 16 matches in the successful 1917/18 campaign when Rangers produced 12 wins and two draws and lost once in their last 15 games to edge Celtic by one point.

Gordon was a cup hero the following season when he scored in the 2–0 Glasgow Cup final win over Celtic played in front of 65,000 spectators. And he was a champion again in 1919/20 – his final season with Rangers – scoring 10 goals, including a hat-trick against Dumbarton.

He played ten times for Scotland between 1912 and 1920 with great success. Undoubtedly his finest hour was when he captained the Scots to a 3–1 victory over the Auld Enemy at Hampden on 14 April 1914 in front of 105,000 supporters. He would have earned more international honours but the SFA put a hold on all matches during the First World War. Gordon was capped three times six years later and his final game was a 5–4 defeat by England at Sheffield Wednesday's Hillsborough ground in April 1920.

On leaving Rangers he played briefly for Dunfermline and then set up in business with former Rangers colleague James Galt to run a series of billiard halls. He died on 22 November 1954.

Chapter 2
The Dominant Force
(1920–1939)

Tommy Cairns
Andy Cunningham
Bert Manderson
Tommy Muirhead
Sandy Archibald
Davie Meiklejohn
Alan Morton
Dougie Gray
Bob McPhail
Jimmy Smith
Jerry Dawson
Sam English
Alex Venters

THE STANDARDS and traditions of Rangers which are still followed today were largely set by the imposing figure of Bill

Struth: the disciplinarian manager whose litany of success between the wars was extraordinary.

Struth, who had joined Rangers as trainer in 1914, became manager in 1920 following the tragic death of William Wilton who drowned in a boating accident. It was the start of a golden period.

Not surprisingly, players from this era feature heavily in the Hall of Fame as Rangers won 14 titles and finally ended their remarkable 25-year hoodoo in the Scottish Cup with a resounding win over Celtic in 1928.

In the 1930s Rangers were virtually unstoppable as they dominated the League championship and the Scottish Cup.

The key protagonists in this purple period are all featured in this chapter and they all have tales of glory and greatness.

Comparing teams from different eras invariably provokes arguments and there is clearly a school of thought that the team from this period was the best Rangers produced. Football boomed in these years with astonishing attendances and Rangers roared to success after success.

Tommy Cairns (1913–1927)

BORN: 30 October 1890, Merryton, Lanarkshire

APPEARANCES: 441

GOALS: 144

HONOURS WON WITH RANGERS

League titles (7) – 1917/18, 1919/20, 1920/21, 1922/23, 1923/24, 1924/25, 1926/27

CAPS: 8 (Scotland)

LONGEVITY IS the key word for Tommy Cairns whose remarkable career took him to within a few months of his 42nd birthday, but it was his 14 years at Ibrox that were the most profitable.

He first made his name in junior football, helping Burnbank Athletic to the Scottish Junior Cup in 1911. He also appeared for Larkhall Thistle before earning an opportunity in the senior leagues. His first professional club was Bristol City where he played for two seasons from 1911. He joined Peebles Rovers in 1913 and had a short spell with St Johnstone before joining Rangers in November 1913.

He made his debut against Hamilton Academical on 27 December 1913 and played a total of nine games in his first season as Rangers finished second to rivals Celtic in Division One. He was a regular the following season, missing just one League game, and he became captain of the team in 1916, an honour he retained for the next ten years. His direct, no-nonsense style and an overwhelming desire not to lose were the qualities that made Tommy one of the top Rangers of his era.

He led the side to their first title in five years in 1917/18, ever present in the starting line-up and contributing 11 goals in the process. Two years later his second winner's medal, the club's tenth title since the formation of the Scottish League in 1890, was even sweeter as the Light Blues won it with a record 71 points and 106 goals.

The 1920 triumph was tinged with sadness because the club's first manager, William Wilton, drowned in a boating accident the day after the season ended. His successor was Bill Struth, the man Wilton had brought in as trainer some six years earlier and whose influence can still be felt at the club today.

Struth's first signing was 27-year-old Alan Morton who arrived at Ibrox from Queen's Park in 1920. The introduction of the left-winger with his quick feet and superb ball control seemed to galvanise the hard-working and persistent Cairns who proved the perfect foil for his talents. Their first campaign marked the start of an astonishing period of dominance for the club, during which time they won 14 out of 19 championships up until the start of the Second World War.

Remarkably, in retaining their title in 1920/21 Rangers improved on their points tally of the previous season, this time finishing with 76 points. Cairns scored 12 times, including one in a 2–1 win at Celtic Park in October.

In contrast, the following season was witness to an agonising last day championship defeat as Rangers drew 0–0 at Clyde and Celtic equalised two minutes from time against Morton at Cappielow to secure the title by one point. There was further agony for the Light Blues in the Scottish Cup final when, despite their status as overwhelming favourites, they lost 1–0 to Morton at Hampden.

Perhaps stirred by failure Rangers went on to win four of the next five League championships, led to each triumph by the evergreen Tommy Cairns. His final Rangers appearance was in a 2–1 win over Queen's Park on 1 March 1927. Though some historians don't credit him with a League win that season, he played in 15 of the 38 matches and so qualified for a winner's medal.

Cairns was also capped at international level, making eight Scotland appearances and never playing on the losing side, winning six and drawing two of the matches. He made his debut in a British Home Championship match against Wales on 26 February 1920 and scored in a 1–1 draw. His final international appearance was on 4 April 1925 in a 2–0 win over England at Hampden Park.

His domestic career was far from over when he left Ibrox. He signed for Bradford City, eventually making 135 appearances for the Yorkshire club and winning a Division Three North winner's medal in 1929. He retired from football in 1932 and later worked as a scout for Arsenal.

A truly great Rangers captain died in 1967.

Andy Cunningham
(1914–1929)
BORN: 30 January 1890, Galston,
Ayrshire

APPEARANCES: 389
GOALS: 182

HONOURS WON WITH RANGERS
League titles (7) – 1917/18,
1919/20, 1920/21, 1922/23,
1923/24, 1924/25, 1926/27
Scottish Cup (1) – 1927/28
CAPS: 12 (Scotland)

IN A move that would seem highly unlikely in professional football today, Andy Cunningham 'gave up' his Rangers career to go and fight for his country for two years in the gory hell of the First World War. Cunningham was a Second Lieutenant in the Royal Field Artillery and regularly saw action on the Western Front in 1916 and 1917 when casualties were horrific.

There are few details of his military career but there is no doubt he was in the heat of battle on a number of occasions as the British Army fought relentlessly with the Germans between trenches in the French countryside. Thankfully, he made it back unscathed and was able to resume his Rangers career and become an important player for the club in the golden era of the 1920s.

Cunningham was already an established player when he signed from Kilmarnock in April 1915, having spent six seasons with the Rugby Park men. Cunningham's play was typified by excellent close control and astute positional awareness. A brilliant inside forward, he was equally adept at scoring goals – with both head and feet – and creating them for others. In his first full season, Cunningham scored 18 goals in 20 games, including two in a 4–0 win over Queen's Park at Hampden in only his second League game, before putting his career on hold when he signed up for service with the Royal Field Artillery.

Andy found it hard to get a game when he returned in 1917 and only played four matches in the 1917/18 season. It was a similar story in the first half of the following season when he played just three times in 21 matches. However, a hat-trick in a 4–0 win over Queen's Park on 18 January 1919 seemed to cement his place in the first team and he scarcely looked back for the next ten years.

The tall, golden-haired Cunningham went on to win seven championships and one Scottish Cup medal, in the famous 1928 final against Celtic when the Light Blues won 4–0. It was a particularly sweet occasion for an Ibrox man who had played in the losing finals of 1921 and 1922. He might not have been given the chance to play had club captain Tommy Muirhead been fit but, in what turned out to be his last year at Ibrox, he deservedly won the honour that Rangers craved the most. Cunningham was also capped at international level, playing 12 times for Scotland and scoring 5 goals.

Cunningham was one of Rangers' most durable players and when he moved to Newcastle United in January 1929 he became the English League's oldest debutant at the age of 38. He began his Newcastle career as player-manager but hung up his boots after one season to concentrate on the management of the club.

He guided Newcastle to FA Cup success in 1932, beating Arsenal 2–1 in the final. However, the club was relegated to the Second Division two years later. Cunningham eventually left

Newcastle in 1935. He is remembered as a moderately successful manager on Tyneside, having won 105 out of 251 games.

After his time with Newcastle, he returned to Scotland where he managed Dundee between 1937 and 1940, before becoming a sportswriter after the Second World War.

Aged 82, he ceremonially kicked off the first leg of the Super Cup between Rangers and Ajax on 6 January 1973 when the winners of the Cup-Winners' Cup met the European Cup holders over two games. Sadly he passed away on 8 May that year.

Bert Manderson (1915–1927)
BORN: 9 May 1893, Belfast

APPEARANCES: 402
GOALS: 5

HONOURS WON WITH RANGERS
League titles (7) – 1917/18,
1919/20, 1920/21, 1922/23,
1923/24, 1924/25, 1926/27
CAPS: 5 (Northern Ireland)

IF THE first great Rangers full back partnership was Nicol Smith and Jock Drummond, the second comprised Bert Manderson and fellow Belfast man Bill McCandless. Manderson joined Rangers in 1915 for the princely sum of £150 from Irish League side Glenavon, having also played for Cliftonville and the now defunct Belfast Celtic. He made his Rangers debut against Aberdeen in March that year and went on to play a major part in the Gers' success story of the 1920s.

Manderson had a superb record of consistency – he appeared in 370 League matches – and at the peak of his career there were few better players in the right-back berth. He teamed up with fellow Ulsterman McCandless in 1920 and the pair formed a Light Blue wall as effective as Smith and Drummond had been two decades earlier.

In the dominant 1920s, the Rangers defence gave away scarcely 25 goals in each of the club's successful League campaigns, a statistic indicative of their efficacy. Manderson's form earned him international honours too, playing five times for Ireland, signing off in a match against Scotland at Ibrox in 1926.

Rangers were irresistible under the management of Bill Struth, who had joined Rangers as trainer in 1919, and become manager after the sad death of William Wilton in 1920. So dominant were they during the inter-war years – ten of the players now stand proudly in the club's Hall of Fame – that Manderson was a member of seven championship-winning teams. The only honour missing from his locker was a Scottish Cup winner's medal as Rangers' famous 'Cup Hoodoo' saw to it that the Light Blues failed to win the trophy for a 25-year period between 1903 and 1928.

Manderson left Rangers for Bradford Park Avenue in the summer of 1927 along with teammate Tommy Cairns. He subsequently returned to Glasgow and worked for a spell as a trainer with Queen's Park.

In retirement he lived in the Mount Florida area of the city near Hampden Park and he collapsed and died on 27 April 1946 when he was preparing to go and watch Rangers face Hearts in the semi-final of the Southern League Cup. Appropriately, Rangers won the game 2–1 and lifted the trophy in what was the last year of wartime football.

Tommy Muirhead
(1917–1924, 1925–1930)
BORN: 31 January 1897,
Cowdenbeath

APPEARANCES: 353
GOALS: 49

HONOURS WON WITH RANGERS
League titles (8) – 1919/20,
1920/21, 1922/23, 1923/24,
1926/27, 1927/28, 1928/29,
1929/30
CAPS: 8 (Scotland)

DAVID BECKHAM'S skills and abilities might be quite different from a man who captained Rangers in a glorious era, but he and Tommy Muirhead have a common bond. Muirhead was one of the original stars of American soccer, some 82 years before Beckham signed his highly lucrative contract with Los Angeles Galaxy in 2007. And, like Beckham, his stay in the States was fleeting as he quickly pined for a better standard of football.

Muirhead had signed for Rangers from Hibs for £20 in May 1917. A fine half back or inside forward, he became a driving force in the engine room of the Rangers team that won six titles in eight seasons. Although Tommy played in a creative position that was by no means the whole story of his game – he simply loved the opportunity to make a biting tackle.

His nickname was 'Horace' and off the field he was quite the dandy, loving to wear the bowler hat and spats that were popular at the time. In 1924 he was seduced by a lucrative offer to become player-manager of the Boston Wonder Workers, who played in the American Soccer League. One of his players was Barney Battles Jr, who went on to become a Hearts legend in the late 1920s and 1930s.

Tommy, however, returned to Rangers after barely a year and got right back into the old routine. He played in the final third of the 1924/25 season as Rangers clinched the title again. League championship success kept on coming, with further titles in 1926/27 and 1927/28, but he was another victim of the club's 'Cup Hoodoo', appearing on the losing side in 1921, missing the 1928 success over Celtic because of a knee injury and then captaining the side the following year when the Gers lost to Kilmarnock in the final.

However, there was solace as Rangers won the League crown in 1928/29 by an astonishing 16 points from Celtic, scoring 107 goals in the process. And he went out on a high, winning the championship again in 1929/30 when Rangers held off the challenge of Motherwell.

Scotland also made use of his services and he was capped eight times between 1922 and 1930. Muirhead left Ibrox in 1930 and went on to manage both St Johnstone and Preston North End before making a switch into sports journalism. He died on 1 June 1979.

Sandy Archibald (1917–1934)

BORN: 6 September 1897, Aberdour, Fife

APPEARANCES: 580

GOALS: 148

HONOURS WON WITH RANGERS

League titles (13) – 1917/18, 1919/20, 1920/21, 1922/23, 1923/24, 1924/25, 1926/27, 1927/28, 1928/29, 1929/30, 1930/31, 1932/33, 1933/34

Scottish Cups (3) – 1927/28, 1929/30, 1931/32

CAPS: 8 (Scotland)

A TOUGH and powerful man who began his working life in the mines of Fife, Sandy Archibald enjoyed an astonishing Rangers career with a British record 13 titles and a club record 513 League appearances, which may never be beaten. Celtic's legendary manager of the era, Willie Maley, once said of Archibald, 'So long as he is on the pitch we can never be sure of victory, no matter the score'.

Over an incredible 17-year period, Archibald proved himself to be a fantastic player, and not just in Old Firm games. He joined Rangers from Raith Rovers as a 19-year-old and won the championship in his first season. Some statisticians have tried to deprive him of the 1933/34 championship success but, in what was to be his last season with the club, he made a significant contribution during his final 15 appearances.

Britain was still at war with Germany when Archibald pulled on a Light Blue jersey in the League for the first time at Kilmarnock on 18 August 1917. He had a highly productive season. He was the only Rangers player to play in all 34 matches during the campaign and scored eight goals, a great return from a man who played on the right wing. Rangers won the championship for the first time in five years. With the title still undecided on the final day of the season – Rangers and Celtic both on 54 points – Archibald scored for Rangers in a 2–1 win over Clyde at Ibrox while Celtic could only draw at home to Motherwell.

The end of the war marked the beginning of a period of dominance for Rangers as they began to assemble a formidable team, first under the guidance of William Wilton and then his successor Bill Struth.

The championship was won in 1919/20, 1920/21, 1922/23, 1923/24 and 1924/25 as Rangers retained an iron grip on the Scottish game's major honour. They had a poor season in 1925/26, finishing in sixth place, the club's worst ever return. Many thought this was because Archibald was injured for the most part of the season.

However, they came storming back the following season. A 2–1 New Year win over Celtic at Ibrox, in which Archibald scored, gave them the momentum they needed and eight wins in the next ten matches enabled them to hold off an impressive challenge from Motherwell to take the title by five points.

Despite his unprecedented success at club level, Archibald had a poor return on the international stage with only eight appearances for Scotland between 1921 and 1932, scoring once in a 2–1 defeat against Wales in 1922. He would have made many more appearances but for competition from Huddersfield Town's brilliant outside right, Alex Jackson.

Archibald's eighth championship medal came in the 1927/28 season, as part of a momentous campaign for the Light Blues. They effectively clinched the League title over the Easter weekend with victories against Hamilton and Dunfermline. And then they turned their thoughts to the cup.

On 14 April 1928 a record crowd of 118,115 assembled at Hampden to watch the 50th Scottish Cup final, between Rangers and Celtic. On what was one of the finest days in Rangers' history they finally put their 'Cup Hoodoo' to rest, getting their hands on the trophy by thumping Celtic 4–0 and ending the club's 25-year wait.

Still level with no goals at half time, it was anyone's game. But a crucial Davie Meiklejohn penalty sent Rangers on their way after 55 minutes, new signing Bob McPhail tapped in a second goal and then Archibald, who had terrorised Celtic all day, smashed two 25-yard shots past Celtic keeper John Thomson to complete the rout. McPhail was in no doubt who the main man was. He said, 'The final belonged to Archibald. He took full advantage of the inexperience of the Celtic full back John Donaghue, who had been pitchforked into the match at the last minute because of an injury to Willie McGonagle.'

Archibald, who used to drive his crosses in from the right side, scored 12 League goals in each the following seasons – 1928/29 and 1929/30 – as Rangers continued their dominance by retaining the title and then making it five in a row the following season.

There was more cup glory too as the hoodoo was firmly put in its place. They won it again in 1930, beating Partick Thistle 2–1 in a replay after a goalless first match. Archibald won the cup for a third and final time in 1932 when goals from Jimmy Fleming, Bob McPhail and Sam English gave Rangers a resounding 3–0 replay win over Kilmarnock after another goalless draw.

Championship medals 12 and 13 were secured in 1932/33 and 1933/34 – the latter in Archibald's final season for Rangers after 17 remarkable years at Ibrox. When he left the club, Archibald returned to his native Fife and took up the post of secretary/manager of his first club Raith Rovers, a post he held for five years. He then took the same role with neighbours Dunfermline before his untimely death in 1946 aged just 49.

Davie Meiklejohn (1919–1936)
BORN: 12 December 1900, Govan

APPEARANCES: 563
GOALS: 16

HONOURS WON WITH RANGERS
League titles (12) – 1920/21,
1922/23, 1923/24, 1924/25,
1926/27, 1927/28, 1928/29,
1929/30, 1930/31, 1932/33,
1933/34, 1934/35
Scottish Cups (5) – 1927/28,
1929/30, 1931/32, 1933/34,
1935/36
CAPS: 15 (Scotland)

THE ENORMITY of the moment was not lost on Davie Meiklejohn as he placed the ball on the penalty spot 55 minutes into the Scottish Cup final at Hampden Park on 14 April 1928. A then record crowd of 118,115 had assembled at Hampden with thousands locked outside to see if Rangers could finally end their 'Cup Hoodoo' when they faced old rivals Celtic, and it was fitting that Meiklejohn should have shouldered the responsibility.

With regular captain Tommy Muirhead injured, Meiklejohn assumed the role and was outstanding in the first half as Celtic pressurised the Rangers defence. The scores were level at half time. With ten minutes of the second half gone, an Alan Morton cross from the left picked out Jimmy Fleming and his shot beat precocious Celtic keeper John Thomson and looked to

45

have clearly crossed the line before Celtic captain Willie McStay punched it away. Rangers were awarded a penalty and their supporters held their breath.

Under enormous pressure, 'Meek' took a short run up and coolly converted the spot kick, drilling it into the corner of the net. He said after the match, 'I saw, in a flash, the whole picture of our striving to win the cup. I saw the dire flicks of fortune which had beaten us when we should have won . . . That ball should have been in the net. It was on the penalty spot instead. If I scored, we would win; if I failed we could be beaten. It was a moment of agony.'

But, with one precise kick, he ended 25 years of hurt and frustration for Rangers, and sent the club on its way back to cup glory. Bob McPhail, who scored the second goal in that famous final, reckoned the game would have been lost had Meiklejohn not scored. But they went on to win 4–0 – a result that had considerable consequences. Rangers were already on a run of supremacy in the League and Celtic were to remain in their shadow for most of the next decade and more.

If ever there was a man who was born to captain Rangers, it was Davie Meiklejohn. Born in Govan, Meiklejohn was one of a long line of great Rangers captains and probably the finest skipper of the pre-war generation. A positionally astute defender and one of manager Bill Struth's 'gaffers on the park', he was a vital member of the highly successful Rangers sides of the 1920s and 1930s. The late Willie Thornton, a Rangers legend himself, paid Meiklejohn the ultimate tribute when he called him 'the greatest player I ever saw'.

Signed from Maryhill Juniors in 1919, Meek spent 18 years at Ibrox before retiring in 1936. During that time, he amassed an astonishing haul of 12 championship medals and five Scottish Cup badges, adding four more to the one he instigated in 1928.

Meiklejohn also won 15 caps for Scotland and twice captained his country against England, most memorably when he led the Scots to a 2–0 win at Hampden in 1931. The Scots were given no chance as England crowed about the abilities of Everton's Dixie Dean, but Meiklejohn shackled Dean and the Scots celebrated.

Meiklejohn retired at the end of the 1935/36 season and initially became a newspaper columnist, working with the *Daily Record*. He returned to football as manager of Partick Thistle in 1947. Tragically, he collapsed in the directors' box at Broomfield after Thistle's game with Airdrie on 22 August 1959 and died on the way to hospital. He was just 58 years old. Over 2,000 mourners attended his funeral at Craigton cemetery near Ibrox. Former teammate and then Rangers director Alan Morton said, 'No cause was ever lost when Davie was behind you. He will go down in history as one of the greatest Rangers to wear the colours.'

Alan Morton (1920–1933)

BORN: 24 April 1893, Glasgow

APPEARANCES: 440

GOALS: 105

HONOURS WON WITH RANGERS

League titles (9) – 1920/21,
1922/23, 1923/24, 1924/25,
1926/27, 1927/28, 1928/29,
1929/30, 1930/31

Scottish Cups (3) – 1927/28,
1929/30, 1931/32

CAPS: 29 (of 31 for Scotland)

ANOTHER PLAYER whose litany of honours illustrates the total domination that Rangers held over Scottish football in the 1920s was Alan Morton. Rangers have always had great entertainers, but Morton – the 'wee blue devil' – was the original. He was pure box-office material the way he teased and tormented opponents on the left wing, regularly finishing each move with a pinpoint cross to one of the forwards. Invariably, Morton was the star of the show.

The diminutive winger was Struth's first signing for the club in 1920 and what an acquisition he turned out to be. Despite a lack of stature – he was 5ft 4in tall – the former Queen's Park man was one of the most devastating Rangers players of all time. His ratio of 105 goals in 440 games was a marvellous return for a man who was supposed to create them for others.

He enjoyed a tremendous career at Ibrox and the zenith has to be the 1927/28 season when the club completed the League and Cup Double for the first time in its history. Rangers ended a 25-year run without success in the Scottish Cup in April when they finally lifted the old trophy, thumping Celtic 4–0 in a momentous final. A week later, they confirmed themselves as League champions, hammering Kilmarnock 5–1 thanks to a Jimmy Fleming hat-trick.

At the end of the previous month Morton had been one of the chief destroyers of England when Scotland famously thrashed the Auld Enemy 5–1 in their own backyard to earn the moniker the 'Wembley Wizards'. Morton ripped England apart in the driving rain that day and set up all three goals for hat-trick hero Alex Jackson while the legendary Alex James scored the other two. It was one frustrated England supporter who inadvertently gave Morton his nickname when he shouted out to him, 'you wee blue devil'. The remark was heard by many around him and the name stuck. The match ball from that incredible day, signed by all of the players, takes pride of place in the Scottish Football Museum at Hampden.

Morton was a superb servant to Scotland. In all, he played 11 times against the 'Auld Enemy' as part of his 31-cap international total. All of his matches were Home Internationals – other than his last one. He played in a friendly match against France in Paris when the Scots, also with Bob McPhail in the team, roared to a 3–1 win with Third Lanark's Neil Dewar scoring all three goals. Morton had been capped twice playing for Queen's Park before his move to Ibrox.

Although born in Glasgow, Morton grew up in Airdrie and when he was turned down by the local team – what a mistake they made – he signed for Queen's Park in 1914 and began studying to become a mining engineer. It was on completion of those studies that the fully qualified Morton turned professional and signed for Rangers. However, he was only ever part-time at

Ibrox. Incredibly, he continued his job as a mining engineer throughout his football career.

Morton was a dapper man – both on and off the field. He regularly walked to Ibrox in his bowler hat with umbrella in hand and people called him the 'wee Society man' – a reference to the insurance company men that collected policy monies from households in Glasgow. He was very self conscious about his appearance and did not like getting his hair dirty when he played. Bob McPhail, who joined Rangers from Airdrie in 1927, once played a head-height pass out to the left wing for Morton and the winger let the ball go over his head. When a startled McPhail inquired what Morton was up to, he told him, 'It's football we're playing. We play on the ground with the ball at our feet, not in the air.'

After playing, he went on to serve Rangers as a director and his 38-year tenure is the longest board service by any individual in the club's history to date. He remained on the board until his death in 1971 at the age of 78. The portrait of Morton in a Scotland strip, which stands at the top of the marble staircase in the Bill Struth Main Stand at Ibrox, is a testament to the esteem in which he is held at the club.

Dougie Gray (1925–1947)
BORN: 4 April 1905, Alford, Aberdeenshire

APPEARANCES: 555
GOALS: 2

HONOURS WON WITH RANGERS
League titles (10) – 1926/27, 1927/28, 1928/29, 1929/30, 1930/31, 1932/33, 1933/34, 1934/35, 1936/37, 1938/39
Scottish Cups (6) – 1927/28, 1929/30, 1931/32, 1933/34, 1934/35, 1935/36
CAPS: 10 (Scotland)

LOYALTY TO one club has become almost extinct in the modern game and it seems fairly certain that no Rangers player in the future will come close to matching Dougie Gray's remarkable record of service at Ibrox. The Bosman ruling, financial gains and shorter careers of managers who like to build their own sides mean players rarely play for Rangers for more than five years these days.

Dougie Gray was there for 22 years, although he didn't play any matches in the final 18 months of his time with the club, which was one of staggering success. Gray is the longest-serving Rangers player of all time having appeared in 940 matches – a figure that has to be reduced by 385 as Southern League and wartime cup competitions are deemed unofficial. He also won six Southern League championship medals during this period so essentially he had been a 'champion' 16 times – but, of course, these too are not included in his statistics. Not bad for a wee laddie from an Aberdeenshire village south of the River Don.

Rangers spotted him playing for junior side Aberdeen Muggiemoss and immediately recognised his talents. They were on the lookout for someone in the right back berth to replace Bert Manderson, who was clearly coming towards the end of his career and Gray seemed to fit the bill.

He joined in the summer of 1925 and he was soon to become a vital cog in the Ibrox machinery. He made his debut on 3 October that year in a 3–1 win over Kilmarnock and by the middle of the season he had effectively taken over from Ulsterman Manderson. But Gray had joined a team in transition and they finished sixth in the table that season, the club's worst ever finish.

However, the next 13 years were a joy to behold as one of the finest Rangers teams of all time claimed the title ten times and Gray played in all of those campaigns. Lacking any real physical advantages, the full back based his game on timely intervention and uncomplicated distribution and also cultivated the habit of making vital goalline clearances on the occasions when his goalkeeper Jerry Dawson was beaten.

He was part of the Double-winning team of 1927/28 – the first time that Rangers achieved the feat. He also featured heavily in the 1929/30 season when Rangers went even further, winning every trophy available to them. The campaign included a famous 2–1 win at Celtic on 1 January 1930 when Rangers claimed their first Ne'er Day win at Parkhead for 28 years on their way to the League title. They beat Partick Thistle in the Scottish Cup final and then put Celtic to the sword in both the Glasgow Cup and Glasgow Charity Cup finals, giving the Gers a 'Grand Slam' season.

Not surprisingly, Gray's talents were utilised by Scotland and he appeared ten times for the national team. He played in the Scotland team – along with Ibrox teammates Tully Craig and Jimmy Fleming – in a 2–0 win over Holland in Amsterdam on 4 June 1929. This came four days after a 1–1 draw with Germany in front of 42,000 fans at the Grunewald Stadium in Berlin.

Possibly the finest tribute that could be paid to Dougie Gray was that legendary Ibrox manager Bill Struth often referred to him as his 'best ever signing'. Given his tremendous service to the club, it is hard to disagree.

Gray left Rangers in 1947 and joined Glasgow neighbours Clyde as a coach. He died on 4 June 1972.

Bob McPhail (1927–1940)
BORN: 25 October 1905, Barrhead, nr Glasgow

APPEARANCES: 408
GOALS: 261

HONOURS WON WITH RANGERS
League titles (9) – 1927/28, 1928/29, 1929/30, 1930/31, 1932/33, 1933/34, 1934/35, 1936/37, 1938/39
Scottish Cups (6) – 1927/28, 1929/30, 1931/32, 1933/34, 1934/35, 1935/36
CAPS: 16 (of 17 for Scotland)

ARGUMENTS OFTEN rage about who was the greatest when it comes to discussing Rangers players but there is little doubt that Bob McPhail would be near the top of most lists. His career at Ibrox was phenomenal as he won the championship nine times and played in six winning Scottish Cup final teams, but it was his goalscoring that really stood out. His League goals return of 230 stood as a record for over 50 years until Ally McCoist managed to post a tally of 251, a number which will surely never be surpassed.

For 13 years McPhail brought joy to the Rangers supporters who gorged on the successes of the period. But his association with the club extended after his playing career was over as he stayed on to coach the reserve players at Ibrox for another 47 years, reporting on the progress of the club's youngsters to Bill

Struth, Scot Symon, Davie White, Willie Waddell, Jock Wallace and John Greig.

A talented young player, McPhail had already displayed his considerable skills with Airdrie, scoring 74 goals in 109 matches and helping them to win the Scottish Cup in 1924 at the age of 18. He was signed by Rangers in April 1927 for what was then the considerable fee of £4,500. His wages were reported to be £8 a week, with an extra £2 for a win and £1 for a draw – apparently among the highest in Britain at the time – and expectations were high. But he gave an early indication of what was to come when he scored two goals in the 4–1 Charity Cup semi-final win over Celtic at the end of that season.

Barrhead-born Bob had a brilliant work ethic but his astonishing eye for a goal was something to behold. During his years at Ibrox he developed an uncanny understanding first with Alan Morton and then Davie Kinnear in a highly productive forward line, which also featured players like Jimmy Smith and Sam English. He earned the rather uncomplimentary nickname of 'Greetin' Boab' for berating teammate Torry Gillick one day and the tag stuck.

McPhail's goals return is all the more remarkable given that he was not the main striker. He was an inside forward, as they were referred to then, and essentially should have linked the play by working from midfield. Perhaps the most crucial of his 261 goals was Rangers' second in the famous 4–0 Scottish Cup final victory against Celtic in 1928. It was a close-range shot and he recalled, 'Jimmy Fleming complained that I took the ball off his toe but I pointed out that it was safer where it was.' He also scored in the cup finals of 1932, 1934 and 1936.

Bob's record of seven Scottish Cup wins, including the one with Airdrie, is shared only by Celtic's Jimmy McMenemy and Billy McNeill and is unlikely to be surpassed in the current climate of continual player movement. McPhail's career mirrored a golden age for the Light Blues. There were a few disappointments, perhaps the strangest being in the 1931/32 season, when Rangers scored their record number of League goals – 118 in 38 matches – yet finished runners-up in the championship to Motherwell. Two years later they scored 118 goals again, this time winning the League and Cup Double.

The 1930s provided an almost unbroken period of fabulous success for Rangers, highlighted by yet another record in the last Old Firm League match at Ibrox before the war. On 2 January 1939, the biggest crowd ever to watch a League football match in the British Isles turned out for the traditional holiday fixture with Celtic. Ibrox was bursting at the seams as 118,567 fans crammed in to watch Davie Kinnear and Alex Venters give Rangers a 2–1 win.

McPhail was also a highly successful Scotland player. He had been capped once just before he joined Rangers and went on to play 17 times, scoring seven goals. His finest performance came at Hampden on 17 April 1937 when a world-record crowd of 149,547, plus at least 10,000 who gained illegal entry to the stadium, watched Scotland beat England 3–1 with McPhail scoring twice.

The outbreak of the Second World War forced the shut-down of the Scottish League just as Bob's career was entering its final phase. He left Rangers in 1940 but was coaxed into playing for St Mirren in the wartime Southern League in 1941 by his brother Malcolm – a successful player with Kilmarnock – who had become a director at Love Street. He played 12 times for the Saints and scored seven goals. Ironically his last match was against Rangers in a semi-final of the Southern League Cup which the Light Blues won 4–1.

After the war, as well as working with the Ibrox youngsters,

Bob formed a successful electrical company, McPhail & Meikle, with his son Robbie for whom he continued to work until his retirement. He died on 24 August 2000 at the age of 94.

Jimmy Smith (1928–1946)
BORN: 24 September 1911, Airdrie

APPEARANCES: 259
GOALS: 249

HONOURS WON WITH RANGERS
League titles (5) – 1930/31,
1932/33, 1933/34, 1934/35,
1936/37
Scottish Cups (3) – 1933/34,
1934/35, 1935/36
CAPS: 2 (Scotland)

THE NUMBERS say it all – Jimmy Smith's goals tally was simply incredible with an average of nearly a goal a game – a statistic that makes him one of the greatest players ever to pull on the Light Blue shirt. Of course, had the war not robbed him of seven years of his career – he was 28 when official football was suspended in 1939 – his record would have been even better.

Smith, a real old-fashioned, bludgeoning type of centre forward, must have been an awesome sight for defenders and goalkeepers. He was 6ft 1in tall and weighed 14 stone and, as the game was considerably more physical then than it is now, was able to use his build to stunning effect. He was undoubtedly as important as anyone during the glorious period of the 1930s.

He was first spotted as a free-scoring youngster with East Stirling, where he had started his senior career, and he was signed by Bill Struth in 1928. But it was two years before he began to make an impact. Jimmy played just twice in the 1928/29 season and once the following year, when he scored in a 3–1 win over Dundee. It was not until the end of the 1929/30 campaign that he made everyone sit up and take notice.

Rangers travelled by ocean liner across the Atlantic in May 1930, sailing from Greenock to Quebec, for their second tour of Canada and the USA in the space of two years. Smith was a revelation. Rangers played 14 matches all over Canada and in the American cities of Chicago, Detroit, Cleveland and New York, winning all of them, with Smith scoring 18 goals in seven starts.

It was clear he was throwing down a major challenge to the regular centre forward of the time, Jimmy Fleming. In season 1930/31 Smith scored 21 goals in 21 League games as Rangers won the title for the fifth season in succession. The situation became even more competitive when the club signed Sam English in 1931, and Fleming responded, scoring 16 League goals and keeping Smith out of the side. Smith only managed eight games but kept his eye in with five goals in those games.

All that changed the following season when Smith took over as the main striker. He retained his place for the next six campaigns, finishing each as the club's top scorer. In 1932/33 he scored 33 League goals in 34 matches as Rangers won back the championship from Motherwell, who finished second.

Incredibly, he netted 41 League goals in just 32 appearances the following season as Rangers held on to their crown with six of them coming at Ibrox on 15 August 1933 in a 9–1 hammering of Ayr United. It was a pity that only 8,000 saw the double hat-trick. The big man also won the Scottish Cup for the first time that season when he scored in the 5–0 drubbing of St Mirren – a match played in front of the rather contrasting crowd of 113,403.

The 1934/35 campaign was just as prolific as Rangers held off Celtic by three points to win their eighth championship in nine years. Smith scored 36 goals in 32 League games – another breathtaking return. That tally included another double hat-trick when he hit Dunfermline for six in a 7–1 win at East End Park on the opening day of the season. The cup final that year also belonged to Smith. He scored both goals to defeat Hamilton Academical 2–1.

The incredible strike-rate continued in 1935/36 when he again scored more goals than games played with 31 strikes in 28 matches and he won the cup for the second time when Bob McPhail's goal defeated Third Lanark. He blasted another 31 goals in the 1936/37 season as Rangers recaptured the championship, and he finished top scorer for the sixth successive season the following year with a return of 22.

With the suspension of football in Scotland in 1939, regional leagues continued and Smith played his part as Rangers featured in the Southern League. If these unofficial matches were counted then Smith went on to reach a tally of 381 goals from 420 games in all matches for Rangers. In that sense he would be the greatest ever – ahead of McCoist and McPhail – but the war was not kind to him. By the time the conflict was over so was his playing career. But he continued to work at Ibrox, for a further 21 years in fact, first as the club's trainer, working the players every day under the watchful eye of Bill Struth, and then as chief scout, a post he retained until his retirement in 1967. The old warhorse passed away on 5 December 2003 at the age of 92 and he is buried at Craigton cemetery near his beloved Ibrox.

Jerry Dawson (1929–1946)

BORN: 30 October 1909, Falkirk

APPEARANCES: 271

GOALS: 0

HONOURS WON WITH RANGERS
League titles (5) – 1932/33,
1933/34, 1934/35, 1936/37,
1938/39
Scottish Cups (2) – 1934/35,
1935/36
CAPS: 14 (Scotland)

NICKNAMES ARE all too predictable in football these days with a 'y' simply added to the end of the player's surname; but Jerry Dawson had the rather grand moniker of the 'Prince of Goalkeepers'. His real name was James but his Rangers teammates had christened him 'Jerry' after the great Burnley and England goalkeeper of the period, Jeremiah Dawson.

Dawson was snapped up by Rangers from Camelon Juniors in November 1929 even though they already had a decent keeper in Tom Hamilton. Indeed, Dawson had to bide his time before he could justifiably claim to be No. 1. He played only once in the next two seasons as Hamilton held on to the jersey. Jerry broke into the side in 1931/32 making 13 appearances before eventually beginning to edge out Hamilton in 1932/33 when Rangers pipped Motherwell for the League title.

More successes followed as Rangers won League and Cup Doubles in 1933/34 and 1934/35. Dawson scarcely missed a match in each of those title successes but was missing from the team when they romped to Scottish Cup glory against St Mirren in 1934. He was struck down with an illness two weeks earlier and Hamilton played as Rangers won 5–0 with Willie Nicholson scoring twice, Bob McPhail, Bobby Main and Jimmy Smith netting the others.

Dawson finally got his hands on the cup the following year as Rangers successfully defended the trophy for the first time in their history when they beat Hamilton Academical 2–1. Bob McPhail captained the side and missed a first-half penalty, but two Jimmy Smith goals gave Rangers the trophy. Dawson was the star of the show in the 1936 final when Rangers made it a hat-trick of victories with a narrow 1–0 win over Third Lanark. McPhail was the matchwinner but Dawson constantly saved Rangers throughout the match.

Jerry was not tall, but like Andy Goram, he had terrific reflexes and tremendous bravery. He was a strong man with large hands – ideal for a goalkeeper – and had great positional sense. His one fault, according to the Rangers front players, however, was his kicking style. He would make a semi-circular run up to the ball so when it arrived upfield there was so much spin on it the forwards found it difficult to control. They pleaded with Dawson to change his style, but he never did.

Dawson was an ever-present in the 1936/37 season when the Light Blues were champions again and he claimed his fifth winner's medal two seasons later.

His emergence as the Rangers regular in 1934 led him to becoming the Scotland keeper for a period of five years in which he collected 14 caps. He only lost two matches, the first one – a 2–1 defeat by Northern Ireland in Belfast – and the last one, a 2–1 defeat at Hampden by England. Dawson also played in a 3–1 win over Holland in Amsterdam, a 3–1 defeat of

Czechoslovakia – as it was then – in Prague's Strahov Stadium and kept out Germany at Hampden as the Scots won 2–0 in 1936.

After the war, with a new Rangers team emerging, he moved to Falkirk where he enjoyed three successful seasons before retiring from playing at the age of 40. He had a spell as a journalist with the *Daily Record* and then became manager of East Fife in 1953, taking over from fellow ex-Ranger Scot Symon who moved south to become manager of Preston North End. Dawson was initially very successful as East Fife won the League Cup for the third time in their history in his first season, 1953/54, beating Partick Thistle 3–2 in the final. However, he left Bayview in 1958 following East Fife's relegation to the Second Division.

He died on 17 January 1977.

Sam English (1931–1933)
BORN: 18 August 1908, Coleraine

APPEARANCES: 72
GOALS: 64

HONOURS WON WITH RANGERS
League title (1) – 1932/33
Scottish Cup (1) – 1931/32
CAPS: 2 (Ireland)

THE STORY of Sam English is undoubtedly one of the saddest in the history of Scottish football and yet his record of 44 League goals in a season makes him an iconic figure at Ibrox. It is the highest tally ever produced by a Rangers player in a League campaign and it will probably never be bettered.

There are a few who have threatened over the years. Jimmy Smith scored 41 a couple of years later, Ally McCoist was on 34 with seven games to go in the 1992/93 season when he broke his leg playing for Scotland in Portugal and Marco Negri rattled 30 goals in the first 19 League matches of the 1997/98 season but could only manage three more during the remainder of the campaign.

It was undoubtedly the greatest achievement of English's all-too-brief Rangers career and it happened in 1931/32 – the same season that saw the tragic death of Celtic keeper John Thomson following the Old Firm match on 5 September 1931 in an incident in which English was blamelessly involved.

It is difficult to comprehend how death can occur as a result of a football match and, thankfully, such incidents are rare. Hibs' full back Jimmy Main died as a result of stomach injuries sustained in a match with Partick Thistle in 1909. The talented West Ham and Lyon player Marc-Vivien Foe collapsed and later died of heart failure when Cameroon played Colombia in the 2003 Confederations Cup. And as recently as December 2007 Phil O'Donnell suffered a seizure playing for Motherwell against Dundee United and died on the way to hospital.

On that terrible day at Ibrox, the second half had just started. Jimmy Fleming had crossed the ball from the right and English was preparing to shoot when Thomson dived at the striker's feet and smashed his head off English's knee. Instantly the players – including Bob McPhail who was two yards away – knew something was wrong and a stretcher was called for. At 9.25 that night the Celtic keeper, aged just 22, died of a depressed fractured skull.

English was devastated. He was completely exonerated of any blame by both Thomson's family in Fife and the subsequent fatal accident inquiry. However, Celtic manager Willie Maley recklessly and unnecessarily cast doubt where there was none when he said at the inquiry, 'I hope it was an accident but I did not see enough to form an opinion.' It was a scandalous thing to say and all the Rangers players never forgave him for saying it. Despite that the entire Rangers team attended Thomson's funeral in Cardenden and captain Davie Meiklejohn read the lesson at one of two memorial services held in Glasgow.

Sam's father wanted him to get out of Glasgow and start a new life in America, because he felt he would never be allowed to forget what happened, and he was absolutely right. There was no escaping the taunts and English was haunted by what had happened. When Rangers went to Parkhead on 28 September for a Glasgow Cup semi-final there were shouts of 'murderer' and 'watch the killer'.

Manager Bill Struth tried to keep him focused on football and the man from Northern Ireland who had settled in Clydebank responded. He scored six hat-tricks as he reached the 44-goals total, but Rangers were pipped to the championship that season by Motherwell. He was equally prolific in the Scottish Cup scoring nine goals in six matches, the last of which was the third goal in the 3–0 cup final replay win over Kilmarnock on 30 April 1932 watched by 105,695 fans.

Such trauma makes it all the more remarkable that he produced a League goals tally that has never been beaten and an overall season return of 53 goals which was not surpassed until Jim Forrest scored 57 in season 1964/65.

English won the championship the next season, 1932/33, but his ratio was not as good with ten goals in 25 matches. At the end of that season he decided enough was enough and he was sold to Liverpool for £8,000. He scored 24 goals in 47 matches over two seasons for the Reds but the taunts about Thomson followed him to England.

He came back to Scotland and played briefly for Queen of the South and then played for Hartlepool United. In 1938 at the age of 28 he retired. He had had enough. Many years later he wrote an article in the *Daily Express* in which he described his career as 'seven years of joyless sport'.

He returned to the Dalmuir area and helped coach Duntocher Hibs and Yoker Athletic, the junior club where he had started his career. He subsequently found employment in the shipyards but fate was to play a heavy hand again. Motor neurone disease – the same condition that also killed Celtic's Jimmy Johnstone – took English in April 1967 at the age of just 58 and he passed away in Vale of Leven Hospital.

Although he only spent two years with Rangers his achievement in that first season means his name is indelibly marked in the club's history. Kris Boyd became the first recipient of the Sam English Bowl in May of 2009, a new award donated by Sam's family and presented to Rangers' leading scorer each season. A plaque has also been put up on the wall of the cottage where he was born in County Londonderry, signifying his achievements.

As a player English had great pace and could finish equally well with either foot and his head even though he was only 5ft 8in tall. As far as teammate Bob McPhail is concerned, he was the best centre forward of them all. He said, 'Sam was better than Hughie Gallacher. Yes, he was better than Jimmy McGrory. Yes, he was better than Jimmy Fleming. Yes, he was better than Jimmy Smith. Though I never played with the great Dixie Dean of Everton, I did play against him. I would have taken English before him.'

That simply exemplifies the tragedy of the situation that a man who could have set incredible striking standards was ultimately wrecked by one moment over which he had no control.

Alex Venters (1933–1946)

BORN: 9 June 1913, Cowdenbeath

APPEARANCES: 201
GOALS: 102

HONOURS WON WITH RANGERS
League titles (4) – 1933/34,
1934/35, 1936/37, 1938/39
Scottish Cups (2) – 1934/35,
1935/36
CAPS: 2 (of 3 for Scotland)

THE OLD Firm have traditionally had their pick of the best young players in Scotland simply because they have the pulling power and the financial muscle to secure most transfer targets. In recent times, for example, Rangers have signed Kris Boyd and Stevie Naismith from Kilmarnock and the Hibs duo of Kevin Thomson and Stevie Whittaker for around £6.5 million. And the situation was no different in the 1930s when Rangers learned about the talents of a young Fifer named Alex Venters.

He first lined up for his local side Cowdenbeath as a 17-year-old, quickly becoming the star of the team. Venters was playing so well for the Fife side that he was selected to play for Scotland against Ireland in September 1933 at Celtic Park in which he lined up beside such heavyweights as Celtic's Jimmy McGrory and Rangers' Bob McPhail.

He scored 37 goals in 95 games for Cowdenbeath, then a top-flight side, but the club had to work hard to resist offers for his services as they were in significant financial difficulties at the time. They finally succumbed a few weeks after his international debut when Rangers offered £2,000 for his services.

He made 15 League starts in Light Blue in the 1933/34 season, which made him a champion in his first six months. But he had to work hard for his place in what was one of the best line-ups in the club's history, and he missed out on cup glory that first season when Bob McPhail was selected for the Scottish Cup final victory over St Mirren at his expense.

However, a year later Venters celebrated a League and Cup Double when he scored ten goals in 28 League matches and seven Scottish Cup goals in eight matches. He won the cup again in 1936 when McPhail's goal defeated Third Lanark and there was further glory when Rangers won the League title in 1936/37 and 1938/39.

The young Fifer was particularly popular on the terraces at Ibrox probably because he scored 18 times against Celtic in various competitions. One of the most famous was in the League derby on 2 January 1939 when he scored the winner in a 2–1 success in front of Ibrox's record crowd of 118,730.

Venters was only 26 when war broke out in September 1939 and, like so many other players of the era, it drastically affected his career. However, success continued to come and his wartime haul of honours was particularly impressive with four Southern League championships and four Southern League Cup wins.

After the war, Venters was transferred to Third Lanark in February 1946. He had scored a total of 207 goals in 420 games for Rangers although more than half of each had been in the war years. A year later, Alex left Cathkin and joined Blackburn Rovers for a £1,000 fee before ending his playing career with Raith Rovers.

For a time he followed the traditional ex-player's route as mine host at the Railway Tavern at Buckhaven. Later, he returned to his original trade in the printing industry as a linotype operator in the Edinburgh office of the *Scottish Daily Mail*. On Thursday 30 April 1959, Venters was preparing to leave for night duty on the paper when he collapsed and died from a sudden heart attack at his home in Park Street, Cowdenbeath.

The locals have never forgotten the impact that he made as a footballer and more recently his career has been celebrated as the playing field near his home was renamed the Alex Venters Memorial Park.

Chapter 3
Silk and Steel
(1946–1955)

Torry Gillick
Willie Thornton
Willie Woodburn
Jock Shaw
Willie Waddell
George Young
Ian McColl
Bobby Brown
Sammy Cox
Johnny Hubbard
Billy Simpson

THE IMMEDIATE post-war period was another golden spell for Rangers when the famous Iron Curtain defence came about and, following the introduction of the League Cup, the first Treble in Scottish football was secured.

With Bill Struth continuing to lead the team, a new group of great players emerged to dominate the late 1940s and then battle with the great Hibs team of the 1950s for the major honours.

The defence of goalkeeper Bobby Brown, full backs George Young and Jock Shaw and the half backs of Ian McColl, Willie Woodburn and Sammy Cox was formidable and regularly kept out the opposition.

However, it was not all about stopping the other team. These men could create attacking moves with equal measure.

Further upfield there were some great characters: Gillick, Waddell and Thornton initially and then Hubbard and Simpson who became great friends and remain so today.

It all came together in 1949 when Rangers became the first team to sweep the boards of all three major trophies.

In 1954 Struth, suffering from ill health, stepped down to hand over the reins to Scot Symon. His legacy is still felt today.

Torry Gillick (1933–1935, 1946–1950)
BORN: 19 May 1915, Airdrie

APPEARANCES: 140
GOALS: 62

HONOURS WON WITH RANGERS
League titles (2) – 1934/35, 1946/47
Scottish Cups (2) – 1934/35, 1947/48
League Cups (2) – 1946/47, 1948/49

MUCH HAS been written and said about Rangers' formidable Iron Curtain defence during the years following the Second World War, but they also had some wonderful attacking players in this period and none more so than Torrance Gillick. A supremely skilful inside forward, Gillick wrote his name into the history books as one of the club's best ever passers of the ball and the only player to be signed twice by manager Bill Struth.

Born in Airdrie, the young Gillick played on the wing for prominent Glasgow junior team Petershill before signing for Rangers in 1933 at the age of 18. He made just a couple of appearances in that first season, as he had joined a club in the midst of a sensational period of success, but his time was not long in coming. The following year, 1934/35, he scored 21 goals in 34 matches as Rangers won the Double for the second successive season.

It was therefore a bit of a shock all round when he was sold to Everton for £8,000 in the same year, a then-record fee for the English club. Gillick was highly successful at Goodison Park where he earned all five of his Scotland caps and won the First Division championship in 1938/39.

However, with war causing the suspension of official competitive football later that year, he returned to Glasgow where he guested for Rangers on a number of occasions. During the various wartime competitions he began to form a highly effective partnership on the left with Willie Waddell. Gillick's delicate and instinctive passes would more often than not find Waddell who would overlap and use his lightning pace to terrorise defences. Gillick's good form prompted manager Bill Struth to re-sign him for the resumption of the Scottish League in 1946.

Gillick had kept all his pace and poise and he chipped in with 17 goals in that first post-war season as Rangers won the League title again and also took the inaugural Scottish League Cup, beating Aberdeen 4–0 in the final with Gillick on the scoresheet once again.

He claimed his second Scottish Cup winner's medal in 1948 as Rangers played in front of phenomenal crowds at last free to enjoy themselves after the dark days of conflict. An amazing 143,570 watched them beat Hibs 1–0 in the semi-final courtesy of a Willie Thornton strike. Then 131,975 saw them draw 1–1 in the final with Morton, in which Gillick scored the Rangers goal, and there was an even bigger crowd assembled for the replay in which Billy Williamson scored the only goal.

Gillick's career at Rangers was coming to an end during the 1948/49 season but not before he picked up another Scottish League Cup winner's medal on 12 March when he scored again and Willie Paton scored another to secure a 2–0 win over Clyde.

Gillick left Rangers the following year but had one more

year at senior level playing for Partick Thistle before moving into a scrap metal business in Lanarkshire.

He passed away on 12 December 1971, a sad day for Light Blues as it also saw the passing of another Rangers great, Alan Morton.

Willie Thornton (1936–1954)

BORN: 3 March 1920, Winchburgh, West Lothian

APPEARANCES: 303
GOALS: 188

HONOURS WON WITH RANGERS
League titles (4) – 1938/39, 1946/47, 1948/49, 1949/50
Scottish Cups (3) – 1947/48, 1948/49, 1949/50
League Cups (2) – 1946/47, 1948/49
CAPS: 7 (Scotland)

WILLIE THORNTON was the original teenage sensation. He signed for Rangers just four days after his 16th birthday, launching an incredible association that lasted until his death in 1991. A brilliant goalscorer, particularly with his head, he formed a deadly partnership with Willie Waddell in the years before and after the Second World War. During the war he fought with distinction in the Italian campaign. After his retirement from playing, he became part of the fabric at Ibrox as an assistant manager to both Davie White and Waddell and then custodian of the famous Trophy Room.

In 1936 Bill Struth sent scout Alec Young to West Lothian to check on a youngster playing for Winchburgh Albion. But he came back raving about Thornton. Despite the presence of another scout, from Hearts, Struth moved quickly to secure the services of the centre forward who became a Rangers player on

17 March that year, signed on the princely wage of £1 a week.

He made his debut on 2 January 1937 against Partick Thistle, making him one of the youngest ever Light Blues. He said, 'They played me on the right wing that day, probably just to break me in.' Famously, Struth was so impressed with the shine on Thornton's boots that day that he immediately doubled his wages to £2. Twenty appearances the following season were the precursor to him being a regular in the side of 1938/39, a season which brought him his first of four championship medals.

However, just five games into the following season war was declared and Willie was off to North Africa and Italy, serving in the British Army's only existent private regiment, the Duke of Atholl's Scottish Horse. Gunner Thornton was on active duty until 1946, serving in Egypt and Libya and he was involved in three landings in Italy. In one such landing, Willie's brave actions earned him the highly prestigious Military Medal.

It is remarkable that Thornton was able to step back in competitive football so easily after six years of war. But he and Waddell were key players in a new Rangers team that had the fans going wild. Overjoyed that the war was over, they relished the football like never before as Thornton and Jimmy Duncanson scored 18 apiece as Rangers won the first post-war championship in 1946/47. The fans were appreciative of Thornton's war efforts too. Indeed, at the first Old Firm derby of the season, both sets of supporters gave him a standing ovation as he came on to the field.

Waddell and Thornton had developed an uncanny connection. Waddell said, 'I could tell where Thornton was with just a quick glance and then know what weight to put on the cross ball . . . He had the instinct to judge the flight and the pace of the ball to get in front of defenders. We just clicked from the day that we came to Ibrox.'

The deadly combination was seen to good effect in front of a staggering 143,570 people when Rangers met Hibs in the 1947/48 Scottish Cup semi-final at Hampden Park. A classic match was decided by a solitary goal, scored with his head by Thornton from a Waddell cross.

Season 1948/49 was even better as Rangers became the first team to complete the domestic Treble when they pipped Dundee by a point for the League, defeated Raith Rovers 2–0 in the League Cup final and then saw off Clyde with a 4–1 win in the Scottish Cup final. And a League and Cup Double came his way again the following season as Rangers held off Hibs by one point in the League. The season was rounded off at Hampden again as Thornton, who had never scored in a major final before, produced two great headers to seal a 3–0 win over East Fife in front of 120,015 in the Scottish Cup final.

Although Hibs prevailed over Rangers in each of the next two League seasons, Thornton's goals still reigned in. He registered 19 strikes in 1950/51 and 27 the following year. By season 1952/53, however, he had become a peripheral figure and did not feature enough to earn a medal even though Rangers regained the crown.

For a man of Thornton's talents seven international appearances seems a paltry return, but there were fewer games then and a host of good Scottish players. Strangely, Thornton's favourite international match was a 2–0 defeat by England in 1948, the reason being that he was able to shake hands with his wartime hero Field Marshall Montgomery who was a special guest at the game.

Never booked or sent off during his career, Willie's talents also stretched to working for the *Glasgow Evening News* during his time at Rangers. He hung up his boots at the end of the

1953/54 season and went into management, initially at Dundee, where he recruited such players as Alan Gilzean, Ian Ure, Andy Penman and Alex Hamilton. Willie then took over from one of his early mentors Davie Meiklejohn at Partick Thistle where he had eight years in the hot seat.

For a legendary goalscorer alleged to have said, 'I don't mind how they go in, as long as they go in for Rangers,' the lure of Ibrox proved too strong in 1968 when manager Davie White asked him to come on board as his assistant. After all, there was work to do as Celtic were enjoying the best spell in their history under Jock Stein. When White moved on in 1969 the old double act was re-united as Willie Waddell took over. During the crossover, Thornton did briefly hold the reins himself. Under him the Light Blues played twice and won twice, making Thornton the only Rangers manager ever to have a 100 per cent record.

Before he died, in August 1991, Thornton also became custodian of the Trophy Room at Ibrox and was match-day host in, of course, the Thornton Suite.

Willie Woodburn (1937–1955)
BORN: 8 August 1919, Edinburgh

APPEARANCES: 325
GOALS: 1

HONOURS WON WITH RANGERS
League titles (4) – 1946/47,
1948/49, 1949/50, 1952/53
Scottish Cups (4) – 1947/48,
1948/49, 1949/50, 1952/53
League Cups (2) – 1946/47,
1948/49
CAPS: 24 (Scotland)

MANY BELIEVE Willie Woodburn to be Rangers' greatest ever centre half – better even than Meiklejohn, McKinnon, Johnstone, Butcher or Gough, and this despite the fact that his career was blighted both by the suspension of official football between 1939 and 1946 and by an incident that occurred during a match against Stirling Albion in 1954.

The Edinburgh-born Woodburn grew up in the shadow of Tynecastle, played junior football for Edinburgh Ashton while training as a plasterer and was expected to sign for Hearts when the time was right. However, Rangers moved in quickly and signed him as a professional in October 1937.

He made his debut on 20 August 1938 in a 2–2 draw in the League against Motherwell and played 12 matches that season as Rangers won the title, although he is not credited as receiving a medal. With Jimmy Simpson at the end of his career, manager Bill Struth saw Woodburn as his natural successor – passionate, competitive, tough and volatile but also a superb footballer who could play with either foot and build the game from the back rather than simply clear the ball the way he was facing.

However, on 13 September 1939 the Scottish football authorities suspended the League after five matches following the British declaration of war against Germany. Although football resumed shortly afterwards, wartime games were deemed 'unofficial' as far as the record books go. It was not a happy time for Woodburn, who suffered a bad knee injury and had to give way to George Young, who kept the No. 5 shirt when the League restarted in 1946/47. But Woodburn quickly reclaimed the shirt, with Young moving to right back, as Rangers won the championship and the inaugural Scottish League Cup that season.

The following season witnessed the emergence of Rangers' legendary Iron Curtain defence – Bobby Brown in goal, full backs George Young and Jock Shaw and half backs Ian McColl, Willie Woodburn and Sammy Cox. Woodburn, more committed than most and an imposing physical presence at just under 6ft, was at the heart of it. Their ability to keep out the opposition was a huge factor in the winning of three more titles in direct competition with the brilliant Hibs team of the time, who boasted the Famous Five forward line of Smith, Johnstone, Reilly, Turnbull and Ormond.

Woodburn had been given the nickname 'Big Ben' but not, as many people thought, in reference to the famous London landmark. Rangers had flown to Portugal in 1948 to play Benfica in a friendly and after the game Woodburn, celebrating the Gers 3–0 win with a glass or two, kept chanting 'Viva Benfica' and the name 'Ben' stuck.

Remarkably, Woodburn was 28 before he earned his first Scotland cap but he quickly made up for lost time and played 24 times for his country. He faced England three times at Wembley and never lost; drawing in 1947 in his debut and winning in both 1949 and 1951 when the Scots won 3–1 and 3–2 respectively.

However, Woodburn's superb career came to a sudden and unexpected halt in September 1954 when the SFA imposed a *sine die* suspension – effectively a lifetime ban – on him for headbutting a Stirling Albion player. It was a move that stunned the whole of Scottish football.

Teammate Ian McColl, who also played in the League Cup qualifying match on 28 August, recalled the incident, 'There was a tackle between Paterson and Woodburn and Paterson went to the ground in a sitting position, although there was nothing untoward at this point.

'Woodburn's leg was caught between Paterson's and as he tried to get away Paterson locked his legs around Woodburn's leg and his knee ligaments . . . Woodburn just picked him up and headbutted him.'

It was his fifth sending off in 17 years as a player. Woodburn was not a dirty player, though he did have a temper and there had been incidents before. In his defence Woodburn claimed that he felt the player was deliberately trying to aggravate a well-documented knee injury that he was carrying at the time, and so he lashed out. Most football historians believe he was made a scapegoat, a man punished in order to deter others, a fact possibly recognised by the Scottish FA when they lifted the ban almost three seasons later.

It was too late, however, for Woodburn to resume playing. His career was over. Woodburn said some years later, 'It was an action that haunted me and I'll never understand why I did it . . . I knew I had to be punished but I never dreamed they would ban me for life.'

By the time the SFA had changed their minds and rescinded the ban on Woodburn he had already started working in the garage business with his brother and was embarking on a new career writing about football in the *News of the World*.

He died on 2 December 2001.

Jock Shaw (1938–1953)
BORN: 29 November 1912,
Annathill, Lanarkshire

APPEARANCES: 242
GOALS: 1

HONOURS WON WITH RANGERS
League titles (4) – 1938/39,
1946/47, 1948/49, 1949/50
Scottish Cups (3) – 1947/48,
1948/49, 1949/50
League Cups (2) – 1946/47,
1948/49
CAPS: 6 (Scotland)

SOME MEN are simply destined to play for Rangers and one such player was Jock 'Tiger' Shaw. He had earned his nickname because his style was tough and uncompromising, and he was just the kind of full back that Bill Struth was after when he went to check out the famous Glasgow junior side Benburb, who played down the road from Ibrox.

It is understood that Struth had an influence in Airdrie signing Shaw in 1933. He spent five seasons at Broomfield where he made a very good name for himself. Finally, in the summer of 1938, Struth decided the Tiger was ready to be unleashed at Ibrox. A fee of £2,000 was laid out for the then 25-year-old and he moved to Glasgow to join the team that had dominated the decade.

He made his debut at left back on the opening day of the 1938/39 League season in a 3–3 draw with St Johnstone and went on to play 28 times in his maiden campaign as Rangers were crowned champions. It was the stuff of dreams for Tiger, whose lifelong ambition had been to pull on the Light Blue jersey. But his dream was shattered later that year with the onset of war and the suspension of all official football competitions.

Unperturbed, Shaw was a terrific wartime player for Rangers, as they won most of the silverware on offer, but he was nearly 34 when the Scottish League restarted in 1946/47. However, his lost years seemed to have done him no harm and he played 28 of the 30 games that first season as Rangers won the title. He also got a Scottish League Cup winner's medal as the Gers beat Aberdeen to win the inaugural competition.

There was a kind of family celebration in April 1947 when Jock won the first of his six Scotland caps as captain of the side that drew 1–1 against England at Wembley. Also on the pitch that day, at right back, was his brother Davie, who played with Hibs and later Aberdeen.

Back at Rangers something special was happening and for the start of the 1947/48 season the new 'Iron Curtain' defence – so-called after the barriers dividing post-war Europe – was being assembled. The backline of Bobby Brown, George Young, Jock Shaw, Ian McColl, Willie Woodburn and Sammy Cox was one of the best ever seen at Ibrox and quickly started to pay dividends.

The next three seasons saw Rangers win two League titles, a hat-trick of Scottish Cups and another victory in the new Scottish League Cup. Shaw was nearly 38 when they won the Double in 1949/50. He was still a key player in the following season and remained club captain until 1953/54, but by then his appearances were few and far between.

When he hung up his boots he became a trainer and he helped a number of young players come through the ranks such as John Greig, Sandy Jardine and Willie Henderson. Another young player who benefited from his experience was former Scotland boss Craig Brown, who joined Rangers as a kid in 1958. He said, 'Jock was in charge of the reserve team when I signed for Rangers and spent a short time at the club. He was someone to look up to, someone you gave instant respect. I know how much he helped me as a young player and I always appreciated that.'

Even when his training days were over he moved on to the ground staff at Ibrox. He simply loved the place. He died on 20 June 2000.

Willie Waddell (1938–1955)
BORN: 7 March 1921, Forth,
Lanarkshire

APPEARANCES: 301
GOALS: 58

HONOURS WON WITH RANGERS
League titles (4) – 1938/39,
1946/47, 1948/49, 1952/53
Scottish Cups (2) – 1948/49,
1952/53
CAPS: 18 (Scotland)

THE INFLUENCE of Willie Waddell will always be felt at Ibrox. His achievements at all levels of the game are legion though it is as a manager that he is most clearly remembered, both in glory and in tragedy. He was in the hot seat when Rangers enjoyed their finest hour – victory in the European Cup-Winners' Cup final on 24 May 1972, almost 100 years to the day that a young Moses McNeil came up with the idea of starting the club. He was also the man who led with authority in the wake of the Ibrox Disaster on 2 January 1971 when horrific crushing on stairway 13 at the Copland Road end of Ibrox resulted in the deaths of 66 supporters.

In a 50-year association with Rangers, he rose from a school-boy player, eager to make his mark, to manager, managing director and vice-chairman of the club. It was his drive and vision which led to Ibrox becoming the magnificent all-seater complex it is today. Its status as one of only a few in Europe with a five-star UEFA rating is testimony to his remarkable Rangers career.

87

Waddell played his first game for the club's reserves at the age of 15. Manager Bill Struth then farmed out the youngster to Strathclyde Juniors to help him gain experience. He turned professional in May 1938 and made his first-team debut at the age of 17 in a friendly against Arsenal at Ibrox three months later. It was a sensational start to his career, Waddell scoring the only goal of the game. A week later he played his first League match in a 4–1 victory over Ayr. Waddell appeared in 27 League games that season, scoring seven goals, as Rangers won the championship.

Waddell seemed to be destined for an illustrious career when the Scottish League was abandoned after just five games of the 1939/40 season because of war. He had broken into one of the great Rangers teams and could have looked forward to a long international run. As it was, he did not receive the first of his 18 Scotland caps until May 1946, making his debut in a 3–1 win against Switzerland.

Rangers played in area divisional leagues during the war and Waddell was a regular and influential performer. They carried off all seven League titles played for in wartime and out of the 34 competitions they entered, they won 25. During these years Waddell was maturing into a strong and powerful winger blessed with a great turn of speed. His acceleration was terrific and it became one of his most potent weapons as he sprinted his way past defences. His crossing ability was legendary. Waddell was capable of providing the most teasing of centres to test opposition nerves.

It was during this time that Waddell scored the first hat-trick of his career in a 4–2 victory over Third Lanark in August 1942. The result was that when the Scottish League resumed in 1946/47, Waddell was a highly experienced and gifted player.

That first season, Rangers picked up where they had left off in 1938/39, winning the first peacetime championship. Waddell scored five goals in his 22 League games. He also scored twice as Rangers reached the new Scottish League Cup final, including one in the semi-final win over Hibernian, though he missed the final itself as Rangers became the first holders of the trophy, beating Aberdeen 4–0 in April 1947.

He didn't appear in the Scottish Cup final win against Morton the following season either, though he had played a crucial part in the semi-final win, again over Hibs. The match was watched by a crowd of 143,570 people and was billed as the 'Famous Five' v the 'Iron Curtain'. Hibs had most of the play, but it was Waddell who broke the deadlock with a run down the wing and a cross for Willie Thornton to head the only goal of the game.

Earlier that season, Rangers had flown to Lisbon to take on Benfica in a friendly match. Rangers won 3–0, but Waddell was also happy for another reason: an air hostess he had met on the flight, called Hilda, became his wife.

Waddell's hard luck story in cup finals continued when he missed Rangers' 2–0 defeat of Raith to win the League Cup in March 1949. He was Rangers' top scorer in the competition, though, getting four in the earlier matches, including a hat-trick against Clyde. But the hoodoo was finally broken later in the season as Waddell was in the line-up as Clyde were beaten 4–1 in the Scottish Cup final.

That was the season that Rangers became the first team to win the Treble. Thornton was again leading marksman with 23 goals in 29 League games as Rangers won the championship and, once more, many of them came courtesy of his chief supplier Waddell.

Though Waddell was a player who usually provided service on a plate for others, he could be a powerful finisher himself.

And perhaps the most important goal he ever scored was the one that won the championship for Rangers in 1952/53. He had an almost telepathic relationship with Willie Thornton who said, 'The great thing about Waddell was his ability to hit a cross on the run and he could do it with either foot . . . We just had this great understanding which was good for ourselves and, of course, the Rangers Football Club.'

Waddell had won his second Scottish Cup medal eight days earlier as Rangers beat Aberdeen 1–0 in a replayed final. But on the last day of the League season they needed a point to make sure of the title and, with 15 minutes left, they were losing 1–0 to Queen of the South. Up popped Waddell to make it 1–1 and Rangers pipped Hibernian to the championship on goal average.

Waddell retired as a player in the summer of 1956. His last appearance in Light Blue was in a friendly against Manchester City. He played on the left wing in that game, his successor Alex Scott taking the right. He immediately turned to management and had a successful spell with Kilmarnock, taking them to a dramatic final-day championship win over Hearts in 1964/65. He then took a job as a sportswriter for the *Scottish Daily Express*, but he was back at Ibrox in 1969 replacing Davie White as manager.

These were difficult times for Rangers as Celtic were enjoying the best period in their history under Jock Stein. But Waddell rose to the challenge. He started to utilise younger players, a policy never more successful than in the 1970/71 League Cup final when 16-year-old Derek Johnstone headed the winner – against Celtic. Two months later Waddell took the leading role in the club's response to the Ibrox Disaster, vowing to rebuild the stadium so that such a tragic event could never happen again.

Eighteen months later, in May 1972, Rangers became kings of Europe when they lifted the Cup-Winners' Cup in Barcelona, a triumph that was, in a large part, testimony to Waddell's preparations and decisions.

Having almost tasted glory in the same competition in 1961 and 1967 but lost out in the final on both occasions, the challenge this time was deemed to be even greater. Rennes, Torino and Sporting Lisbon were all put to the sword before the semi-final against old foes Bayern Munich. A 1–1 draw in Germany was followed by a 2–0 home win and the Gers were off to Barcelona to face Moscow Dynamo.

It was Waddell's finest hour and Rangers 3–2 victory brought home a European trophy that the club and its supporters had craved so badly and it set the seal on his managerial reign. He handed the responsibility over to Jock Wallace but remained a very influential figure behind the scenes until the mid-1980s.

Waddell died in 1992 but his influence at Ibrox remains as strong as ever.

George Young (1941–1957)
BORN: 27 October 1922, Grangemouth

APPEARANCES: 428
GOALS: 31

HONOURS WON WITH RANGERS
League titles (6) – 1946/47, 1948/49, 1949/50, 1952/53, 1955/56, 1956/57
Scottish Cups (4) – 1947/48, 1948/49, 1949/50, 1952/53
League Cups (2) – 1946/47, 1948/49
CAPS: 53 (Scotland)

RANGERS HAVE been fortunate to have had some fantastic captains in their history and there are many who believe that George 'Corky' Young was the greatest of them all. He earned his nickname because of the lucky champagne cork he carried in his pocket, but it hardly seems an appropriate nickname for a man who stood 6ft 2in tall and weighed 15 stone. Young was a massive man in every sense and his influence on both Rangers and the national team was colossal.

Originally a centre half, Young moved to right back to allow Willie Woodburn to fill the central area. They were two of the six men who comprised the famous Iron Curtain defence. He had many qualities – most obviously as a tough defender. He was awesome in the air and a fierce tackler, his long legs often preventing the opposition breaching the Rangers back line. His fitness was such that between the autumn of 1948 and the summer of 1953 he missed a mere five League games out of the 150 that Rangers played.

But perhaps his greatest ability was to turn defence into attack with incredible speed. He could launch a ball 60 yards or more with the minimum of effort and it invariably found the front men, and players like Willie Waddell and Willie Thornton thrived on the breakaway. Young and Rangers won six titles in ten years, including the Treble in 1948/49, mostly battling with the great Hibernian team of the era. The Edinburgh club won three titles and finished runners-up to Rangers on three occasions.

Young also collected two Scottish League Cup and four Scottish Cup winner's medals – none quite so fulfilling for him as the 4–1 victory over Clyde at Hampden on 23 April 1949 when he scored twice from the penalty spot.

Such a career is bound to earn admirers. Eric Caldow, a teammate initially and subsequently a great captain himself, is in no doubt about Young's standing in the grand scheme of things, 'He had a fantastic presence at the back and was a natural leader. Every player looked up to him and had everything you could wish for in a defender . . . He was a big man who was good in the air, was a fierce tackler and also had a lot of skill. He was a truly great Rangers player.' John Greig, a fantastic skipper in his own right in the 1960s and 1970s, added, 'George epitomised what being a Rangers captain was all about. He was known as the "Gentle Giant" as well as "Corky" and although he was a very imposing player, he was a fair one.'

Young played 53 times for Scotland, appearing in 34 consecutive matches at a time when there were far fewer international matches than there are today. Indeed, it took nearly two decades for his caps record to be surpassed.

He led Scotland a record 48 times but his influence was far more substantial than any captain of the modern day. Basically, Young ran the Scottish side in the days when committees picked teams and there was no manager. Remarkably, he arranged training, theatre visits and even booked local transport for the team. He announced he would play his final game for Scotland against Spain in Madrid on 26 May 1957 – but, cruelly, the selectors did not pick him.

During his playing days and beyond he also ran a coffee shop with goalkeeper George Niven in Glasgow's Hope Street which was a popular haunt. And when he left Rangers at the end of the 1956/57 season, and stopped playing the game, he began to concentrate on his hotel business. He returned to football for a few years in the early 1960s to manage Third Lanark.

There was considerable controversy in 1985 when Rangers refused to allow a testimonial match for George to be played at Ibrox, believing that if they did it would spark a spate of requests from other former players. Rangers also banned their players from taking part and the game went ahead at Brockville with a Scottish League XI beating an Anglo Select XI, managed by Don Revie. Fortunately, the rift was healed seven years later when chairman Sir David Murray invited George to be his special guest at Ibrox for the match against Hibs in 1992.

He died in January 1997.

Ian McColl (1945–1960)

BORN: 7 June 1927, Alexandria,
West Dunbartonshire

APPEARANCES: 526

GOALS: 14

HONOURS WON WITH RANGERS
League titles (7) – 1946/47,
1948/49, 1949/50, 1952/53,
1955/56, 1956/57, 1958/59
Scottish Cups (5) – 1947/48,
1948/49, 1949/50, 1952/53,
1959/60
League Cups (2) – 1946/47,
1948/49
CAPS: 14 (Scotland)

THE WORD 'legend' is widely used without foundation these days; inappropriately attached to many who are undeserving of the accolade. However, it is entirely applicable when used to describe John Miller McColl, better known as Ian, who is without question one of the greatest players ever to ply his trade with Rangers.

McColl spent 15 years at Ibrox playing in 526 matches, scoring 14 goals and winning 14 major honours – seven League titles, five Scottish Cups and the League Cup twice. He played in the first Rangers team to take part in European competition and, having been an excellent international player who gained 14 caps, he became the Scotland manager in 1961 where he won 16 of 27 matches. However, the statistics don't really tell the full story of someone who was not only a magnificent player but a true gentleman.

Sadly, McColl passed away in October 2008 at the age of 81. He was one of the last remaining links to a golden era for Rangers in the aftermath of the Second World War when football boomed. The period was dominated by Rangers and Hibs. From 1946 until 1953 they had a stranglehold on the title; Rangers winning in 1946/47, 1948/49, 1949/50 and 1952/53 and Hibs triumphant in 1947/48, 1950/51 and 1951/52.

During those years of rivalry, matches between the sides were often billed as the Hibs Famous Five – Gordon Smith, Bobby Johnstone, Lawrie Reilly, Willie Ormond and Eddie Turnbull – v the Rangers Iron Curtain of Bobby Brown, George Young, Jock Shaw, Ian McColl, Willie Woodburn and Sammy Cox. Though Rangers were far from toothless up front at the time, with Willie Waddell, Torry Gillick, Willie Thornton and Jimmy Duncanson among the forwards, during the ten-year period from 1946 to 1956 the defence conceded less than a goal a game – an almost unprecedented defensive record.

In those days the formation as 2–3–5 – two full backs, three half backs and five forwards (two wingers, two inside forwards and a centre forward). McColl played at right half beside the mighty Woodburn, with Cox on the right with Young at right back and Jock Shaw at left back.

But McColl was not just a defender, he could play the game too, a fact that was not lost on goalkeeper Brown, who, coincidentally, also became Scotland manager in his later years. He recalled, 'I remember Ian was very strong in defence but he was also good on the ball and was adept at turning defence into attack. My great memory of him was his fastidiousness at improving his passing. In those days training was basic and all we had was the running track around the pitch. Ian used to play one-twos against the wall and did other things to try to improve his game. He was very dedicated in that regard.

'We had many fine moments in the League and the cups but my abiding memory is a bleak November day when we went to Methil to play East Fife, who were a powerful team at that time and regularly finished in the top five. The game had a 2 p.m. kick-off to help the local miners in terms of their shifts. They would be down the pits at five that morning so they could see the game in the afternoon – a game that had been sold out for weeks. Ian was superb that day. I think he cleared two off the line, but he was wonderful in defence and we won the match 2–1.

'There is no doubt he was a great servant to Rangers. He didn't have the greatest quality of life in his latter years and that saddened me.'

His last title triumph came in the 1958/59 season and though still club captain his role had become rather peripheral. He was, however, recalled for the 1960 Scottish Cup final as a replacement for the injured Harold Davis and was a steadying influence as two Jimmy Millar goals gave Rangers a 2–0 win over Kilmarnock.

He was still officially a Rangers player the following season when he was appointed manager of Scotland, a position he held for four years. One of his finest matches in charge was the 1963 clash with England at Wembley when Rangers legend Jim Baxter scored both goals in a 2–1 win. The victory was all the more remarkable as Eric Caldow broke his leg and Davie Wilson had to move to left back as there were no substitutes in these days.

In 27 matches as Scotland manager he won 16 times which is undoubtedly a record to be proud of. But in 1965 he moved south to manage Sunderland, deciding to take Baxter's mercurial talents with him. Sadly, the move was not successful as Slim Jim had started to have more fun off the field than on it.

Another Scotland manager Walter Smith remembers watching McColl in action, and summed up his 15 years at Ibrox, saying, 'Ian was a fantastic stalwart for Rangers as part of the Iron Curtain defence . . . He is someone I can remember coming to watch playing for the club when I was a boy and he later went on to have a successful career in management as well . . . Anyone who goes and plays over 500 games for Rangers has made a significant contribution to the club and Ian was no different.'

Bobby Brown (1946–1956)
BORN: 19 March 1923, Dunipace, nr Falkirk

APPEARANCES: 296
GOALS: 0

HONOURS WON WITH RANGERS
League titles (3) – 1946/47, 1948/49, 1949/50
Scottish Cups (3) – 1947/48, 1948/49, 1949/50
League Cups (2) – 1946/47, 1948/49
CAPS: 3 (Scotland)

A HIGHLY talented goalkeeper, Bobby Brown was the last line in the famous Iron Curtain defence and was undoubtedly a fantastic player for the club both in terms of consistency of appearance and performance. He missed only one League match in six years and played in 179 consecutive matches during a wonderful period for Rangers and football in general as massive crowds flocked to enjoy it all in the post-war environment. Brown achieved 109 clean sheets during his 296 appearances – a statistic that reveals much about his abilities between the posts.

Brown was a key figure in Bill Struth's side – one of the strongest in the legendary manager's 34 years at Ibrox – but even he sometimes felt the full force of the boss's wrath, for example, following a mistake in front of 131,975 people during the 1948 Scottish Cup final against Morton. Brown recalled, 'There was a tremendous gale blowing up and down Hampden, and it was emphasised clearly that not only had I to be in charge of the six-yard box but also ready for any high balls coming down within the 18-yard line.

'Morton kicked off and within 30 seconds their left half Whyte got the ball and, bearing in mind the wind, he launched this ball into the air towards my goal. I flew out to try to reach it but sadly misjudged it and it not only went over my head but it bounced once, twice, three times into an empty net . . . There was dead silence from the Rangers supporters, not to mention the players, as you can imagine, as I was lying on the turf.

'We managed to get to half time with no further scoring. We were in the dressing room and suddenly, as I stood up to tie my laces, Mr Struth, who always carried a stick, hit me across the backside. I think I must have jumped about three feet in the air. He shouted at me, "Pay attention to your work."

'We went out on the second half and I prayed that we would get an equaliser. Thankfully we did when, with about six or seven minutes to go, Torry Gillick scored.

'We had earned a replay and we duly won it when Billy Williamson scored the only goal. I was very much a relieved man.'

Brown had been a Queen's Park player before the war and had served in the Fleet Air Arm, a branch of the Royal Navy responsible for the operation of aircraft, during the conflict, guesting for Portsmouth, Plymouth, Chester and Chelsea during those years. Tall, blond and agile, Brown had actually played for Scotland against England before he joined Rangers in a wartime international at Villa Park. The Scots lost 3–2 but Bobby was judged to have played well.

He turned professional when he signed for Rangers in May 1946 but only as a part-time player. At other times he worked as a PE teacher at Denny High School in Falkirk. He recalled those early years at Ibrox, 'I came out of the services in 1946 and it gave me a great deal of pleasure to find that Rangers wanted me to sign. I was privileged to become part of the Iron Curtain defence which was legendary and I had the fortune to play in front of incredible crowds – sometimes as many as 150,000 people.

'We had a great rivalry with Hibs at that time. We had fantastic games against them in the 1940s and 1950s. They had the Famous Five forward line and we had the Iron Curtain defence. Many said they would have loved to have seen the two combined in the Scotland team but it never quite happened that all of us played at once. We used to go to Easter Road and play in front of crowds in excess of 50,000 and that could be doubled when they came to Ibrox.

'Of course, we had brilliant forward players then too, like Waddell, Thornton and Duncanson as well as Jimmy Caskie. But there was something special about the Iron Curtain defence. We all seemed to click perfectly and we got on well together. It seemed natural to us.'

Rangers and Hibs traded the title for seven years following the resumption of official competition after the war, with Rangers winning on four occasions and Hibs winning three crowns. Brown won three of these championships, playing in every game during 1948/49 when Rangers secured their first ever domestic Treble. He also earned three Scottish Cup and two League Cup winner's medals.

Following a 5–0 defeat at Tynecastle in the League Cup at the beginning of the 1952/53 season, Brown lost his place to new recruit George Niven who kept him out for the rest of that season. Brown won the jersey back for most of the following season – Struth's last as manager – but Niven became No. 1 thereafter and in May 1956 Brown was transferred to Falkirk for £2,200.

Within a year he had retired from playing and later became manager of St Johnstone, guiding them into the top division on two occasions and then keeping them there. In February 1967 he was appointed manager of Scotland. Incredibly, his first match in charge was against England in a European Championships qualifier at Wembley, a match that is remembered to this day. The fact that Scotland beat England – then world champions – 3–2 on their own patch does not really tell the story of how the Scots, captained by John Greig, humiliated the old enemy with Jim Baxter as protagonist in chief.

Brown had mixed fortunes as national team manager, winning nine games, drawing eight and losing eleven, but he was often hampered by withdrawals as clubs 'encouraged' their players to pull out of international squads. He left the Scotland post in the summer of 1971 and moved into business but continued to have an involvement in football by scouting for Plymouth Argyle before his retirement.

Sammy Cox (1946–1955)
BORN: 13 April 1924, Darvel,
Ayrshire

GAMES: 310
GOALS: 18

HONOURS WON WITH RANGERS
League titles (3) – 1948/49,
1949/50, 1952/53
Scottish Cups (3) – 1947/48,
1948/49, 1949/50
League Cup (1) –1948/49
CAPS: 25 (Scotland)

IF YOU happened to bump into any Rangers supporters in Canada and mentioned the name Sammy Cox you would immediately command their undivided attention. The man – who played in the left-half slot in the legendary Iron Curtain defence of the 1940s and early 1950s – is honorary president of most of them! Cox emigrated to Canada in 1959 at a time when thousands of Scots were doing so and he has been a key figure in the North American Rangers Supporters Association.

They awarded him life membership in 2001 and they have relished having such a celebrated figure in their midst. He said in 2002, 'When you walk into these Rangers clubs it's like walking into a bar in Glasgow. Close your eyes and you are sure you're there.'

Cox had been a promising young player and turned out for Queen's Park, Third Lanark and Dundee during the Second World War. He lived in Darvel in Ayrshire, just along the street

103

from former Light Blue Alex Smith, and he signed professional forms for Rangers in Smith's house. Cox joined the club in the summer of 1946, on the same day as goalkeeper Bobby Brown, the last two pieces of what would become the Iron Curtain defence, and they became great teammates in a great Rangers side.

Cox made his League debut at right back in August 1946 in the 4–2 win at Motherwell. He played 13 League games that season in four different positions, also appearing at right half, left half and inside right. He had good technical ability and a quick football brain which gave him a tremendous positional sense. However, it was his tigerish tackling which made him a key player for Rangers.

By the 1947/48 season he had established himself in the side and played in every League game, including one on the left wing against Clyde. Cox even got the winner in a 2–1 victory. He won the first of his club honours with Rangers that season, a Scottish Cup winner's medal after a replay in the final against Morton.

By the following season he had moved to left half and George Young had switched to right back to complete the legendary defence which also included keeper Bobby Brown, left back Jock Shaw, right half Ian McColl and centre half Willie Woodburn. That Iron Curtain laid the foundations for Rangers to become the first Scottish team to win the Treble, which they did in 1948/49. Cox missed only one League game as Rangers took the title by a point from Dundee. He also picked up his one League Cup medal in March that season with a 2–0 victory over Raith Rovers and his second Scottish Cup winner's medal in the 4–1 defeat of Clyde in April.

It was a momentous year for Cox as he also won his first Scotland cap, playing an inside forward role, in a 3–0 defeat against France in Paris. He moved to left back a month later and played in a 3–1 win over England at Wembley. In a distinguished international career, he appeared 24 times for his country and was made captain for his farewell appearance, against England in 1954.

Back at Ibrox, Cox was ever-present again in 1949/50 as Rangers retained the League title. Cox also got his third and final Scottish Cup winner's medal that season as East Fife were beaten 3–0 in the final.

The next two seasons were barren as Rangers failed to win a major honour. Cox played fewer games, varying between left half and left back. But in 1952/53, he was back in favour at left half and won the last of his three championship medals, though he missed out on a fourth Scottish Cup winner's medal as he was not selected for the final against Aberdeen.

Halfway through the 1953/54 season he was switched again to left back and by the next season his appearances were down to 12 League games. He played his last match in a Rangers jersey in the 2–1 defeat by Aberdeen in the sixth round of the Scottish Cup on 19 February 1955.

A modest man, he said of his time in one of the footballing world's most famous defences, 'In all honesty Bill Struth did not know that much about football tactics, but he knew if you were playing badly! He put together the team and we took it from there. Jock Shaw and I used to decide who we were picking up and we just got on with it . . . I was lucky to be a part of that defensive system.'

Cox spent a few seasons with East Fife before making the move across the Atlantic where he is still held in the highest esteem.

Johnny Hubbard (1949–1959)

BORN: 16 December 1930, Pretoria, South Africa

APPEARANCES: 236
GOALS: 109

HONOURS WON WITH RANGERS
League titles (3) – 1952/53, 1955/56, 1956/57
Scottish Cup (1) – 1952/53
CAPS: 1 (South Africa)

RANGERS CAN boast some superb strikers over the years whose achievements are revered by supporters of all ages. From Bob McPhail, Willie Thornton through Jimmy Millar, Jim Forrest, Colin Stein, Derek Johnstone, Ally McCoist and Mark Hateley, the opposition net bulged with regularity. These great men grabbed cup final winners, crucial League strikes and vital goals in the European arena.

However, there is one thing they cannot boast and it is a record which has stood since 1955 and held by a diminutive South African. Remarkably, Johnny Hubbard is the last Rangers player ever to score a League hat-trick against Celtic and he remembers it as if it was yesterday. Can you imagine? New Year's Day at Ibrox, a full house and you contrive to pop the ball into the Celtic net three times – and you're a winger? It's Roy of the Rovers stuff.

Hubbard can't believe that his record still stands but he is fiercely proud of it. It is perhaps unusual that, given there have been high scoring wins for both sides over the years, so few hat-tricks have been achieved. Stevie Chalmers is the last Celtic player to score three in an Old Firm League match and that was in 1966.

Of course there have been trebles in other matches and McCoist can boast two – in the 1983/84 League Cup final and the 1986 Glasgow Cup final, which was played by full-strength sides in front of a sold-out Ibrox. However, Hubbard is still the daddy after all these years. The great pity is that there is no video evidence of his remarkable achievement but those who were there – including Sir Alex Ferguson – feel privileged. Ferguson recently rated Hubbard's first goal as the greatest he has ever seen so that gives you some indication of its quality.

Hubbard said, 'It's amazing to think that my hat-trick still stands when you consider all the strikers who have played with Rangers since. I can't believe it is the last time a Rangers player scored a hat-trick in a League match against Celtic. Six years earlier Jimmy Duncanson did the same thing when he scored three against Celtic on New Year's Day. It's a great record to have and I wonder when it might be beaten.'

So what happened that fateful day? It had been a fairly uneventful match with honours even after the first 45 minutes and it was late in the game that Hubbard wrote his name into the history books. He remembers, 'It was quite a quiet game. It was 1-1 at half time and Billy Simpson had scored for us. Then with 14 minutes to go John Little passed the ball to me just outside our box and I just went on a run from there.

'I beat Bobby Evans, Willie Haughney, Jock Stein and Meechan and a couple more besides. Suddenly I only had the goalkeeper to beat, I waltzed around him and I walked the ball into the net. It was just a lucky run! I heard that Sir Alex Ferguson thought it was the best goal he has ever seen. That was a great thing to hear.'

The Rangers fans could scarcely believe what they had witnessed, but Hubbard gave them more. 'The second goal was a little bit unusual too,' he continued, 'because I didn't use my feet or head to score it. I passed the ball to Billy [Simpson] and went off down the left wing. I ran into the box, he crossed the ball over and I chested the ball into the net.'

With one minute of the match left, Hubbard used another of his great skills – he scored 54 out of the 57 penalties he took for Rangers – when Derek Grierson was pulled down in the box, and chalked up his historic hat-trick from the spot.

Hubbard came to Scotland in 1949 and was the first South African to play for Rangers. Although a small man, he was a key player in the 1950s team, winning the Double in 1952/53, top scoring in 1955/56 with 27 goals and playing a key role in the 1956/57 title triumph, scoring 15 goals in 33 games.

Although he had a tremendous scoring record for the Gers, Hubbard had not always been a goalscorer, 'Originally I was an inside right, but when I was 16 I was told to play outside left and that's where I stayed. I was naturally right-footed, but Mr Struth used to say to me, "I want you to get down the left, beat your back and get your cross in." When I made my debut against Partick Thistle in September 1949 we beat them 2–0 and both goals came from my crosses. I was good at doing what I was told!'

Hubbard was also in at the beginning of Rangers' adventures in European football, when the club played in only the second European Cup competition in 1956/57, and he scored in the away leg against OGC Nice.

He was transferred to Bury in 1959 for £6,000 and scored 29 goals in 109 appearances for the Shakers. He returned to Scotland in 1962 and signed for Ayr United where he spent two seasons before retiring in 1964. He settled in Ayrshire and became a PE teacher though he was also involved in football development. In keeping with his long-term relationship with Ibrox, one of the young players who benefited from his expertise was Steven Naismith, who joined Rangers in 2007 from Kilmarnock for £2 million.

Billy Simpson (1950–1959)
BORN: 12 December 1929, Belfast

APPEARANCES: 239
GOALS: 163

HONOURS WON WITH RANGERS
League titles (3) – 1952/53,
1955/56, 1956/57
Scottish Cup (1) – 1952/53
CAPS: 12 (Northern Ireland)

ALL BOYS steeped in football pretend to be their hero as they kick a ball about, whether it is on a cobbled street, in a public park or on an indoor synthetic surface. They try to copy their idols, either in the way they play or perhaps the way they celebrate a goal. One Belfast kid fell into this category but the huge difference was that his emulation became reality. Billy Simpson actually lived the dream when he sailed across the water to sign for Rangers in the autumn of 1950 and became a fantastic player for nearly nine years.

Simpson recalled, 'As a wee boy I used to play football in the streets of Belfast and we all kidded on we were one of the Rangers players. I was always Willie Thornton because I loved the way he played. Little did I know that I would not only play beside him but I would replace him in the side when he retired.'

Rangers needed fresh blood up front at the time and manager Bill Struth sent Torry Gillick to Belfast to check out Simpson, who was playing for Linfield. When a more than favourable report was returned, Struth sanctioned what was then a record transfer fee of £11,500 to beat off Everton who were also in contention to sign the exciting striker.

It proved to be a bargain. Simpson's goals return of 163 in 239 games was sensational. His first goals for the club came in the form of a hat-trick in a 5–0 win over East Fife on 23 December 1950. It was the start of a goals trail that would last nearly a decade. Initially, he played as an inside forward but the No. 9 jersey soon became his because he was a natural finisher. He might not have had the same elegance as others but his courage was commendable and his positional sense even better.

Like Thornton, the man he replaced, Simpson was a fantastic header of the ball. If the delivery was right he would get his head on it and invariably score. Struth, though, felt there was something that needed tweaking when Billy first joined the club. The legendary manager was a former athlete of some renown and he noticed that Simpson's speed was being affected by the length of his strides. He sent him to nearby Bellahouston Harriers where the sprint coach taught him to take shorter strides so that he would be quicker over the first 10 or 15 yards. Struth is not credited with being a master tactician but he certainly knew how to enhance the components of his team.

It was season 1952/53 that it all came together for the former Linfield man when he played a huge part in leading Rangers to a League and Cup Double. Rangers reached the Scottish Cup final and were due to face Aberdeen on 25 April and Billy could not wait for the showpiece game. He was shattered, therefore, when Struth – who demanded the best from his players at all times – told him he was being left out because he had been sent off in a League match a week earlier. John Prentice was brought into the team and Willie Paton played centre forward. Simpson watched on with envy from the old Main Stand at Hampden. Perhaps it was fate, but the game finished 1–1 and a replay was ordered for 29 April. Simpson was brought back in and he scored the only goal of the game.

The League race was incredibly tight and in the end it needed goal average to separate Rangers and Hibs. Simpson had scored 21 goals in the campaign, including one in a 3–1 win against Dundee three days after the cup final. Needing a final point from the last match of the season against Queen of the South, Willie Waddell equalised 15 minutes from time to secure the title.

Struth retired at the end of the following season, ending an astonishing 34 years as manager at Ibrox, a time in which he had won 18 of the 27 titles Rangers had contested. Scot Symon took over and needed time to freshen the side, but Simpson remained and flourished. He helped Rangers to the title in 1955/56 and then the following season he was equally influential as the Light Blues held off Hearts to retain their crown.

The Tynecastle men had enjoyed a seven-point lead at one point but Rangers produced a fantastic run of form in the second half of the season and, when Simpson headed the only goal at Tynecastle on 13 April 1957, it seemed to break the Edinburgh outfit. Later that year Simpson also experienced the kudos of scoring the winning goal for Northern Ireland at Wembley when he headed the third goal in a 3–2 victory over England. Northern Ireland have only ever recorded one other win in the famous stadium.

Hearts gained revenge on Rangers in the 1957/58 season and although the Light Blues reversed the trend again the following season, Simpson had left by the time the title was won. He moved to Stirling Albion initially and then teamed up with Willie Thornton again, who was manager at Partick Thistle.

Simpson also had a short spell with Oxford United but

when a knee injury ended his career he returned to Glasgow where he got a job working for Remington Rand in Govan. Always a keen Rangers man and having never lost his Belfast brogue, Simpson still visits Ibrox regularly, usually in the company of his close friend Johnny Hubbard.

Chapter 4
A Classic Team
(1956–1966)

Eric Caldow
Ralph Brand
Alex Scott
Bobby Shearer
Billy Ritchie
Jimmy Millar
Harold Davis
Davie Wilson
Davie Provan
Ronnie McKinnon
Jim Baxter
Willie Henderson

SUPPORTERS WHO followed Rangers in the Scot Symon period still insist that the team he built and moulded in the early 1960s was peerless.

Rangers enjoyed lavish success at the time with six championship wins and five Scottish Cup successes and they also reached the European Cup-Winners' Cup final in 1961 having made the semi-final of the European Cup the previous year.

They had fantastic entertainers like Jim Baxter and Willie Henderson and sensational strikers in Jimmy Millar and Ralph Brand.

There was power and poise at the back in the shape of Bobby Shearer, Ronnie McKinnon and Eric Caldow while Davie Wilson was a winger whose goals return was quite spectacular.

Harold Davis, who came close to death in the Korean War, and Alex Scott were in at the beginning of the Symon era and were hugely important in his early successes.

As if dominating the scene was not joyful enough for the Rangers supporters, great rivals Celtic were very much in their shadow and regularly put to the sword.

The zenith was the 1963/64 season when the Light Blues scorched to the second Treble in their history, holding off Willie Waddell's Kilmarnock in the league, hammering Morton 5–0 in the League Cup final and defeating Dundee 3–1 in the Scottish Cup final.

Eric Caldow (1953–1966)
BORN: 14 May 1934, Cumnock, Ayrshire

APPEARANCES: 407
GOALS: 25

HONOURS WON WITH RANGERS
League titles (5) – 1955/56, 1956/57, 1958/59, 1960/61, 1962/63
Scottish Cups (2) – 1959/60, 1961/62
League Cups (3) – 1960/61, 1961/62, 1964/65
CAPS: 40 (Scotland)

A SENSE of pride and joy enveloped Eric Caldow as he walked out at Wembley Stadium on 6 April 1963 to face England, and with good reason. He was captaining his country for the 14th time in what was his 40th appearance for Scotland. He was also captain of one of the greatest Rangers teams of all time who were on their way to the championship again and with the promise of Scottish Cup glory to come. Having already won eight major trophies at Ibrox at the age of 30, the boundaries seemed limitless for the immensely talented full back.

Wham! Tottenham striker Bobby Smith smashed into Caldow with such severity that he broke his leg in three places. The injury ended his international career and denied him greater glories with Rangers. It may seem strange to open a chapter on a great Ranger on such a negative note but the incident was undoubtedly pivotal in his career. Caldow was prevented from being part of only the second Rangers team to win the Treble the following season and, by the time he did make it back into the team, many of his teammates were starting to leave. But football was different then and challenges that would now be considered something akin to grievous bodily harm were commonplace.

Despite all that, Eric Caldow had the distinction of playing in two great Rangers sides having been destined to play for the club since he was 14. A brilliant full back, who was equally at home on either side, he made his debut in 1953 at the age of 19 in the company of players such as Woodburn, Cox and Waddell, and ended his Ibrox days in 1966 alongside Greig, Henderson and McKinnon. He was a good tackler who would time his challenges well. But his greatest gift was his speed. He always had enough pace to recover and get back at his man if beaten on the ground.

He recalled how it all began, 'I was playing football for my school and also for a local youth team when a schoolteacher, Alex Sloan, saw me play and recommended me to Rangers director George Brown who was a friend of his.

'Initially, Rangers farmed me out to play for Muirkirk Juniors for a couple of seasons but I was brought back to Ibrox in 1952. It took me about a year to get into the team but, by the end of my second season, I was an established first-team player.'

He made his debut in a 4–2 League Cup win over Ayr in September 1953. He played eight League games that term, standing in for the great George Young – the man he admired the most. By 1955/56, when he won his first championship medal, he had become a regular at right back. But the following season, when he won his second title, he began to play more at left back, forming a partnership with Bobby Shearer.

The penalty spot played a major part in Caldow's career. Firstly by bringing the skipper great joy as it gave Rangers a vital win in their pursuit of the 1958/59 championship. He said, 'My favourite goal for Rangers was the penalty I took against Celtic on 1 January 1959. I remember the match very well as it was close to being abandoned as the conditions were so bad.

'We went a goal down after 15 minutes but we managed to equalise four minutes later. We were then awarded a penalty on 63 minutes and I stepped up to take it . . . As I was preparing myself for the penalty I remember that Celtic's Bobby Evans tried desperately to distract me by saying that the game should be called off because you couldn't see the penalty spot. Anyway, I went ahead and took the penalty and it gave us a memorable 2–1 victory.'

But he felt differing emotions in the spring of 1961 when he led Rangers into their first European final – the Cup-Winners' Cup final – having disposed of Ferencvaros, Borussia Mönchengladbach and Wolverhampton Wanderers, then one of the strongest teams in England, along the way. Skipper Caldow, however, was unable to lift the trophy, as Rangers lost 4–1 on aggregate to Fiorentina. Sadly Caldow also missed a penalty.

However, there was compensation in both the Scottish Cup and the League Cup in 1961/62. Hearts were beaten 3–1 in a replayed League Cup final and St Mirren 2–0 in the Scottish FA Cup. His fifth and final championship came in 1962/63.

Before the horrific incident with Smith at Wembley, Caldow had been an automatic choice for Scotland since his debut in April 1957 – also against England at Wembley – and had missed only two games for Scotland in six years.

It took Caldow a long time to recover from his broken leg and the following season he played only three League games. His place at left back was taken by Davie Provan. By 1964/65

Caldow had fought back and re-established himself. Provan switched to right back and Caldow played 26 League games on the left. He got his third League Cup winner's medal as Rangers beat Celtic 2–1 to lift the trophy once again. But that was to be his swansong. Caldow was 32 and played only three games in his final season of 1965/66. Remarkably for a defender, he was never booked once while playing for Rangers.

He played one season with Stirling Albion and then moved to England where he ran Corby Town for two years. He returned to Ayrshire in 1970 to become manager of junior side Hurlford United and his successes there led him to becoming manager of Stranraer in 1973 and he had two seasons at Stair Park. Always immaculate and engaging, Caldow is still a regular at Ibrox on match days working for the hospitality department.

Ralph Brand (1954–1965)

BORN: 8 December 1936,
Edinburgh

APPEARANCES: 317
GOALS: 206

HONOURS WON WITH RANGERS
League titles (4) – 1958/59,
1960/61, 1962/63, 1963/64
Scottish Cups (3) – 1961/62,
1962/63, 1963/64
League Cups (4) – 1960/61,
1961/62, 1963/64, 1964/65
CAPS: 8 (Scotland)

IN 1999 Rangers supporters voted Ally McCoist and Mark Hateley as the best striking partnership in the club's history – and there are few reasons to argue with their selection. However, if you talk to fans of a certain vintage they will tell you that the double act of Ralph Brand and Jimmy Millar from the all-conquering 1960s team was equally as good – if not better.

In four seasons between 1960/61 and 1963/64 Rangers ruled the roost. During this devastating spell, the Light Blues won the League title three times, the Scottish Cup three times and the League Cup three times. And it was in 1964 when it all came together as the remarkable Scottish Cup final triumph over Dundee gave Rangers the Treble – a clean sweep of the honours which had only been achieved once before, in 1949, also by Rangers.

Brand was a player ahead of his time; a man who thought

deeply about football when tactics were sparsely employed in the Scottish game. The chemistry between him and the courageous Jimmy Millar was perfect and during this period of Rangers' dominance they scored an awesome 254 goals. Brand explained, 'Jimmy came by train from Edinburgh like me and we ended up travelling together. In those days the journey would sometimes take as long as two hours so it gave us time to chat. We would discuss what had gone on in matches and hopefully take things from this to make things better the next time.

'I used to think about the game a lot. I always felt that to spend only two hours training with hardly any ball work was not enough to improve one's play. I used to go back out on to the pitch myself but that was a bit lonely and not much use as I was only kicking the ball about myself. I had nobody to pass to. Then I persuaded Jimmy to go back with me and things clicked from there.

'Our trainer at that time, Davie Kinnear, had his training programme mapped out for weeks at a time. It was good but I didn't think it was enough for us. But we had to be inventive to get the chance to do extra training. We had to boot a ball right across the terracing to hide it and then we could go and get it after training was finished.

'Jimmy and I developed a good understanding. In those days the centre halves were able to come right through you to win the ball, so Jimmy and I worked on playing wall passes to get past defenders rather than risk injury! It was little things like that which contributed to the overall picture and it certainly worked for us at the time.'

Bill Struth spotted the 15-year-old Brand on TV when he played for Scotland against England in a schoolboy international at Wembley in 1952 and swiftly signed him on a provisional contract that summer. He turned professional in the spring of

1954 and made his debut at the age of 17 at outside right against Kilmarnock on 6 November. It was some debut. Brand scored twice as Rangers won 6–0.

He spent the next two years on National Service and returned in December 1957 to forge his partnership with Millar. In 1960/61 he was ever-present in the League and scored 24 goals in 34 matches. He finished the season with 40 goals in all competitions – the highest mark of his career – including five in the run to the European Cup-Winners' Cup final. Millar added a further 23 goals in all competitions that year.

Brand had great balance, was fearless and possessed great speed off the mark. And though only 5ft 7in tall, he was also good in the air. He used all his skills to score goals for fun. He scored four in a match three times – against Hibernian in a 6–1 League Cup win in 1959, in a 6–0 League victory over Raith in 1961 and against East Stirling in a 7–2 Scottish Cup tie in 1963. Such was his form in that 1962/63 season that he also scored hat-tricks in consecutive League games against Kilmarnock and Raith.

Brand played in four championship winning teams – 1958/59, 1960/61, 1962/63 and the Treble-winning side of 1963/64. But it was in the Scottish Cup that he left a record goalscoring mark. In the 1962 final, he scored the opener as Rangers beat St Mirren 2–0. In the following year's final, he scored in a 1–1 draw with Celtic. In the replay Jim Baxter gave one of his memorable performances as Celtic were torn apart. Brand scored twice – one of them from 25 yards – as Rangers won 3–0. Then, in 1964, Brand wrote himself into the history books by getting another goal as Dundee were beaten 3–1 in the final. He became the first man to score in three consecutive Scottish Cup finals.

It's a record that still stands. He is modest about his

achievement, 'I was not really aware that my record would be something that would stand for years and still stands to this day. When we played the responsibility for scoring goals was shared and nobody really kept tabs about who did what season by season.'

Brand also won four League Cup winner's medals – scoring goals in the final against Kilmarnock in a 2–0 victory in 1960/61, and again as Hearts were beaten 3–1 in a replay in 1961/62. In all, Brand played in seven cup finals for Rangers, scoring six goals and never finishing on the losing side.

He won eight Scotland caps, making his debut against Northern Ireland in 1961, and scored eight times. He would have had more had not Denis Law been in possession of the No. 10 jersey for Scotland at the time.

His last match for Rangers was on 23 April 1965 when he scored the only goal in a 1–0 defeat of Third Lanark in the last League game of the season. Brand was transferred to Manchester City in August 1965 for a £30,000 fee. Two years later he moved to Sunderland and ended his career at Raith Rovers.

He used to drive a taxi in Edinburgh before retiring and now works for the hospitality department at Ibrox on match days.

Alex Scott (1954–1963)

BORN: 22 December 1936, Falkirk

APPEARANCES: 331

GOALS: 108

HONOURS WON WITH RANGERS
League titles (4) – 1955/56,
1956/57, 1958/59, 1960/61
Scottish Cup (1) – 1959/60
League Cups (2) – 1960/61,
1961/62
CAPS: 11 (of 16 for Scotland)

THERE WAS a sense of déjà vu about the arrival and departure of Alex Scott as a Rangers player as he displaced a legend and then made way for a young upstart. Willie Waddell was essentially winding down his career when the teenage Scott burst on to the scene in the mid-1950s, and it was the precocity of Willie Henderson that ultimately forced Scott's transfer to Everton in February 1963.

However, in eight years in the Rangers first team, Scott was a hugely effective player both at home and in Europe, which was new territory in those days. He had been signed provisionally aged 17 from Camelon Thistle in 1954 and then officially moved in the spring of the following year. Remarkably, the powerful, pacy and productive winger scored a hat-trick on his debut – a 4–1 win over home town team Falkirk.

He won a championship-winner's medal in his first full season, 1955/56, playing in all 34 matches and scoring nine goals. It seemed as though the transition from Waddell to Scott was seamless.

He was just as effective the following season as Rangers held on to their crown, Scott chipping in with 12 goals this time as well as creating more than twice that number for others. Alex won his third championship medal in 1958/59 when Hearts were pipped by two points and, again, he never missed a match.

His last title came in 1960/61 and it was as thrilling a finish as you can imagine. Needing a victory in the final game of the season against Ayr United to hold off nearest challengers Kilmarnock, manager Scot Symon played Scott at centre forward and he blasted a hat-trick as Rangers won 7–3.

Perhaps it was his style, but Scott also seemed to thrive on the nascent European stage. He scored against Anderlecht and Red Star Bratislava as Rangers reached the semi-finals of the European Cup in 1960, only to succumb to Eintracht Frankfurt who ensured their place in the historic final, which Real Madrid famously won 7–3 at Hampden.

The following season, with Rangers in the Cup-Winners' Cup, Scott scored four times in a campaign which saw the Light Blues become the first British team to make it to the final, where they met Fiorentina. The Italians, managed by the legendary Hungarian Nandor Hidegkuti, were too cute for Rangers winning 2–0 at Ibrox and then 2–1 in Florence in a two-legged final. Scott scored Rangers' consolation goal, one of 12 European goals he registered – a record he shared with Ralph Brand and Jimmy Millar until it was later surpassed by the prolific Ally McCoist in 1997.

Scott found more consolation in domestic cup competitions. Earlier that season he had scored the clinching goal in the League Cup final when Kilmarnock were beaten 2–0. He won the same trophy again the following season when Hearts were beaten 3–1 in a replay. But by then Alex's reign at Ibrox was all but over as a young precocious Willie Henderson was fast emerging as one of the club's most exciting talents. Incredibly, the following year, 1962, Scott was playing for Rangers reserves – having been replaced by Henderson – when he was selected by Scotland to face England at Hampden on 14 April. The Scots had not beaten the Auld Enemy at Hampden for 25 years and Scott was one of four Rangers players in the side – Baxter, Caldow (the captain) and Wilson the others – as they recorded a famous 2–0 victory. Wilson scored the first goal and Caldow clinched the victory with a late penalty.

It was one of 16 caps Scott collected during his career and his inclusion by manager Ian McColl, a Rangers legend in his own right, was no doubt influenced by the fact that he had scored a hat-trick in a 6–1 win over Northern Ireland in October the previous year.

With few chances for first-team football once Henderson was in the Rangers team Scott moved to Goodison Park in February 1963 for £39,000, as Everton beat off interest from Tottenham Hotspur, and the ploy paid rich dividends. Within a few months Everton were champions.

At Goodison, Scott was known as 'Chico' because of his swarthy appearance and dubbed the 'Head Waiter' by teammates because of his habit of running with one arm held out stiffly, as if carrying a tray of drinks. He contributed to a memorable era on Merseyside, accompanied by his compatriot Alex Young, for whom he set up countless goals. Though his own goalscoring became more sporadic in England – he scored 26 in 176 games for Everton – he provided several during the club's FA Cup success in 1966.

It was during his time on Merseyside that Scott made his last appearances for Scotland against the world champions

Brazil who were warming up for the 1966 World Cup finals in England. The Scots achieved a creditable 1–1 draw.

In September 1967 he returned to Scotland, joining Hibs just as his younger brother, Jim, also an international, was leaving the Edinburgh club to join Newcastle United. His football circle was completed when he joined Falkirk in 1969/70 and he played for his home town side until he retired in 1972, this time alongside his brother with whom he later went into business. Alex passed away in September 2001.

Bobby Shearer (1955–1965)
BORN: 29 December 1931, Hamilton

APPEARANCES: 407
GOALS: 4

HONOURS WON WITH RANGERS
League titles (6) – 1955/56, 1956/57, 1958/59, 1960/61, 1962/63, 1963/64
Scottish Cups (3) – 1961/62, 1962/63, 1963/64
League Cups (3) – 1960/61, 1961/62, 1963/64
CAPS: 4 (Scotland)

RANGERS FOOTBALL Club has had its fair share of leaders in its time but few have matched the passion, commitment and unbridled loyalty to the cause shown by Bobby Shearer. In basic terms he was a Rangers fanatic – long before he joined the club in 1955 – and it was the ultimate honour for him when he received the captaincy in 1963. He was a man bursting with pride as he led the team to a glorious Treble in 1963/64 as they cleaned up the domestic honours with a fantastic team.

Shearer was a tough guy in every sense of the expression and did not earn the nickname 'Captain Cutlass' for nothing. His tackling was fierce and players knew they had been in a game when they came up against Shearer, who played right back for Scot Symon's all-conquering team.

Indeed, there is a story that one tackle in particular in a pre-

129

season friendly was so severe that he carried through and crashed into a substitute who was on the sidelines – they were only allowed in non-competitive games in those days – and just about cut him in two! The poor substitute had to be taken away for treatment.

Shearer was maybe not the quickest of players but he was strong and influential on those around him – especially emerging young players. John Greig, who became a marvellous captain in his own right, said, 'I have a lot to thank Bobby for. He was the captain of the team when I came in and he really helped me settle. He was a great captain because he led by example. He personified the Rangers spirit with his will to win and it rubbed off on everyone.'

Willie Henderson shares the same view and counts him as a great influence and guide when he was breaking into the team. He said, 'I was 17 when I made my Rangers debut and he was captain at the time. There were not many people I listened to but he was one of them. He was one of those people who, when I look back at my time at Ibrox, was a real true blue Ranger. He played for the jersey and he loved the club.'

Shearer was signed for £2,000 from Hamilton in 1955 having spent five seasons with his local team. He played 16 times in his first season as Rangers held off Aberdeen to win the 1955/56 championship. He learned much during his first campaign playing alongside experienced players like George Young and Ian McColl and the following season scarcely missed a match as the Light Blues retained their crown, this time edging out Hearts. Strong and fit, he put together a run of 165 successive games as Rangers dominated the Scottish scene in the late 1950s and early 1960s.

He was also in at the beginning of the Light Blues' European adventures when he played in the European Cup games in the autumn and winter of 1956. In all he appeared 30 times in Europe for Rangers including the semi-finals of the European Cup in 1960 and the final of the Cup-Winners' Cup the following year when they lost to Fiorentina.

But his sweetest success was probably the title victory in the 1958/59 season because it was Celtic who helped Rangers win it. Rangers were two points clear of Hearts going into the final day but the Tynecastle side had the better goal average. The Light Blues promptly lost 2–1 at home to Aberdeen and the Ibrox fans booed loudly thinking their team had blown the title. However, the jeers turned to cheers when it was announced that their old rivals came to the rescue by defeating Hearts 2–1.

The following season, Shearer proved his commitment to the cause when he ended up as the last line of defence taking over from the injured keeper George Niven after only eight minutes of a League meeting with Hearts. Rangers ran out 3–1 winners.

Sandy Jardine, then a young apprentice at Ibrox, used to clean Shearer's boots as part of his duties and remembers the full back's influence at the club, 'He was a great character. Bobby might not have been the silkiest of soccer players but for commitment, drive and enthusiasm he was faultless. Bobby was a supporter as a kid. He understood the history and the tradition of the club and when he went on the park he had a fantastic will to win . . . In football you can face better players and better teams but if you have that desire to succeed then many times you will.'

Shearer left Rangers in 1965 having spent ten magnificent years with the club. He played one season with Queen of the South before his retirement but then moved into management, becoming Third Lanark's manager in what was to be their last fateful season, 1966/67, following that with a spell as boss at Hamilton Academical in 1970/71. A regular at Ibrox in the intervening years, Bobby passed away on 6 November 2006 aged 74.

Billy Ritchie (1955–1967)
BORN: 11 September 1936,
Newtongrange, Midlothian

APPEARANCES: 340
GOALS: 0

HONOURS WON WITH RANGERS
League titles (2) – 1962/63,
1963/64
Scottish Cups (4) – 1961/62,
1962/63, 1963/64, 1965/66
League Cups (3) – 1961/62,
1963/64, 1964/65
CAPS: 1 (Scotland)

EVERY GREAT team needs a solid base and the all-conquering outfit of the 1960s had Billy Ritchie to rely upon as the last line of defence. For the first few years of his Rangers career he had to battle with George Niven for the No. 1 jersey; but then in an incredible three-year period he played in a European final and won seven major honours.

Those were halcyon days for Rangers but Ritchie earned his place the hard way having his career interrupted by National Service and a severe injury. He recalls, 'I actually first went to Rangers in 1954 but it was not until 1955 that I signed a contract for the first team. Bobby Brown was still there when I joined and, of course, George Niven was another great keeper who was my rival for the position. George and I were great friends though. We got on very well even though we were both after the same thing.'

Billy made his debut on 25 August 1956 at Methil in a League Cup tie against East Fife, a match which Rangers won 4–1. But it was not until the following season that he won the gloves for any length of time, playing in most matches but luckily missing out on the 7–1 thrashing that Celtic imposed on the Light Blues in the League Cup final that season.

Ritchie was then called up for National Service in Cyprus and effectively missed two seasons. He returned in a 2–1 win against Raith Rovers in March 1960 and then played in the Scottish Cup semi-final replay against Celtic a month later, which Rangers won 4–1.

Despite fighting his way back into the No. 1 shirt, fortune did not favour him when he suffered a chipped bone in his ankle in a 3–1 win at Tynecastle on 26 October 1960. He said, 'I couldn't believe it. I had won my place, then gone on National Service and had to win it back again, and then when I suffered the injury I had to do it all again. It was a bad injury which kept me out until the end of March but I managed to win my place back.'

Rangers won the title that year but the injury restricted his League appearances and he was not eligible for a medal. He also missed out on the League Cup final against Kilmarnock in October. But, if that was untimely, his first game back in the first team was the first leg of the semi-final of the Cup-Winners' Cup against Wolves in March 1961.

Ritchie was outstanding in both legs as Rangers won 2–0 at Ibrox and drew 1–1 at Molineux. He recalled, 'It was incredible. I played a reserve game at Motherwell on the Saturday and I was in for the Wolves game on the Wednesday!' That victory meant that Rangers became the first British club to contest a European final. However, they were outmanoeuvred over two legs by Fiorentina, who lifted the trophy after a 4–1 aggregate victory. Ritchie said, 'We attacked both at home and away but the

Italians were more tactically aware than us. I don't think they were any better but they were better tactically . . . In saying that their flying winger Kurt Hamrun was some player – he gave us so many problems.'

Finally, Billy earned some silverware the following season, 1961/62, as the great Rangers team of the period won the cup Double. He claimed medals in the League Cup and Scottish Cup with wins over St Mirren and Hearts respectively. There was more silverware in 1962/63 as Rangers won the title by nine points from Kilmarnock, with Ritchie absent only once. Celtic were hammered 3–0 in the Scottish Cup final and only Kilmarnock stopped a Light Blue Grand Slam when they beat Rangers 3–2 in the semi-final of the League Cup.

But the zenith of what was a tremendously successful Rangers team, as stars like Willie Henderson and Jim Baxter dazzled the Rangers fans and goals rained in from Ralph Brand, Jimmy Millar and Davie Wilson – was 1963/64 when Rangers swept the board for only the second time in the club's history. Billy Ritchie was between the sticks for all 50 games. Again Kilmarnock were their nearest challengers in the League as Rangers produced some irresistible displays. Morton were thrashed 5–0 in the League Cup final in which Jim Forrest scored four – a record which has yet to be beaten.

It was at Hampden on 25 April 1964 in the Scottish Cup final that Rangers had the chance of the Treble. Standing in their way was the excellent Dundee team of the period who had pipped Rangers for the League title two years earlier. Ritchie rates it as his greatest memory – even if the keeper from the other team got all the plaudits! He said, 'If I had to pick one game it would be that Scottish Cup final against Dundee. It was a fantastic game and it's true that the match belonged to Bert Slater. He was superb that day.

'We eventually won 3–1 with two late goals and the Treble was ours. I remember walking off and the referee told me it was the best game he had ever handled.' In summary of Rangers' dominance that season Ritchie said, 'We had great players at that time, no doubt. However, I think it was a team effort more than individuals. We had good balance in the team and every man did his job.'

Ritchie won the League Cup again the following season when two Forrest goals beat Celtic 2–1 and his last honour came in the 1966 Scottish Cup final when the boot of Kai Johansen famously decided the Old Firm replay in favour of the Light Blues.

Sadly, he lost his place in the early part of the 1966/67 season to Norrie Martin. He even found himself omitted from the reserve team and so he left for Partick Thistle. He said: 'I thought I still had something to offer. I was completely out of the picture so, like George Niven before me, I signed for Thistle.'

He had three decent years with the Jags and then moved to Motherwell as their goalkeeping coach, but ended up playing in the first team. Billy takes up the story, 'The idea of a goalkeeping coach was fairly new in those days and I went to Motherwell to work with a good young lad called Keith MacRae, who was later sold to Manchester City for £100,000.

'Keith got injured and the manager Bobby Howitt told me I was playing. Even when Keith got fit again I kept my place for a while and we played against Coventry City in the Texaco Cup and knocked them out. Joe Mercer was their manager at the time and he asked me to join them!'

Ritchie may not have gone to Coventry but he was not finished. He turned out for Stranraer at the age of 40 before his retirement from playing. He worked for nearly 30 years at

Motherwell College and gets through to Ibrox for the odd game these days, but the goalies of today don't thrill him. He says, 'I can't believe how poor they are at cross balls. For me it was like picking apples from a tree.'

Jimmy Millar (1955–1967)
BORN: 20 November 1934,
Edinburgh

APPEARANCES: 317
GOALS: 162

HONOURS WON WITH RANGERS
League titles (3) – 1960/61,
1962/63, 1963/64
Scottish Cups (5) – 1959/60,
1961/62, 1962/63, 1963/64, 1965/66
League Cups (3) – 1960/61,
1961/62, 1964/65
CAPS: 2 (Scotland)

WALTER SMITH and diehard Rangers fan comedian Andy Cameron probably disagree on a number of issues, but they share a common bond when it comes to their favourite player. There is only who tops the bill for the famous manager and talented entertainer – Jimmy Millar.

It is entirely possible that the two of them were not standing far from each other on the Ibrox terracing watching the great man in action during the glory days of the early 1960s when the supporters revelled in the delights of one of the greatest sides in the club's history. Millar was tough, brave, quick and brilliant in the air for someone who was only 5ft 8in, and he found the net with stunning regularity.

However, he had to bide his time before he made it at Rangers, but it was certainly worth the wait. He was actually a midfield player – a half back in those days – when he started out with Dunfermline under manager Bobby Ancell but when he was moved up front and scored 20 goals in the first half of the 1954/55 season, Rangers came in for him. Scot Symon paid £5,000 for his services in January 1955, and personally handed Millar his £20 signing-on fee from the Ibrox safe.

However, no sooner had Millar started his Rangers career than he was off on National Service and was posted to Cyprus with the Royal Scots Fusiliers. It was two years before he really got going and even then his chances were limited. It was really the summer of 1959 that changed his career in a dramatic way as Symon began putting together a team that would dominate for over five years. Regular striker Max Murray was injured when Rangers were due to play in Denmark in an end-of-season friendly against Staevnet. Millar was drafted in and he scored all four goals in a 4–0 win.

From the start of the 1959/60 season Millar was Rangers' regular No. 9. He scored 21 goals in 30 League games that season, including four against Arbroath, a hat-trick against Clyde and the only goal of the game to beat Celtic in the New Year's match.

His partnership with Ralph Brand was sensational. They linked superbly together and it was a double act that terrorised defences for years. Millar recalled, 'Ralph was way ahead of his time. He would always go on at me to go back out in the afternoon for more training. We would practise one-twos and generally just get used to each other's play so that we would know where we would be on the park during a match.

'In our time it was Millar and Brand and people tend to compare us with McCoist and Hateley because they were another great striking partnership. I have no doubt they were as good as us – maybe better. I suppose it's up to the fans to decide.'

He was also lethal in the Scottish Cup that year. Seven matches, seven goals, including two headers in the 2–0 victory over Kilmarnock in the final, a result that produced his first winner's medal. Millar was on fire and his final tally for the season was 40 goals in 54 games, including three in the European Cup in which Rangers reached the semi-final before falling to Eintracht Frankfurt – an astonishing total for a first season centre forward.

After scaling the dizzy heights, 1960/61 was a setback for Millar, even though Rangers won the championship. He played in 21 successive League games from the start of the season and won his first League Cup winner's medal when Rangers beat Kilmarnock 2–0 in the final in October. But he suffered a slipped disc and did not appear again in domestic competition that season after mid-January.

Before his injury, Millar had scored five goals in five games in the early rounds of the Cup-Winners' Cup, including two in the 8–0 thrashing of Borussia Mönchengladbach. He recovered from his back problems in time for the second leg of the final at Fiorentina in May 1961 when Rangers lost 2–1 and failed to secure the trophy.

The following season, 1961/62, Millar scored Rangers' first goal in the 3–1 victory over Hearts in the League Cup final replay in December. And he was in devastating form in the Scottish Cup too, scoring seven goals in five games en route to the final, including four for the second time against Arbroath. Rangers beat St Mirren 2–0 in the final, though Millar didn't get on the scoresheet that day.

Rangers were champions again in 1962/63, in large part due to Millar's 27 League goals, his highest tally. He scored four in a match for the fourth time in his career in the 5–0 hammering of Dundee United, also hitting two important hat-tricks that season. The first was against Sevilla in the European Cup-Winners' Cup and the second took Rangers past Dundee United in the Scottish Cup semi-final to set up a meeting with Celtic. Rangers won the final 3–0 in a replay. Millar's goals count that season was even better – 45 in 55 games – his best ever haul.

The next season was to be a glorious one in Rangers' history with the winning of the Treble. Millar, however, was missing for a long spell at the start of the season and Jim Forrest took his place with great success, especially in the League Cup in which he scored 16 goals in ten games including four in the final against Morton. Millar scored just six goals in his 22 League games, but saved his best for the classic Scottish Cup final encounter with Dundee.

Dundee's keeper Bert Slater had a memorable match and Rangers only sealed the victory in the last few minutes, Millar scoring twice in a 3–1 win. Millar recalled, 'I have been told a few times it was one of the best cup finals ever. Dundee had a lot of international players at that time but I think on the day we had the edge on them.

'The best player on the field was Bert Slater. He was the man of the match. I scored two that day and Ralph scored one but if Bert had not put the shutters up we could have won quite handsomely.

'It was Willie Henderson who set up my first goal but I was a bit surprised when he set up the second. He had moved on to the left side, which was unusual because he had been playing down the right all game, and produced a good cross to the back post. I managed to get on the end of it and my header looped into the net. Ralph sealed it all in the dying seconds and we were overjoyed when the final whistle sounded.'

Millar was to win two more trophies in his 12 years at Ibrox

– the League Cup in 1964 and the Scottish Cup in 1966, both against Celtic.

He joined Dundee United in the summer of 1967 and it was there that a young Walter Smith had the pleasure of playing beside his idol. Millar had a brief spell as manager of Raith Rovers in season 1969/70 – and even signed his old mate Brand – but that side of the game was not for him. He had already opened up a pub, the Duke's Head in Leith, and he quit football to concentrate all of his efforts in that.

He is still a popular figure at Ibrox where he entertains guests in the hospitality suites on match days.

Harold Davis (1956–1964)
BORN: 1933, Cupar, Fife

APPEARANCES: 261
GOALS: 13

HONOURS WON WITH RANGERS
League titles (4) – 1956/57,
1958/59, 1960/61, 1962/63
Scottish Cup (1) –1961/62
League Cups (2) – 1960/61,
1961/62

THE MACHINE-GUN fire from North Korean forces ripped into Harold Davis's body in no-man's-land and he was lucky to survive, somehow crawling 200 yards with blood pouring from his wounds to reach a first aid post. An American 'bubble' Bell H-13 helicopter – like the ones made famous in the TV series *M.A.S.H.* – led him to safety and the next thing he knew he awoke in a British military hospital in Japan.

He had suffered terrible abdominal injuries and shrapnel wounds to his leg and foot. He spent the next two years in hospitals and rehabilitation centres as surgeons and physiotherapists fought to repair the massive damage that had been caused. It is therefore incredible to think that this hero of the Korean War – a largely forgotten conflict – became a stalwart player of not just one great Rangers side but two. Modern mercenary badge-kissers and those who feign injury would surely shrink with embarrassment in the very presence of such a man.

It was a link with Scot Symon that proved to be the catalyst for Davis's career as Symon had signed the youngster when he was manager of East Fife, although he was soon called up for National Service and sent to the Korean War in 1951 where he was a corporal with the Black Watch.

He recalled the fateful moment when he came close to making the ultimate war-time sacrifice, 'Night-time was when most of the shelling and shooting took place. I just happened to be in a place I should not have been. A flare went up and I got caught in no-man's-land . . . I was hit by machine-gun fire in the abdominal area and on the leg and the foot. They missed my Achilles by inches.

'The first thing you think about is survival. I was strong enough to drag myself back a couple of hundred yards and I was pulled into a first aid post . . . An American helicopter then picked me up and took me back behind the lines to an emergency hospital. It was the Yanks who saved my bacon.'

Although born in Fife, Davis had been brought up in Perthshire and it was during his rehabilitation at Bridge of Earn that he met Davie Kinnear who took a vested interest in the young war veteran. Kinnear had won championship medals with Rangers in 1936/37 and 1938/39 and had become one of the leading physiotherapists in the country and he returned to the club to work for Symon soon after he had replaced Bill Struth as manager in 1954. He mentioned Davis to the manager, who clearly remembered the young half back and when Davis returned to playing for East Fife – they had kept him under contract during all that time – Symon moved in to sign him for £1,750 in October 1956.

Davis said of his early days at Ibrox, 'I was in awe because I was joining men like Ian McColl, George Young and George Niven. Young was a giant in every sense and he could kick a leather ball just about as far as they can kick these lightweight balls now.

'I also played with Ian McMillan and Jim Baxter and they were great to play with. McMillan was clever and thoughtful and Jim was just a class act. He might have two or three bad games and then he would go out and win a game on his own.'

Davis was tough but he was also very quick. No one at Ibrox could beat him over 100 yards. He worked harder on his fitness than any other player because of the injuries he had suffered in action and he was a vital player in a defensive-midfield role. Not many won tackles against him. He won the title in his first season and he went on to claim three more in his time at Ibrox.

Davis was also involved in Rangers' first tentative ventures into European football, first playing OGC Nice in the European Cup in October and November 1956 but losing in a play-off. There was much better to come in 1959/60 when the club reached the semi-finals of the same competition, going all the way to the final of the Cup-Winners' Cup the following year, again losing to European opposition this time in the shape of Fiorentina.

The match was played home and away over two legs in these days and Rangers were outthought by Fiorentina who won 4–1 on aggregate. Davis was blamed for the opening goal in the 2–0 Ibrox defeat when he was short with a pass back but he reckons keeper Billy Ritchie was too slow to come off his line! The real lesson for him, however, was the way the Italians played. He and a few others in the Rangers team knew they had to change their ways but they were not encouraged to do so. He said, 'If I had to criticise Scot Symon it would be that he was reluctant to change with the times. Football was evolving in Europe but we were still playing the same way.

'It was a pride in playing for the jersey that got Rangers through a lot of the time but the Continental teams were expressing themselves better with inter-passing and good movement. There were a few occasions, however, when we took the law into our own hands and disobeyed his orders.

'I remember we were down to ten men at Tynecastle one day when Ritchie went off injured and Bobby Shearer had to go in goal. We got together and said, "Right, let's play football." We played some great stuff and won 3–1.'

The emergence of John Greig in the early 1960s limited Davis's appearances and, during the 1963/64 season as Greig took over at right half, Davis moved to Partick Thistle before becoming a trainer at Queen's Park for four years. He returned to Rangers as a trainer under Davie White in 1969 but the move was short-lived as White was sacked in October that year and Harold went with him. They teamed up again at Dundee and Davis was on the coaching staff when the Dark Blues won the League Cup in 1973.

He said, 'The thing I am most proud of is that when I went to Ibrox I went into a team that included McColl, Young, Alex Scott, Johnny Hubbard and Billy Simpson, and when I finished up I was playing with Baxter, Greig, Ralph Brand and Willie Henderson . . . There is only one or two who can say that they played with both sets of stars and that's what I treasure the most.'

In the late 1970s he and his wife Vi moved north to Gairloch where they ran a hotel. He still lives there today, perhaps entirely appropriately, working hard to raise money for Erskine, the charity for ex-servicemen and women.

Davie Wilson (1956–1967)

BORN: 10 January 1939, Glasgow

APPEARANCES: 373

GOALS: 157

HONOURS WON WITH RANGERS

League titles (2) – 1960/61, 1962/63

Scottish Cups (5) – 1959/60, 1961/62, 1962/63, 1963/64, 1965/66

League Cups (2) – 1960/61, 1961/62

CAPS: 22 (Scotland)

RANGERS FANS have enjoyed watching some fantastic strikers in their time and one of those – diminutive blond-haired winger Davie Wilson – holds a scoring record that might never be beaten. It came on 17 March 1962 at Brockville where Falkirk were put to the sword as Wilson scored six times in a 7–1 victory to become the only Rangers players to hit a double hat-trick since the war.

Remarkably, bludgeoning striker Jimmy Smith achieved this feat twice – against Ayr United on 15 August 1933 and Dunfermline on 11 August 1934. Others have come close since. Marco Negri scored all five in the famous 5–1 win over Dundee United back in August 1997 while Kenny Miller also hit five goals in a 7–1 hammering of St Mirren in November 2000. However, Celtic's Dixie Deans is the only other Scottish player to have notched six goals in Scottish football's top-flight when

Partick Thistle were the victims in a 7–0 defeat in November 1973.

Wilson recalled his big day, 'I remember I was switched to centre forward against the Bairns because Doug Baillie was ruled out through injury and Jimmy Millar was moved back into midfield. I had played in attack before and Scot Symon knew I could score goals so he probably reckoned I would fit in fine. Alex Scott played on the right wing and a young Willie Henderson took the No. 11 jersey for the day.

'That game at Brockville was special for me. There was a full house of just under 20,000 inside the ground, including my father who went to all the matches. It was a ground I really liked and I had some happy memories there. I even recall going there as a youngster and being passed over the heads to the front so I could see the game and get a closer view of my Rangers heroes.

'Anyway, the crowd that day also included the Falkirk chairman Duncan Ogilvie and his family. They were personal friends of ours but at the end of the game Duncan's daughter could hardly bear to look at me because I had just scored a barrowload of goals that destroyed her team!

'It was just one of those days. I scored three with my right foot and three with my left. I even had a goal disallowed near the end because Alex Scott was in an offside position.

'Strangely, it was only 1–0 at half time and I went on to score four in a 15-minute spell after the break . . . My last goal came ten minutes from the end and that caused a problem for the Saturday evening sports papers. I think it was the *Green Citizen* that concluded my scoring at five and carried the headline "Wilson Goes Nap!" . . . After the game Mr Ogilvie gave me the ball, a white-laced, leather ball which I still have.

'Today I am a proud member of the six-goal club along with Celtic's Dixie Deans who scored the same number of goals past

Alan Rough of Partick Thistle on 17 November 1973. I was really hoping that Marco Negri or Kenny Miller could have scored six as opposed to five in recent years as our wee club is crying out for new members!'

Wilson joined Rangers from Baillieston Juniors in May 1956 but, vying with Andy Matthew and Johnny Hubbard, it was really three years later before he made the No. 11 jersey his own. He was a mere 5ft 6in tall but was fast and a very direct sort of player. One of his trademarks was to drift unseen into the box towards the far post when Alex Scott or Henderson was raiding down the right flank and successfully pick up on their crosses.

He is only credited with two League championship medals, but he played 15 of the 34 games in the 1958/59 season and 16 in the Treble season of 1963/64 – statistics that would be more than enough for a gong these days. He won his first silverware in April 1960 when he played in the Scottish Cup final in which Rangers beat Kilmarnock 2–0. In the 1960/61 season, Wilson played in all 60 matches and scored 23 goals, winning his first championship winner's medal and a League Cup winner's medal too as Rangers beat Kilmarnock 2–0 in the final.

Another player who experienced the club's early forays into Europe, Wilson found the net three times in eight matches as Rangers reached the semi-final of the European Cup in 1959/60, including one against their eventual conquerors Eintracht Frankfurt. He also took part in the Cup-Winners' Cup run that saw Rangers to their first European final. He played in all eight games and scored the crucial away goal that took them past Ferencvaros in the first round. But it was a loser's medal that awaited him as Rangers went down 4–1 to Fiorentina in May 1961.

Wilson was now reaching his peak as a goalscorer and his

six-shooting performance at Falkirk was among a haul of 29 goals he scored in 53 games during the 1961/62 season. But the following season was even better. His 23 in the League, putting him second only behind Jimmy Millar's 27, proved vital as Rangers regained the championship. Rangers scored 94 goals in the title race and Wilson, Millar and Ralph Brand accounted for 69 of them. Wilson scored all four as Rangers beat Partick Thistle 4–0 in April and hit five in seven games in the Scottish Cup, including one in the 3–0 win over Celtic in the final. His final haul for the season was 33 goals in 55 games.

But as Rangers headed towards their first trophy in their Treble season of 1963/64, Wilson's luck turned against him. He broke his ankle in the 3–1 League Cup semi-final victory over Berwick Rangers and had to sit out the final, which Rangers won 5–0 against Morton. The injury kept Wilson out from October to February. His comeback game was against St Mirren. Wilson scored, but Rangers lost 3–2.

He then played in all ten remaining League games, scoring five times as Rangers took the title by six points from Kilmarnock. He got the only goal of the game against Dunfermline to put Rangers through to the Scottish Cup final and received his fourth winner's medal in the competition as Rangers triumphed 3–1 over Dundee.

He won one final Scottish Cup medal in 1966 when Celtic were beaten 1–0 in a replayed final before moving on the following year to Dundee United as part of a player exchange deal for Swedish international winger Orjan Persson. He had five seasons at Tannadice.

Wilson was capped 22 times by Scotland. Arguably his best display was when he had to move to left back when Eric Caldow broke his leg at Wembley in 1963 and two Jim Baxter goals gave ten-man Scotland a 2–1 win over England.

After his retirement from playing he had spells in management at Dumbarton, Queen of the South and Kilmarnock, before quitting the game altogether and working for a financial company.

Davie Provan (1958–1970)
BORN: 11 March 1941, Falkirk

APPEARANCES: 262
GOALS: 11

HONOURS WON WITH RANGERS
League title (1) – 1963/64
Scottish Cups (3) – 1962/63,
1963/64, 1965/66
League Cups (2) – 1963/64,
1964/65
CAPS: 5 (Scotland)

IT MAY seem a strange way to describe Davie Provan's Rangers career, but it was bookended by a couple of broken legs. The talented defender had to wait five years before he got his chance in the Rangers first team. It came when former captain, Eric Caldow, suffered a leg break at Wembley playing for Scotland against England in April 1963. Caldow was on the sidelines for the best part of a year and Provan took his place at full back. There was a cruel irony, however, when a crude challenge from Celtic's Bertie Auld badly broke Provan's leg in the first Old Firm game of the 1967/68 season, an injury that spelled the end of his time at Rangers.

Provan recalled, 'I played in Rangers reserves basically for five years; such was the quality of the team at the time. It was only when Eric Caldow broke his leg at Wembley playing for Scotland that I got my chance to come into the side, and in my first full season we won the Treble!'

'Of course, it was really unfortunate for Eric that his broken leg put him out and got me in but a broken leg ended my career so you have to take the good and the bad in football.'

Rangers were irresistible in the early 1960s and Provan had adaptability, playing either right back or left back with some aplomb. He did play for the first team on a few occasions before Caldow's injury, earning his first winner's medal when Celtic were thumped 3–0 in the Scottish Cup final replay in 1963. But 1963/64 was a fairytale season for a man who had shown a great deal of patience since signing for the Light Blues in 1958. He only missed one match in the League, played in all six Scottish Cup matches and all ten League Cup games as the Light Blues swept the board for only the second time in their history.

The tall and powerful defender won further silverware in 1964/65 and 1965/66, beating Celtic first in the League Cup and then in the Scottish Cup where his fellow full back Kai Johansen memorably scored the only goal of the game. But that was his last honour for Rangers. He played in the Cup-Winners' Cup final against Bayern Munich in 1967, but the Light Blues lost 1–0.

Provan's impact at Rangers in the mid-1960s resulted in international recognition and he was capped five times. It gave him something to cherish. He said, 'I think my greatest memory in football was getting capped for Scotland in the World Cup tie against Italy at Hampden when we won 1–0 and John Greig scored the goal.'

The day his leg was broken – 11 September 1967 – is obviously still a painful reminder that his career was cut down in its prime. He recalled, 'Having played in a League international in Belfast I was in line to get back into the full Scotland side, and then I broke my leg when I was challenged by Bertie Auld.

'The funny thing is that Bertie and I often play golf together now. It's unbelievable how things work out but it was he who broke my leg and it really finished me at Rangers.'

He fought his way back to fitness but he was not the same player any more and his appearances became sporadic, with Sandy Jardine and Willie Mathieson holding down the full back berths. He moved to Crystal Palace in 1970 and also played for Plymouth Argyle in England before returning to Scotland where he finished his career at St Mirren in 1975.

He never lost his Rangers connections, however, as Alex Ferguson, a teammate at Ibrox, made him his assistant when he took over as manager at Love Street. He also worked for John Greig when he was Rangers manager, mostly as chief scout, and currently you will find Davie a gregarious host in the hospitality suites of Ibrox on match days.

Ronnie McKinnon

(1960–1973)
BORN: 20 August 1940

APPEARANCES: 473
GOALS: 3

HONOURS WON WITH RANGERS
League titles (2) – 1962/63,
1963/64
Scottish Cups (4) – 1961/62,
1962/63, 1963/64, 1965/66
League Cups (3) – 1963/64,
1964/65, 1970/71
CAPS: 28 (Scotland)

THE EVENTS of 3 November 1971 will always be remembered as some of the most remarkable in Rangers' history, but for Ronnie McKinnon it was the night his Rangers dream died.

On an amazing night in Lisbon, Rangers lost 4–3 after extra time to Sporting in the José Alvalade Stadium in the second leg of their European Cup-Winners' Cup second-round tie. Having won the first leg at Ibrox 3–2, the tie had finished 6–6 on aggregate and Dutch referee Laurens van Raavens wrongly ordered a penalty shoot-out. Rangers promptly missed four of their five penalties and the Portuguese celebrated what they thought was a dramatic victory.

On the advice of John MacKenzie, a former colleague at the *Scottish Daily Express*, manager Willie Waddell checked his rulebook which confirmed that extra-time goals counted double in the event of a level aggregate score. The rule had just changed that summer and the referee had forgotten. The penalty shootout verdict was overturned, Rangers were declared the winners and the rest is history as the Light Blues went on to win the trophy in Barcelona the following May.

It was a night of unbridled celebration in the Portuguese capital, but for McKinnon it was as if his world had completely collapsed. The centre back, who had been a rock for Rangers and Scotland during the 1960s, suffered a double fracture of his right leg and never played for the club again.

He won nine major honours and played 473 games for Rangers and was undoubtedly a main element in the great side of the early 1960s which fans of the time can recite in their sleep: Ritchie; Shearer, Caldow; Greig, McKinnon, Baxter; Henderson, McMillan, Millar, Brand and Wilson. And although he was devastated to have his career cut short at the age of 31, McKinnon was philosophical enough to recognise what he had achieved. He said, 'I was very lucky and privileged to play in a great Rangers team. The half back line of Greig, myself and Baxter, in my opinion, was probably the best the club has ever had.

'Of course there were many other great players in the team too. I won medals galore and I won caps because I played for Rangers . . . People have often asked me, "Did you like playing for Rangers?" and I always say, "I didn't like playing for Rangers – I loved it."

'I was also fortunate to be involved in some fantastic matches for Scotland – none more so than the 3–2 win over England in 1967. England were the world champions and when we went down to Wembley to play them we were branded no-hopers, we didn't have a chance. So to play against a team of that quality away from home and beat them so convincingly was a fantastic achievement . . . The thing was we didn't just beat them, we played them off the park. "We beat them nae bother," as they say in Glasgow. We showed the world champions.

'I was lucky because I had so many highs. I broke my nose twice but the second time actually straightened it so that worked out in my favour! I think every player that plays football, his one dread, the one thing at the back of his mind is "I hope I don't break my leg".

'There are some breaks that heal well and there are others that take a long time. I was supposed to be back in six months after my trouble in Lisbon, at least that's what the surgeon Archie McDougall told me, but I was out for 18 months . . . I got a real bad one and I never really made it after that. I tried hard to come back but that was effectively the end of my career.

'The club did me a great favour in taking me over to Barcelona for the final because I obviously couldn't play. In fact I still had stitches in my leg. Colin [Jackson] had picked up an injury over there and he was ruled out of the match, so we were both feeling a bit sorry for each other. We went out and commiserated in our own way – and I won't go into specific details.

'The next thing we know, Jock Wallace came in and had a go at Colin because he might have been needed for a potential replay so we had to sober him up quickly, but Rangers won the cup so everything was fine – although we had sore heads the next day!'

McKinnon remained with Rangers for the next 18 months but he never played for the first team again. He remembers, 'I went to the club and said that my career was over and I asked for a free transfer or something of that nature. I was no good any more to them. Happily that's what happened and I decided to go to South Africa and I played for two more years for Durban United.

'I went into the dressing room for my first game and I looked at the strips and they were green and white. I said to the guy, "I'm not playing in this strip, no way!" I said that he'd not told me about playing in green and white before I agreed to sign. All of a sudden he was in a real flap. The next thing he is saying things like, "Can we get another kit?" and, before he had a heart attack, I said, "I'm only kidding!"

'I had two good years with them and it was good fun. Then after that I started selling cars and that sure beats working for a living! I ended staying in South Africa for 30 years and I loved it. It's a beautiful country.'

Ronnie, whose father was from the Western Isles, is back in Scotland now and lives on the Isle of Lewis.

Jim Baxter (1960–1965, 1969–1970)
BORN: 29 September 1939, Hill o'Beath, Fife

APPEARANCES: 254
GOALS: 24

HONOURS WON WITH RANGERS
League titles (3) – 1960/61, 1962/63, 1963/64
Scottish Cups (3) – 1961/62, 1962/63, 1963/64
League Cups (4) – 1960/61, 1962/63, 1963/64, 1964/65
CAPS: 24 (of 34 for Scotland)

TINA TURNER'S anthem 'The Best' has been booming around Ibrox since the mid-1990s. The writers Mike Chapman and Holly Knight are probably blissfully unaware that their song perfectly encapsulates the talents of Jim Baxter.

A multitude of footballers have been described as world class over the years, but most were not fit to lace Jim Baxter's boots. For five years he was the king of the all-conquering Rangers side put together by Scot Symon and he relished the adulation. The bigger the stage the better it suited 'Slim Jim'. However, as with contemporaries George Best and Jimmy Greaves, Jim's love of life off the field proved to be his downfall.

Baxter in full flow was like an orchestra conductor. He had beautiful ball skills, an exceptional left foot and the vision and time to make space for others to play in. He also had his own style. There was a rule that Rangers players must have their shirts tucked inside their shorts. Baxter, however, always left a little piece of his shirt hanging out over his left hip. It was a distinctive trademark and went with the swagger that marks out only a few as being of the highest class. Naturally, the fans adored him.

He simply loved to embarrass the opposition – especially Celtic, and England on the international stage. He had an incredible Old Firm record. In 18 games – ten League, five League Cup and three Scottish Cup – he only lost twice. There is scarcely a more enduring image than Baxter keeping the ball in the air with his priceless left foot during Scotland's 3–2 win in 1967 over then world champions England at Wembley.

Others, like Denis Law, wanted to try to score more goals and inflict more pain on England – Baxter just wanted to take the mickey. Four years before, he had scored both goals in the 2–1 defeat of England and later said he was thinking about scoring a third goal in his own net to give himself a hat-trick!

Born in the Fife mining village Hill o'Beath on 29 September 1939, he worked as a coalminer before coming to Ibrox from Raith Rovers in June 1960. The 20-year-old was signed for a then record fee of £17,500.

Those who were fortunate enough to see him play will never forget the formidable sight of Slim Jim, a truly world-class player in all his pomp. A player of style and arrogance, but one blessed with sublime skills. He won three titles, three Scottish Cup and four League Cup winner's medals in five years. But off the field he was a rogue. There is a famous story, which he happily confirmed some years later, that he took the legendary Hungarian Ferenc Puskas 'out on the batter' in Drumchapel. Rangers had just played the all-conquering Real Madrid side at Ibrox in the first round of the European Cup on 25 September

1963 and Puskas scored the only goal of the game.

Baxter and Puskas ended up boozing all night as Jim recalled, 'Puskas was a great guy. Drumchapel was funny because he was absolutely sozzled. I remember thinking, "Puskas is steamboats!" He could hardly speak a word of English and I just remember this wee squeaky voice saying, "Jeemmy, Jeemmy, wheesky, wheesky," that's all he'd say. We ended up downing whisky all night!'

In the last season of his first spell at Ibrox, Baxter broke his leg during a 2–0 European Cup victory over Rapid Vienna in December 1964. He was out for three months and by the time he returned he had become restless. He made his last appearance in April 1965 in a 1–0 League defeat to Dundee and the following month he was transferred to Sunderland for £72,500. He moved on to Nottingham Forest for £100,000 in 1967, but by then he was better known for his off-the-field activities. His return to Rangers in 1969 was unsuccessful and in December 1970 he hung up the boots forever at the age of 31.

Sadly, Jim lost his fight with cancer at the age of 61 on 14 April 2001, and football lost one of its greatest sons. Glasgow Cathedral was packed for a moving and entertaining funeral service – just as Jim wanted – and he will forever be etched into the folklore of Rangers and Scottish football.

John Greig said, 'Money simply could not buy him. He was perhaps more noticeable because he played with his left foot and I always feel that left-footed players are more artistic and better to look at. Basically, Jim was unbelievable. He was so immaculate in the way he played the game. He could land the ball on a sixpence if he wanted to.

'I remember vividly he used to chip the ball from the 18-yard line and hit the bar every time, usually collecting a fair amount of money in bets in the process. His game was all about self-confidence as well as ability. He wanted the ball in any area of the park and he was afraid of no one.

'Of course, he couldn't tackle a fish supper and he was more delighted when he did make a tackle than any defence-splitting pass he produced in a game. In saying that, Jim was a real competitor. He didn't like losing to anybody. He was as strong a character as anyone else at that time.'

Greig knows that Baxter had the same impact as other 'entertainers' like Davie Cooper, Brian Laudrup and Paul Gascoigne, and the fact that he was still revered so many years after giving up the game speaks volumes for his status in the history of Rangers. He added, 'You can't kid the fans on. They are the judges and when he died the number of scarves and other tributes that were placed at the Ibrox gates showed just how much Jim Baxter meant to the fans – even although he stopped playing over 30 years earlier.

'Many great players have graced this club, but there is no doubt that Jim Baxter was one of the best ever. He had charisma and he had astonishing ability And one thing I have always remembered, he never once publicly criticised Rangers Football Club.'

Manchester United manager Sir Alex Ferguson, who played alongside Baxter in his short second spell at Rangers, said, 'Baxter was Rangers' greatest ever player and would have been a great player in any era.' He even suggested the Fifer was 'arguably the best player to play in Scottish football. He had immense skill, balance, confidence, grace and the ability to pass and hold the ball. He was just a fantastic footballer. Fantastic.'

Willie Henderson

(1960–1972)

BORN: 24 January 1944, Baillieston

APPEARANCES: 426

GOALS: 62

HONOURS WON WITH RANGERS

League titles (2) – 1962/63, 1963/64

Scottish Cups (4) – 1961/62, 1962/63, 1963/64, 1965/66

League Cups (2) – 1963/64, 1970/71

CAPS: 29 (Scotland)

IN FOOTBALL these days the word 'vision' is used a lot but in the 1960s football was a more entertaining place and no one was blind to the talents of Willie Henderson – apart from maybe Willie himself. A fantastic winger with incredible pace, great skill and the knack of creating and scoring vital goals, Henderson was the teen star of the era. However, his eyesight was not the best. The joke of the time was, 'What a player Willie would be if only he could see!'

This was never more apparent than late on in a crucial Old Firm match in which Rangers were chasing a winner. Henderson said, 'Bobby Shearer asked me to find out how long there was to go and I went over to the bench and asked the question. I saw a hand go up with five fingers showing and promptly told Bobby there were still five minutes left.

'He said, "Great, let's see if we can get a goal."

'Then 30 seconds later the final whistle sounded and, as we were walking down the tunnel, Bobby slapped me on the back of the head and said, "I thought you said there were five minutes to go?"

'I replied that I had gone to the dugout to ask the question and he said, "That was the Celtic dugout, you bloody idiot."'

Teammate and fellow entertainer Willie Johnston said, 'In some floodlit matches I'm sure he couldn't see the ball. I think he must have had radar in his head or something.'

Whatever it was it worked. Henderson was an instant success and he was coveted by a number of top clubs before Rangers got him. He said, 'I had played for Scotland at youth level and a lot of scouts came to watch me. I think there were about 40 over a period of about six months. There were offers to go here, there and everywhere but I always felt my father wanted to see me in that blue shirt.'

He had been inspired by the great Brazilian Garrincha who had dazzled millions with his skill at the 1958 World Cup, and Willie had a similar impact on the Rangers fans, who adored him. His swaggering style encapsulated the spirit of the Swinging Sixties. In football terms he had the same appeal as any of the Rolling Stones or the Beatles.

Known as 'Wee Willie' – hardly the most inventive nickname for someone standing just 5ft 4in – Henderson was an original boy wonder. He made his Rangers debut aged just 17 and played for Scotland a year later. He forced Alex Scott out of the side and on to Everton, and the fans lapped up his glittering array of talents.

Many of those who saw him, and most notably those who played against him, say they have never encountered a quicker player, but there was more to his game than lightning pace. His skill at beating defenders was a joy to watch, while he could deliver crosses with pinpoint accuracy and pop up, just when needed, to score crucial goals.

He made his breakthrough in the 1961/62 season and played in the Scottish Cup final that year as Rangers comfortably defeated St Mirren 2–0. He also got his first taste of football in the European arena that season and scored his first goal against Vorwaerts of East Germany in bizarre circumstances.

The Cold War was very much alive in those days and the East German authorities would not allow the Vorwaerts players to play at Ibrox in case they sought political asylum so Rangers' 'home' game had to be played in Malmo, Sweden. Henderson scored but the match was abandoned because of fog and the teams tried again the next day. Rangers won 4–1 and Willie was on the scoresheet again.

Henderson was part of the famous early 1960s side that many regard as the finest Rangers have ever had and the successes came thick and fast with Henderson showing blistering pace and impossible trickery on the right wing. He was heavily involved in the League and Cup Double in 1962/63 and was then part of the clean sweep of the honours in 1964, which finished with the Scottish Cup final win over Dundee.

He scored one of the most talked about Old Firm goals en route to that final when Rangers met Celtic in the quarter-final at Ibrox. Rangers were leading 1–0 when John Greig played the ball from just outside his box to the halfway line where Jim Forrest tapped it back to Henderson. Suddenly he took off, leaving opposing players for dead with pace, poise and terrific close control. His run took him into the Celtic box and he fired a left-foot shot past John Fallon. It was a stunning goal and he goaded the Celtic fans by holding his arms aloft in front of them.

Henderson was equally productive in the classic 1963/64 Scottish Cup final with Dundee which was settled in the last few moments. It was Willie's corner that was headed into the net by Jimmy Millar to give Rangers the lead but Dundee equalised almost immediately through Kenny Cameron.

A replay was beckoning when Henderson decided to intervene. He recalled, 'It was 1–1 and I asked an ambulance-man who was sitting on the sidelines how long there was to go and he told me four minutes, I said, "Right, it's time I went to work."'

Henderson popped up on the left wing to take a short free kick from Jim Baxter, beat Alex Hamilton and sent a cross to the back post from where Jimmy Millar looped a header into the net. A minute later Ralph Brand scored a third goal and the Treble was secured in the most dramatic way possible.

His skills dominated the game in the first half of the decade, until Jimmy Johnstone assumed the mantle in the late 1960s as part of a resurgent Celtic. They were very similar players and Scottish football was a hugely entertaining place with the two on fire at the same time.

As the great Rangers team began to break up, trophies were harder to come by. Henderson played in the Scottish Cup-winning team of 1966 when Kai Johansen's goal beat Celtic, but it was four years before Rangers won any more silverware.

Henderson's final season at Ibrox seemed destined for glory; he played a leading role in helping Rangers on their famous 1972 European Cup-Winners' Cup adventure, most notably with an extra-time goal in the quarter-final against Sporting Lisbon.

But it was all to end under a cloud, as Henderson missed out on becoming a European winner when he left the club before the final in Barcelona. He had a fall-out with manager Willie

Waddell and was sitting on a beach in South Africa as his former teammates wrote their names into the club's history, beating Moscow Dynamo 3–2.

After leaving Rangers he had a spell with Sheffield Wednesday and then Hong Kong Rangers. He played briefly for Airdrie then retired and had a spell in Spain where he ran a bar. He has been running a hotel in Lanarkshire successfully for a number of years now. In addition, Henderson has retained his contacts with Rangers and on match days he can be found working for hospitality, invariably lighting up proceedings with stories and quips from his many, many glory days of the 1960s.

Chapter 5
European Glory and Treble Triumphs (1972–1978)

John Greig
Willie Mathieson
Colin Jackson
Sandy Jardine
Willie Johnston
Dave Smith
Alex MacDonald
Colin Stein
Alfie Conn
Peter McCloy
Derek Johnstone
Tommy McLean
Tom Forsyth
Davie Cooper
Bobby Russell

Almost 100 years to the day that four young men gave birth to Rangers Football Club, the Light Blues enjoyed their finest hour when they lifted the European Cup-Winners' Cup on 24 May 1972 in Barcelona.

The 11 men who were on duty that night in the Nou Camp Stadium made history so it is hardly surprising that they are all included in the Hall of Fame. It was undoubtedly one of the toughest campaigns that any team has faced in search of European glory; Rangers had to defeat Stade Rennes of France, Portugal's Sporting Lisbon, Torino of Italy and then the mighty Bayern Munich. They went three goals up in the final against Moscow Dynamo and, although they lost two late goals, they held on to lift the trophy.

It sparked a fantastic spell in the 1970s when Rangers not only won the Treble for a third time but achieved the feat twice in the space of three seasons under Jock Wallace.

Hampden became their second home as they appeared in cup final after cup final during the period which is still revered by so many fans.

And, of course, John Greig, the man voted the Greatest Ever Ranger, was at the heart of it all as the inspirational captain.

John Greig (1961–1978)

BORN: 11 September 1942, Edinburgh

APPEARANCES: 755
GOALS: 120

HONOURS WON WITH RANGERS
League titles (5) – 1962/63, 1963/64, 1974/75, 1975/76, 1977/78
Scottish Cups (6) – 1962/63, 1963/64, 1965/66, 1972/73, 1975/76, 1977/78
League Cups (4) – 1963/64, 1964/65, 1975/76, 1977/78
European Cup-Winners' Cup (1) – 1971/72
CAPS: 44 (Scotland)

IF YOU were to pick one man to accurately reflect the essential spirit of Rangers Football Club then John Greig would top the list every time. Players and staff at Murray Park, the Rangers training centre since 2001, call him 'The Legend', while the Ibrox supporters voted him their 'Greatest Ever Ranger' in 1999. It is hard to argue with either title. It wasn't just his ability, although he was a devastatingly strong and influential player; it was also his passion, his drive and his undeniable will to win. He was a magnificent captain and he remains a superb ambassador for the club in his role as a director.

Greig was part of two great Rangers sides, the all-conquering 1960s team and the Treble winners of the 1970s. And, of course, he was captain when Rangers enjoyed their finest hour on 24 May 1972 in Barcelona by winning the European Cup-Winners' Cup. In between those glorious times he showed fantastic leadership when Rangers lived in the shadow of Jock Stein's Celtic. He was equally influential on the international scene, captaining Scotland to their famous 3–2 'humiliation' of world champions England in 1967 among 44 appearances for his country. After playing for the club for 17 years he was thrust into the manager's chair following Jock Wallace's resignation in 1978. He wasn't as successful in management as in his playing days, but he still claimed four trophies in five years.

Greig had come from a Hearts-daft family, but it was his family who convinced him to sign for Rangers in 1961. He said of his first visit to Ibrox, 'I remember walking into the manager's office when I came to sign for the club and I wondered what I was letting myself in for because I had never seen a club this size.

'I have to be honest and say that I wasn't a Rangers supporter as a boy. My brothers and I were all Hearts fans but it was they who told me to sign for Rangers and it was the best advice I ever got. I never looked back from the day I put pen to paper and despite what they say about the modern-day players and how much they earn I wouldn't change my career for anything.'

He made his debut in September 1961 in a League Cup tie against Airdrie and went on to play 11 games that season, mostly as a dashing inside forward. He contributed seven goals that campaign as the Light Blues won both the League and the Scottish Cup.

However, for the following season he moved to half back

and that's where he found his place in a side that dominated the Scottish game – winning six major trophies in a row – a League and Cup Double in 1962/63, the Treble in 1963/64 and the League Cup in 1964/65. Greig recalls, 'The team just gelled together. We played a 4–2–4 system before it became commonplace. When I came in I played as a sweeper and that allowed Jim Baxter and Ian McMillan to play in the middle of the park and support the front players . . . And our forward line of Willie Henderson, Jimmy Millar, Ralph Brand and Davie Wilson scored a heck of a lot of goals – especially Millar, Brand and Wilson.

'We also had two great full backs in Bobby Shearer and Eric Caldow with Ronnie McKinnon at centre half. So it was a great side and we all complemented each other. I owe so much to that team because they taught me so much on the field. They were all a huge help to me. I used to travel through to Glasgow on the train with Ralph and Jimmy, which was an education in itself.

'Bill Shankly used to say that if you have two or three men in your team who were deep thinkers about the game then you have a chance of a really good team. Here was I as a young boy sitting beside two top-class players listening to them talking expansively about the game we had just played or the game we had coming up. It was a fantastic learning situation for me and I never forgot that.'

That great side began to break up in the mid-1960s and Celtic emerged to enjoy the greatest period in their history. These were tough times for Rangers but Greig, despite offers from England, remained resolute and determined. He became captain in the 1966/67 season and in that first campaign led the club to the Cup-Winners' Cup final where Rangers were narrowly defeated 1–0 in extra time by Bayern Munich in Nuremburg.

Given that Celtic had won the European Cup the week before it was a difficult time for everyone at Ibrox. Domestically, Rangers were in the shadows. They won just one major trophy between 1966 and 1973 – the 1970/71 League Cup and Greig missed the final because he was injured. He said, 'We lost a couple of managers on the road, we lost a lot of players on the road and probably the biggest problem was that we were up against the best Celtic team ever – the team that won the European Cup. Those were not easy years.

'One of the things about that time was that if you were in the international team, nine times out of ten you would go to England to play but I never had any thoughts about that and I was happy to stay. I think the supporters appreciated that. Don't get me wrong, I'm a terrible loser but through all that time, having had all the success that I had had in the early 1960s, I felt bad for the supporters.'

He had more to deal with than on-field disappointment. In the dark days following the Ibrox Disaster in 1971, when 66 people died, he played the captain's role in leading the players as they attended the victims' funerals. A statue of Greig was erected at the Copland Road end of Ibrox Stadium on 2 January 2001 – the 30th anniversary of the disaster – as a memorial to those who lost their lives in the crush on stairway 13.

Within 16 months of the tragedy Rangers were kings of Europe when they defeated Moscow Dynamo 3–2 in the Nou Camp to claim the club's first European trophy. Sadly, due to the fans invading the pitch, Greig had to be presented with the trophy in a small room below the main stand. Despite this, it remains his greatest achievement. He said, 'It was tense at the end because we allowed Dynamo to score two goals but we got there and it was so important for the club and the fans . . . It was disappointing that I couldn't get presented with the cup in the normal way but the achievement was huge.'

Following European glory Willie Waddell stepped aside as manager, leaving Jock Wallace to take over the hot seat, a move that heralded a marvellous revival in the fortunes of the club and a chance for the captain to write his name in the history books. The next trophy was the Scottish Cup which arrived on 5 May 1973 after a classic final against Celtic. But it was the League that really mattered and, finally, after 11 long years, the trophy returned on 29 March 1975, clinched at Hibernian's Easter Road ground. Greig was injured for the match but, in a pre-arranged move, Wallace allowed the only survivor from the 1964 championship team to join in the celebrations by replacing Sandy Jardine with a minute to go.

That victory sparked a glorious few years at Ibrox. Rangers swept the board in two of the next three seasons, making Greig the first and only player to be part of three Treble-winning campaigns. He was named Scotland's Player of the Year in 1976, having also received the accolade in 1966, and was awarded an MBE in 1977 for his services to football. Remarkably, just weeks after lifting the Scottish Cup in 1978 after a 2–1 win over Aberdeen Greig was thrust into the manager's job at the age of 35 when Wallace resigned in a row over money.

He went desperately close to retaining that Treble in his first season of management. Rangers won the League Cup, beating Aberdeen 2–1 in the final, and conquered Hibernian 3–2 in the Scottish Cup final second replay. However, the League championship eluded them, with the title returning to Celtic following their 4–2 win at Parkhead in the Old Firm derby on 21 May 1979. Greig's men finished runners-up.

Rangers were to win another Scottish Cup and a League Cup under Greig, but in October 1983 he resigned to be replaced by the returning Jock Wallace. Greig's heart, however, belonged to Rangers and he came back to Ibrox in 1990, initially in the public relations department. He went on to work closely with Dick Advocaat and then Alex McLeish before taking a role in the youth development department, becoming a director of the club in 2004.

His tally of 498 League appearances is second in the all-time list behind Sandy Archibald, and his influence over Rangers will never be forgotten.

Willie Mathieson (1962–1975)
Born: 30 January 1943,
St Andrews

Appearances: 276
Goals: 3

Honours Won with Rangers
Scottish Cup (1) – 1972/73
European Cup-Winners' Cup (1) –
1971/72

FOR MOST Rangers supporters 24 May 1972 represents the greatest moment in the club's history and every one of the players from that night in Barcelona deserve inclusion in the club's Hall of Fame simply for being part of the iconic team that lifted the European Cup-Winners' Cup. Willie Mathieson was one of the last 'Barcelona Bears' to be inducted into Hall of Fame in 2007, but for a man who had been working down the pits ten years earlier the events of that day are as fresh as if it were yesterday.

The 3–2 victory over Moscow Dynamo in the Nou Camp remains Rangers' greatest result, even if the scenes at the end were chaotic as brutal Spanish police beat the over-exuberant Rangers supporters who had spilled on to the pitch. Amid the crazy scenes, one fan tried to make a special presentation to Mathieson in the form of a chocolate cake he had transported from one side of the world to the other.

Willie said, 'I remember the final being quite easy at the start. Early in the second half we were 3–0 up and could hardly believe it. Then Sandy Jardine and I between us lost a goal

175

which brought them back into it and then they got a second which started the panic a wee bit. The fans then started to come on the park which made it worse. So there were a few nervy moments at the end before the final whistle went.

'The scenes at the end were incredible. One lad ran over to me and he had a big chocolate cake in his hand. He had come all the way from Australia just for the game and wanted to present me with this cake for some reason. He was originally from Scotland, had travelled to Spain from Australia just to see the game and was then heading back down under without even going to see his family in Scotland. The dedication of some of the fans was unbelievable.'

Becoming a European winner was unimaginable for Mathieson who was working at Dundonald Colliery as an apprentice electrician when the opportunity arose to sign for Rangers as a part-time player in 1960. Two years later he became a full-time player and made his debut in the first-team three years on from that in 1965.

He was one of just five players to feature in every round on the way to that famous victory in the Nou Camp and followed that success by claiming a Scottish Cup winner's medal a year later in the match best remembered for Tam Forsyth's six-inch winning goal against Celtic.

If his was an unflashy career played largely in the shadows of those with greater ability and egos, then it was no less worthy as a result. A Rangers scout had gone to watch a teammate at St Andrews United – Willie Penman who subsequently signed but played just two games – and left impressed with left back Mathieson. Preston North End and Raith Rovers were also interested but the chance to join the best team in the land and work with players like Jim Baxter was too good to turn down.

Mathieson's father insisted that he finished his apprenticeship as an electrician so it was 1962 before he signed full-time. Willie would work down the mines until his shift ended at 2 p.m., catch a train to Glasgow for training at Ibrox and then rush to make the last train back.

It was February 1965 that Mathieson made his Rangers debut against Hamilton Accies in the first round of the Scottish Cup and it was a comfortable day as Rangers won 3–0 with Ralph Brand scoring inside the first 15 seconds of the game. Unlike the modern game where clubs pick from huge squads, football in the 1960s was very much about the first team and the reserve team with the reserves filling in when required until they were deemed first-team material.

To that end, it was the 1967/68 season before he managed to hold down a regular place in the side. However, his emergence coincided with Celtic's stranglehold on the domestic scene in what was the best period in their history. He said, 'I was in and out the team after my debut. Eric Caldow was holding down the left back position at that time. He broke his leg and Davie Provan came into the first-team and when he broke his leg I got my chance. So it was through two unfortunate incidents that I got my chance. But you just have to make the most of these opportunities.

'It was a difficult time for Rangers as Celtic were quite a force. Between around 1967 to 1973 Celtic were really on a high. But, in saying that, we got to two European finals, a semi-final and a quarter-final in those five years, which isn't bad going!'

Mathieson was extremely left-footed which prompted one Ibrox fan to call him 'Willie Wan Fit', a rather uncreative observation but one that stuck during his days at Ibrox.

Mathieson left Ibrox in 1975 for spells at Arbroath and his local team, Raith Rovers, before hanging up his boots. After a brief stint coaching at Berwick Rangers, where he worked with his fellow Barcelona Bear Dave Smith, he drifted away from football but still maintains an interest from afar. He lives in Inverness where he still does some part-time electrical work and regularly smiles about that chocolate cake in Barcelona.

Colin Jackson (1963–1982)
BORN: 8 October 1946, London

APPEARANCES: 506
GOALS: 40

HONOURS WON WITH RANGERS
League titles (3) – 1974/75, 1975/76, 1977/78
Scottish Cups (3) – 1975/76, 1977/78, 1978/79
League Cups (5) – 1970/71, 1975/76, 1977/78, 1978/79, 1981/82
CAPS: 8 (Scotland)

IF PATIENCE is a virtue then Colin Jackson is undoubtedly one of the most virtuous Rangers players of all time as he had to wait nearly seven years, after signing as a 16-year-old, before he became a first-team regular. Although born in London, he was raised in Aberdeen. Rangers signed him from Sunnybank Athletic in 1963, allowing him to continue playing for his local club before bringing him back to Ibrox full time. But he only made a handful of appearances during the remaining years of the decade.

However, in the 1970s he flourished as a reliable stopper who read the game well, tackled strongly and was terrific in the air – at both ends of the ground.

In season 1971/72 he finally found favour with Willie Waddell, missing only one game during the campaign and earning a League Cup winner's medal into the bargain. But it was under Jock Wallace that his career really took off, scoring the winner against his home town club, winning two Trebles and eight Scotland caps during the next ten years at Ibrox.

His biggest regret was missing out on the 1972 Cup-Winners' Cup final in Barcelona. Jackson had only dropped one match during the run to the final as Rangers eliminated Rennes, Sporting Club of Portugal, Torino and Bayern Munich. But he went over on his ankle in the build-up to the final against Moscow Dynamo and was ruled out to be replaced by the 18-year-old Derek Johnstone.

Jackson recalled, 'I was devastated. Ronnie McKinnon had broken his leg against Sporting and was already ruled out and he and I went out drinking. We ended up in a bit of state. Jock Wallace went mad and threw me under a cold shower, screaming that there could be a replay and that I had better be fit for it. I was so despondent I hadn't even thought about that.'

But eventually it all came right for the tall centre half. Invariably partnering Tom Forsyth in the centre of defence, he played over 50 games in both Treble campaigns – 1975/76 and 1977/78 – when the Light Blues' dominance of Scottish football was almost unchallenged. The following season Jackson's last-minute header gave Rangers a 2–1 win over Aberdeen in the League Cup final. Jackson said, 'That cup final winner was special but, being from Aberdeen originally, I wasn't allowed back in the city for about five years after that!'

The club went on to win the Scottish Cup that year, albeit after two replays with Hibs, during a campaign when the powerful defender reckons Europe's ultimate prize could also have been plundered. By then under the management of John Greig, Rangers reached the quarter-finals of the European Cup having eliminated Juventus and PSV Eindhoven, two of the favourites. Jackson remembers thinking that they should have gone on to win it. 'My big regret is that we didn't win the European Cup in 1979. We were good enough to do it and we slipped up, in my opinion, as a result of over-confidence.

'We lost out to Cologne in the quarter-finals and it was galling. We lost the first leg 1–0 and then we could only draw 1–1 at Ibrox and that was us out. Notts Forest put them out in the semi-finals and they went on to win it, of course. We would have fancied our chances against Forest. Indeed, I feel sure we would have beaten them. If we had just managed to keep our feet on the ground, I feel we could have gone all the way.'

Today, Jackson is a man who looks back on his career with pride. He has an active role in the Rangers Former Players Club, helping to raise funds for any ex-player who experiences difficulties. So, to be part of the Hall of Fame is a genuine thrill for him. He says, 'I consider it to be a great achievement. I often look up at the board at Ibrox and read through the names on it. It's great that my name is on there too.

'I only once felt like leaving Rangers and that was after a fall-out with Willie Waddell in 1972. Wolves, Coventry and Tottenham were all in the market but he wouldn't let me leave . . . I was also actually tapped up by Leeds United a few times but I chose not to go down and in the end they went for Gordon McQueen instead.

'I was glad that I stayed because I was part of a very good Rangers team that went on to win two Trebles in 1976 and 1978. I was also fortunate enough to play in some huge games, like the Cup-Winners' Cup semi-final against Bayern Munich in 1972 and a number of cup finals. I played for Scotland in a winning side against England at Hampden and I scored the winner in the 1978/79 League Cup final. I'm happy with that.'

Sandy Jardine (1964–1982)
BORN: 31 December 1948,
Edinburgh

APPEARANCES: 674
GOALS: 77

HONOURS WON WITH RANGERS
League titles (3) – 1974/75,
1975/76, 1977/78
Scottish Cups (5) – 1972/73,
1975/76, 1977/78, 1978/79,
1980/81
League Cups (5) – 1970/71,
1975/76, 1977/78, 1978/79,
1981/82
European Cup-Winners' Cup (1) –
1971/72
CAPS: 38 (Scotland)

CLASS, ELEGANCE and composure are just three words that fit perfectly with a man who was not only a fantastic player but also a great ambassador for Rangers. Only John Greig and Dougie Gray made more appearances for the club and yet it took nearly four seasons of first-team football before Sandy Jardine settled into the right back position – a role in which he was to excel. Of course, he went on to become a vital member of the side that won two Trebles in three years in a long career that marked him down as one of the greatest Rangers players of the post-war era.

Jardine came to Rangers from school at the age of 15. He

had just turned 18 when he made his debut at right half against Hearts in February 1967. He retained his place for the rest of the season and scored a screamer in a 2–2 draw against Celtic in the last League match of the campaign. But joy turned to disappointment when he played in the European Cup-Winners' Cup final later in May. Rangers lost 1–0 to an extra-time goal against Bayern Munich.

At the start of the 1968/69 season, on the instructions of manager Davie White, Jardine found himself playing centre forward. He had some striking success, scoring 11 goals in 12 consecutive appearances. But when Willie Waddell took over from White towards the end of 1969/70 he moved Jardine again, this time to full back. He was a natural. A reliable tackler with attacking instincts and armed with the skill and pace to get past people, he became one of the first exponents of the overlapping full back role.

He won his first major trophy in October 1970 in the 1–0 defeat of Celtic in the League Cup final and the following month he made his first appearance for Scotland, coming on as a substitute against Denmark at Hampden. His first international start came in October 1971 in a European Championships qualifier against Portugal. He marked the great Eusebio out of the game and Scotland won 2–1.

That was the beginning of what was to be a remarkable spell for Jardine. On 19 April he scored a crucial goal in the European Cup-Winners' Cup semi-final against Bayern Munich. A week later, on 27 April, he started a run of 171 consecutive appearances for the club, which continued until 30 August 1975, speaking volumes about his outstanding ability and his fitness. On 24 May that year he won a Cup-Winners' Cup winner's medal against Moscow Dynamo in Barcelona. He won a Scottish Cup winner's medal the following year and in 1974 he was selected for Scotland's squad for the World Cup in Germany.

After the tournament Jardine and Celtic's Danny McGrain, who represented Scotland together in 19 internationals, were spoken of as the best full back pairing in the competition. Scotland were undefeated, beating Zaire 2–0 and drawing with Brazil and Yugoslavia. They failed to qualify for the later stages only by virtue of having an inferior goal average to that of Brazil. But the Scots were impressive, and none more so than Jardine who played in all three matches.

Back home, the next season saw Rangers take the championship for the first time in 11 years. Jardine was again ever-present, scoring nine goals in 34 League games. He captained the side at Easter Road on the day that Colin Stein's header gave Rangers the point they needed to be champions – even if Sandy hit the post with a penalty! And he made way for the injured John Greig to come on in the final seconds as a substitute to savour the moment.

There was even more success to come, however, with two Trebles in three years in seasons 1975/76 and 1977/78. The trophies include two League Cup final victories over Celtic, 1–0 and 2–1, and Scottish Cup final wins against Hearts 3–1 and Aberdeen 2–1. During that 1975 League Cup run, Jardine scored five goals in seven games including a hat-trick against Airdrie.

He was again selected for the World Cup in Argentina in 1978. But he was troubled by injury and played only in the 1–1 draw with Iran. However, there was compensation in the 1978/79 season as Rangers retained both the Scottish and League Cups, beating Hibernian 3–2 after a second replay and Aberdeen 2–1 in the respective finals.

At the start of the 1979/80 season Jardine scored what was

probably the goal of his career. Facing Celtic in the Drybrough Cup final, he won possession in a tackle on the edge of his own penalty area then ran almost the length of the field, beating defender after defender. As he reached the Celtic box, he cut inside and unleashed a left-foot shot that rifled into the back of the net. It was a glorious goal – yet one which didn't quite get the credit it deserved. Rangers' final goal in that 3–1 victory was scored by Davie Cooper, who flicked the ball in the air four times over Celtic defenders before slotting it home. It was a breathtaking moment and as Jardine himself has said with wry humour, 'I hardly got a mention in the papers the following day.' But Jardine's strike remains one that any player would be proud to have locked away in his bag of memories.

There were two more cup winner's medals to be had – a 4–1 victory over Dundee United in a replayed Scottish Cup final in 1981 and, later in the year, a 2–1 League Cup final win over the same opponents. But the final break with the team that had won those two Trebles was soon approaching and, after playing in every League game in 1981/82, Jardine was released by the Light Blues and joined Hearts.

With Jardine as their sweeper, Hearts went close to honours in 1985/86, finishing runners-up in both the championship and the Scottish Cup. There was heartbreak in the League; they lost 2–0 at Dundee while Celtic beat St Mirren 5–1 to steal the title on goal difference. Jardine was chosen as Scotland's Player of the Year. He was 37 and it was the second time he had received the honour though he will tell you it was his third such award as he was part of the World Cup squad in 1974 who jointly received the accolade.

When he retired from playing, he became player-assistant manager and then joint manager at Hearts where he remained until 1988. He has been back at Ibrox for over a decade working first in the sales department and now in charge of scouting and player liaison. A man who is acutely aware of the club's history, Sandy is heavily involved in the Hall of Fame and has worked wonders expanding the club's archive.

Willie Johnston (1964–1973, 1980–1982)

BORN: 19 December 1946, Glasgow

APPEARANCES: 393

GOALS: 125

HONOURS WON WITH RANGERS

Scottish Cup (1) – 1965/66

League Cups (2) – 1964/65, 1970/71

European Cup-Winners' Cup (1) – 1971/72

CAPS: 9 (of 22 for Scotland)

EXPLOSIVE IS an entirely accurate description of the career of Willie Johnston – who is revered by Rangers fans all over the world for his goals in Barcelona but reviled by others for being sent home from the 1978 World Cup finals. He was explosively fast on the pitch but his temper had the same speed; most estimates reckon that he was sent off an incredible 22 times in his colourful career. Willie will tell you, 'I liked to get my retaliation in first!'

It had all started so peacefully when he arrived on the scene at Rangers as a dashing inside forward with a terrific nose for goal. Johnston had only played three first-team matches when Scot Symon selected him to face Celtic in front of 91,423 fans on 24 October 1964 in the League Cup final. To say he was nervous about the prospect is an understatement. 'Jim Baxter was my mentor that day because I was nearly too scared to go out of the dressing room,' recalled Johnston. 'I was only 17 and

I didn't think I should be there but Jim looked after me and settled me down. I will never forget it.

'Jim was the captain that day and he told me to just think of it as a game at the Albion training ground. He was so calm. Then he said to me, "Listen, if it's 0–0 in the last minute and we get a penalty, you go up for the cup and I'll take care of the penalty."

'He settled me down and it was a great game to play in. We had a few changes to our team that day because of injuries but it was a terrific win for us. Jim Forrest, who was on fire in that period, scored twice for us then Jimmy Johnstone got one back, but we did enough to win the cup. It was a fantastic occasion . . . Scot Symon showed faith in me that day and thanks to Jim I coped with it all.'

The whole season was a tremendous one for the teenager. Within a few months he played against Celtic again in the New Year game when Jim Forrest once more made the difference by scoring the only goal. Johnston also played four times in the European Cup during the campaign – including a thrilling match with Inter Milan who went on to win the trophy.

He was unfortunate that his breakthrough with Rangers coincided with the beginning of the best period in Celtic's history. So there was some irony that their manager Jock Stein handed Johnston his international debut in a World Cup qualifier against Poland in October 1965 when he was also in temporary charge of the national team.

By this time he was a regular in the Rangers team and he had begun to edge out Davie Wilson for the left-wing berth and he was in the Rangers team that won the Scottish Cup in 1966 when Kai Johansen's strike settled the replay with Celtic. Little did he know that he would not win another honour for over four years, such was Celtic's dominance of the period.

Johnston was a 'veteran' of 21 when that honour came along in the 1970/71 League Cup final when Derek Johnstone became an instant Rangers hero. Indeed it was Willie who supplied the cross from the right flank for 16-year-old 'DJ' to get between Billy McNeill and Jim Craig to head the only goal. Willie had played in losing finals to Celtic in 1965/66 and 1966/67, so he was pleased to even up the score with his second winner's medal.

Rangers had a decent side but Celtic's was better and when Rangers lost the European Cup-Winners' Cup final in 1967 to Bayern Munich just a week after Celtic had been crowned European Cup winners, it was a bitter pill for the Light Blues to swallow. Willie often said that if Rangers had had someone like Jock Stein in charge their results would have been different. So, when Rangers navigated their way to the 1971/72 Cup-Winners' Cup final, Johnston, John Greig, Sandy Jardine and Dave Smith – the survivors from 1967 – knew the importance of winning. Between them they were determined to make sure that this time there was to be no mistake. Willie – known as 'Bud' because of a coat he wore that made him look like Bud Flanagan – scored two superb goals as Moscow Dynamo were beaten 3–2. The first was a clever header from a Dave Smith cross and for the second he latched on to a huge Peter McCloy kick-out before calmly placing a left-foot shot beyond the Dynamo keeper.

Goalscoring seemed natural to Johnston, whose haul of 125 puts him in the club's top 20 scorers. Two of his most important strikes came during the run to the final that year. A vital equaliser against Rennes in France and another strike on foreign soil, this time in a 1–1 draw in Italy against Torino. But it was his indiscipline that ultimately convinced Rangers to sell him in December 1973 to West Bromwich Albion after yet another sending off – this time against Partick Thistle – which resulted in a nine-week suspension.

It took a then record fee of £138,000 to take him to the Hawthorns where he was a great success. His pace and trickery on the wing made him a fan favourite and eventually won him a Scotland recall just in time for the World Cup in 1978. However, the trip to Argentina turned into a nightmare for him. He tested positive for the banned substance fencamfamin after the dismal 3–1 defeat by Peru. The substance was in two tablets of Reactivan, a drug you could buy over the counter in the UK to boost patients who were feeling low or debilitated. Johnston was sent home in shame and he had to flee the country shortly afterwards because of abuse and press interest, moving to Canada where he played for the Vancouver Whitecaps.

John Greig brought him back to Rangers in 1980, paying £40,000 for his services, and Willie acquitted himself well for two seasons. He played 37 games in his first season back but was dropped for the Scottish Cup final replay against Dundee United, which Rangers won 4–1. His old mate Alex MacDonald signed him for Hearts and he prospered there for another two years before moving into coaching with East Fife, even turning out for them at the age of 39.

These days you're likely to find him in the Portbrae bar in Kirkcaldy where he still talks a great game.

Dave Smith (1966–1974)
BORN: 14 November 1943, Aberdeen

APPEARANCES: 303
GOALS: 13

HONOURS WON WITH RANGERS
European Cup-Winners' Cup (1) – 1971/72
CAPS: 1 (of 2 for Scotland)

SOME PEOPLE follow the mantra that you get all you deserve in life but that rule does not apply to a hugely gifted footballer who only achieved one major success in his career and undoubtedly deserved much more. In saying that, when the only success is generally regarded as the greatest in Rangers Football Club history then there has to be some comfort in that.

It is inevitable that all 11 players who took part in the European Cup-Winners' Cup final against Moscow Dynamo on 24 May 1972 would be given their place in the Hall of Fame and Dave Smith, along with Willie Mathieson and Alfie Conn, completed the inductions in 2007. Playing as a sweeper behind 18-year-old Derek Johnstone, centre half that night because Colin Jackson and Ronnie McKinnon were both injured, Smith was superb, nursing the talented youngster through the game. But he was also instrumental in two of the Rangers goals during that famous victory, setting up Colin Stein to smash in the opening goal and then producing a precision cross from which Willie Johnston found the net with a glancing header.

Smith said, 'I really thought we were on easy street all the way through the match. People might say that we panicked at the end, but we were 2–0 up at half time before making it three in the second half. I honestly thought we were pretty comfortable even though the second goal we lost with three minutes remaining was a bad mistake. But we never felt we were in any danger . . . The end of the game was a bit of an anticlimax as all the Rangers fans ran on and we had to sprint back to the dressing room . . . The cup was then presented to John Greig and Willie Waddell in a small room at the back of the Nou Camp so the party started when they came back.

'For me, the bigger game was the semi-final against Bayern Munich as they had beaten us in the 1967 final. I always felt that they were a bigger team than Moscow as they had more star players. Franz Beckenbauer and Gerd Müller were both in the squad and we overran them in the semi-final. That was a great result.'

An elegant, composed player with terrific ability, Smith signed for the Light Blues in August 1966 from Aberdeen for £50,000. It turned out to be a great bit of business for the club, but the move was in doubt right up to the last minute. Although discussions between the clubs were ongoing right up to the start of the 1966/67 season, Aberdonian Dave was worried that another 'Smith' might prevent his transfer as Rangers had moved for Dunfermline's Alex Smith a couple of days earlier. Aberdeen had made it clear that they were keen to keep a player they regarded as one of their biggest assets.

Dave Smith recalls the run up to his move, 'When I saw that Rangers had signed Alex Smith I thought my chance of moving to Ibrox had gone because he was also a midfielder. I had already turned down moves to Spurs and Everton and I remember thinking that if I was not moving to Rangers I would stay at Aberdeen.

'As it was, the team-sheet went up for Aberdeen's first game of the season and I was on it but Davie Shaw, who was the chairman at Pittodrie at that time, came to see me and said that I had to speak to the boss. So I went up to his office.

'The manager, Eddie Turnbull, told me that if I wanted to move to Rangers I had to be at Perth at 1.30 p.m. to meet them. It was 12 noon at the time so I knew I would struggle to make it. He didn't really want me to go, that's why he told me so late. But I went anyway and met up there with Scot Symon.

'To be honest I didn't even discuss terms with Symon. He just said that he would look after me and that was good enough for me. Mr Symon was a real gentleman and it was a pleasure to sign for him. I signed the day before the start of the season for £50,000, which was a top fee at the time.

'The funny thing was that the players at Rangers never really saw that much of him during the week, although he did occasionally come down to watch a bit of training. Normally we would just see him on a Saturday before the game and even then he didn't really tell us how to play, he just encouraged you really and that is what a lot of managers did at that time.

'I am probably from the old school but I am a great believer that managers are only as good as the players on the park. There is a lot of talk about tactics and things like that but if players don't perform to their best, it doesn't matter what the manager says, there is a good chance you will not win.'

In common with a number of other members of the Rangers Hall of Fame, Smith moved to Glasgow at a time when Celtic were dominant, so silverware was hard to come by. To compound matters he was injured for the League Cup final of 1970/71 and then left out of the Scottish Cup final team in 1973. He feels Rangers should have been more successful in his period because they had the players but simply lacked consistency. He said, 'If you look at the team we had when I was at the club Peter McCloy was as good a goalkeeper as you could get at that time as was Sandy Jardine at full back. John Greig was the heart of the team while Alex McDonald, Colin Stein and Willie Johnston, to name just a few, were all really good players. I am surprised that we didn't win the league because on paper we definitely had the players to match Celtic.'

Smith's performances in the 1971/72 season earned him the Scottish Football Writers' Association Player of the Year and, despite his lack of silverware he believes that he was lucky to be a part of a great Rangers team and always looks back at his time at Ibrox with great pride. He said, 'Of course it was great to win the Player of the Year award but for me the best thing about being a footballer was about pulling on the Rangers jersey. That was a great feeling and I was always proud to do that whether I was playing for the first or the second team.

'Speaking to fans now so many tell me how much it would mean to them to play one game for Rangers but I was lucky enough to make several hundred appearances for the club. I will always treasure my time at Ibrox and, deep down, I wish I hadn't left when I did.'

Smith moved on to Arbroath in November 1974 for £12,000 as player/coach. He later went on to become player/manager of Berwick Rangers and Peterhead and also enjoyed spells in America and South Africa. Of course, today he always loves to get back together with the Barcelona Bears.

Alex MacDonald (1968–1981)
BORN: 17 March 1948, Glasgow

APPEARANCES: 503
GOALS: 94

HONOURS WON WITH RANGERS
League titles (3) – 1974/75,
1975/76, 1977/78
Scottish Cups (4) – 1972/73,
1975/76, 1977/78, 1978/79
League Cups (4) – 1970/71,
1975/76, 1977/78, 1978/79
European Cup-Winners' Cup (1) –
1971/72
CAPS: 1 (Scotland)

PLAYERS HAVE come and gone at Ibrox – especially in recent years – and never really grasped what it means to pull on the blue jersey. For Alex MacDonald it was a joy and honour every time. Born in the Kinning Park area of Glasgow and a supporter for as long as he can remember, the flame-haired midfielder lived the dream and was an integral part of Rangers' successes in the 1970s.

MacDonald took time to settle, but emerged as the heartbeat of the team that triumphed in Europe in 1972 and went on to win two Trebles in the space of three seasons. He was combative and his energy was boundless. He became a terrific box-to-box player and had the uncanny ability of getting ahead of the strikers to score vital goals.

This scenario was perfectly illustrated at Hampden Park on

25 October 1975 when MacDonald scored the winner in the Old Firm League Cup final to set up what would be a clean sweep of the honours. Derek Parlane got away from his marker Roddy MacDonald to fire a cross into the Celtic box. Johannes Edvaldsson headed it out but only as far as Quinton Young who headed it back in and Alex dived to send a header past Peter Latchford. He said, 'It was the ultimate for me. It really was a dream come true. To score the winner against Celtic in a major final is something you can't really describe. I was doing what every one of my mates would have died to do – and I was getting paid for it.'

It is Willie Waddell who should take the credit for shaping MacDonald's career. He had started at St Johnstone where he first worked under Rangers' legendary Iron Curtain goalkeeper Bobby Brown and then Willie Ormond. Davie White signed him on 19 November 1968, paying £50,000, and MacDonald scored in his third match – a 3–0 away over Raith Rovers – but he was a peripheral figure at Ibrox in that first season.

When Waddell took over the following year, he encouraged the midfielder to change his game to become a 'push and run' player and the seeds of his future success were sown. At the time, though, Rangers were living in the shadow of Celtic and that was especially difficult for a diehard like 'Doddie'. Maybe his emotions got the better of him when he was sent off in a Scottish Cup third-round tie at Parkhead on 21 February 1970, for going in late on Celtic keeper Evan Williams.

However, nine months later he was involved in the move that gave him his first winner's medal and Rangers their first trophy in over four years. With 40 minutes gone in the League Cup final against Celtic, he swept a great ball out wide for Willie Johnston whose cross into the box was headed into the net by 16-year-old Derek Johnstone for the cup-winning goal.

It was a rare moment of joy for the success-starved Rangers fans. But while domestic bliss was still a few years away, glory in Europe came the following season and MacDonald was as responsible as anyone for delivering it. He played in all nine matches as Rangers knocked out Rennes of France, Sporting Club from Lisbon, Torino of Italy and then German giants Bayern Munich before defeating Moscow Dynamo in the European Cup-Winners' Cup final in Barcelona. It was MacDonald's goal at Ibrox which clinched a 2–1 aggregate win over Rennes and he did it again in the quarter-final against Torino when he stole in at the back post to bundle Tommy McLean's cross over the line.

MacDonald will never forget the memories of Barcelona and he still wears his winner's medal around his neck. He said, 'I had tickets for my brother-in-law and I had to actually throw the tickets out of the team bus to him. He didn't get to the hotel because they wouldn't let him in. He had travelled quite a distance like the rest of the Rangers supporters and I didn't want to let him down. It was just a sea of blue and it was great to see. That's one of the memories that stands out for me.'

Rangers seemed to be romping to victory in the final after Colin Stein's strike and two Willie Johnston goals put them three up, but Moscow scored twice late on. Rangers held on and the fans could not contain themselves when Spanish referee José Maria Ortiz de Mendibil blew for full time. But MacDonald's euphoria of winning was coupled with a fear of over-jubilant supporters endangering his well-being.

As he fought arduously through the crowds in an attempt to get to the Nou Camp tunnel, he suddenly felt himself being hoisted into the air and carried to safety. As he looked down he saw that one of the men carrying him was none other than his best pal who had arrived to be his saviour. Alex said, 'I had a couple of friends at the match who I grew up with in Kinning Park. One of them was Stuart Daniels and he helped look after me on the pitch at the end. I was lifted up and shunted across to the tunnel . . . Big Stuart was great but the whole situation was unbelievable. I've never seen so many people.

'When we flew home and got back to Ibrox a great memory for me was seeing Bobby Shearer in the crowd. He was standing in the pouring rain and it was fantastic to see him in there with the fans.'

MacDonald won his first Scottish Cup medal in 1973 when Celtic were beaten 3–2 in the final and he was in the team at Easter Road in March 1975 when a draw with Hibs gave Rangers the title for the first time in 11 years to end Celtic's stranglehold on Scottish football.

The next three years were phenomenal. Rangers swept the board in 1975/76 and MacDonald scored the second goal – a low volley through a ruck of players – in the 3–1 Scottish Cup final win over Hearts which sealed the Treble. They did it again in 1977/78. MacDonald only missed three games as Celtic were beaten in the League Cup final, the title was clinched on the last day with a 2–0 win over Motherwell and then MacDonald scored in the 2–1 Scottish Cup final win over Aberdeen.

He won his last medal the following season, when Hibs were beaten in the second replay of the Scottish Cup final, and then moved to Hearts in 1980. Two years later he took over as manager at Tynecastle and in 1986 he was seven minutes from winning the Premier Division title when Albert Kidd scored against Hearts for Dundee and Celtic won the pennant on goal difference. He was hugely successful as Airdrie boss too, taking them into the top division, two Scottish Cup finals and European football.

These days, having retired from football, he is back to being simply Alex MacDonald, Rangers fan. Having been at the hub of so many famous Rangers triumphs, he can be proud of his achievements. But he is as humble as ever, 'It's something that you can't really explain. From childhood and going to school you dream about playing for Rangers and you think that doing that would be the ultimate.

'But then, so many years on I was actually voted into the Hall of Fame to join people like Jimmy Millar and Jim Baxter. It was absolutely unbelievable.'

Colin Stein (1968–1972, 1975–1978)
BORN: 10 May 1947, Linlithgow

APPEARANCES: 206
GOALS: 97

HONOURS WON WITH RANGERS
League Cups (2) – 1970/71, 1975/76
European Cup-Winners' Cup (1) – 1971/72
CAPS: 17 (of 21 for Scotland)

A RECORD transfer, hat-tricks, punch-ups, a brand new house and two of the most important goals in the club's history – it all happened at Rangers for Colin Stein. He was the darling of the fans in the late 1960s and early 1970s for his aggressive all-action style and, but for another Stein across the city, he would have been considerably more successful during his time with Rangers.

Of course, he will forever be revered for his thunderous right-foot shot which screamed into the Moscow Dynamo net in the Cup-Winners' Cup final as Rangers sealed European glory in 1972. And it was Stein's header which tore into the roof of the Hibs net on 29 March 1975 that clinched Rangers their first championship in 11 years. Though, cruelly, he did not get a medal that time.

Rangers paid what was then a record fee of £100,000 to sign Stein from Hibs on 31 October 1968, and his impact was immediate and spectacular. He scored a hat-trick on his debut –

a 5–1 win over Arbroath at Gayfield on 2 November – and seven days later he scored another triple as his former club were thrashed 6–1. The bookies were worried he was going to make it three in a row when Rangers travelled to face Dundalk in the Fairs Cup. Stein scored twice and was only denied a treble when his shot came off one post, ran along the line and hit the other post.

However, Stein's problem was that his temper was as explosive as his goalscoring and he regularly fell foul of officials. Indeed, there is little doubt that suspensions in his first season at Ibrox were hugely costly to Rangers. He was involved in a scuffle with Tommy McLean – who subsequently joined Rangers himself – at Kilmarnock on 4 January 1969 and Billy Dickson charged in to assist McLean. Stein and Dickson ended up trading punches and both were sent off. In those days suspensions were time periods rather than matches and Stein was banned for 28 days, though he only missed one match on that occasion due to postponements.

His second suspension was much more damaging. He had scored his third hat-trick for Rangers in a 6–0 trouncing of Clyde on 16 March when he was roughly challenged by Clyde defender Eddie Mulheron. Mulheron had two or three kicks at Stein and eventually the Rangers striker retaliated. He was suspended until 1 May and therefore the rest of the season and Rangers suffered badly. They missed his presence and goals in the League run-in, winning just three of their last seven games and handing the title to Celtic, and also in the Scottish Cup final when Celtic won 4–0 to continue their dominance of Rangers at the time.

Ironically, when his suspension was over he went on to star for Scotland. He scored against Wales, Northern Ireland and England and then struck four times in an 8–0 win over Cyprus.

That remains the last time a Scotland international player has scored a hat-trick.

In the following season there was some apparent interest from English clubs, most notably Everton, and Stein managed to secure a meeting with Rangers chairman John Lawrence to talk about his contract. This was highly unusual but, as Stein sat at one end of a long table and building tycoon Lawrence sat at the other end, the player managed to negotiate for himself a £10,000 payment and a brand new house!

He finally tasted success as a Rangers player in the 1970/71 League Cup final, a match made famous by his teenage strike partner Derek Johnstone who scored the only goal of the game against Celtic. Stein said, 'The pressure was on in that game because we hadn't won a major trophy for four years. We were a very good team then but we lacked consistency. We seemed to be unable to put runs together and that's what cost us. We would play really well for two games and then average the next.

'I remember Willie Waddell going up to Derek and telling him he was playing and I think Derek was more surprised than anybody. It turned out perfectly, of course, because he was in the right place at the right time. It was Willie Johnston who crossed the ball and big Derek went in between Jim Craig and Billy McNeill to head the only goal of the game. I had only played with him in bounce games [friendlies] before that.'

Stein finished as Rangers' top scorer that season with 20 goals in all competitions including a strike against Bayern Munich in the Fairs Cup. The Germans prevailed on that occasion, winning 2–1 on aggregate but Stein and Rangers were to have their revenge.

But the season was blackened by the Ibrox Disaster on 2 January 1971 when 66 people were crushed to death after a dramatic conclusion to the traditional New Year derby. With the game seemingly going to finish goalless, Jimmy Johnstone scored for Celtic in the 89th minute then Stein equalised for Rangers with just seconds left. It is still wrongly reported in certain quarters today that the carnage occurred as fans tried to get back in to celebrate Stein's goal. The terrible accident did not happen until five minutes after the final whistle.

It was a tribute therefore that a little over a year later Rangers were kings of Europe and Stein was at the hub of the glorious run. He played in all nine matches on the road to the final in Barcelona. Perhaps he was most effective in the amazing second-round tie with Sporting Club. He scored twice at Ibrox in a 3–2 win and then twice in Lisbon in a 4–3 defeat after extra time. With the aggregate scores level, the referee wrongly awarded penalties and Rangers missed all of theirs. However, he rectified his mistake immediately and awarded the tie to the Light Blues on the away-goals rule that had come in that season.

Stein's goal in the final was a great piece of finishing. He latched on to a long ball from Dave Smith and, stretching, managed to fire a right-foot shot into the net. Stein recalled, 'It was an incredible time and one I will never forget. That European run was obviously the highlight of my Rangers career and looking back I think it was a fantastic achievement. The teams we beat to get to the final were of the highest calibre.'

His close friend Willie Johnston scored the other two in the famous 3–2 win over Moscow Dynamo. Amazingly they both left Ibrox for England within a matter of months of the Barcelona triumph. Stein joined Coventry City in a deal worth £140,000 which included Quinton Young moving from Highfield Road to Ibrox.

Stein did well in the English First Division, scoring 20 times in 80 games. However, he came back to Ibrox in March 1975 – largely due to the fact that Coventry could not continue making their payments on the transfer fee – and scored that crucial goal at Easter Road which won the title. The following season he won the League Cup for the second time when he played up front with Derek Parlane while Derek Johnstone played in midfield in the 1–0 win over Celtic.

However, the two Dereks were the regular strikeforce and Stein's involvement was limited. The following season he played just two games and, not enthralled at the thought of reserve team football, he jumped at the chance to go to Kilmarnock on loan in the 1977/78 season, even though they were in the First Division at the time. Remarkably, he helped Killie knock Celtic out of the Scottish Cup and then, ironically, lost 4–1 in the quarter-finals to Rangers at Ibrox.

He was released by Rangers at the end of the season and, aged just 30, he retired from playing. He said, 'When I went back to Rangers I was getting close to my sell-by date. In the end I was sick of the reserves so I gave up. However, I have memories I will cherish forever.'

Alfie Conn (1968–1974)

BORN: 5 April 1952, Kirkcaldy

APPEARANCES: 149

GOALS: 39

HONOURS WON WITH RANGERS

Scottish Cup (1) – 1972/73

League Cup (1) – 1970/71

European Cup-Winners' Cup (1) – 1971/72

THE BOLD and brave decision to cross the Old Firm divide at a time when the rivalry between Rangers and Celtic was as fierce as ever means Alfie Conn's actions are still debated by Rangers fans to this day. Conn's swashbuckling style made him an icon for many young supporters in the early 1970s and he played a considerable part in the major successes of Rangers at the time. By the tender age of 21, Conn had collected the League Cup, scored in an epic Scottish Cup final victory over Celtic and forever etched his name into Ibrox lore by being a member of the team that achieved European glory in Barcelona.

Enough, you might think, to be highly thought of for the rest of his days. Conn, however, committed the cardinal sin of crossing the great divide and signed for the Parkhead club after three years in England with Tottenham. Such is the rivalry in the world of the Old Firm, his decision was seen as treacherous.

Even now there are those who are unforgiving, but time has been a great healer and Conn has made it plain that Rangers are still his first love. So why on earth did he sign for Celtic in 1977? 'It was a case of wanting to play for Jock Stein. Looking back, if it had been any other manager I don't think I would have crossed the divide,' revealed Conn. 'I had a mortgage to pay and although there were a couple of offers from England they were not really suitable.

'So I came back to Scotland. I never had the chance to say "yes" to a return to Ibrox because I was never asked. I supported Rangers from when I was boy and when I look back now on the time I signed for Celtic, I wonder if I did the right thing.

'As I say, I had a mortgage to pay and a family to look after. I think some of the fans have forgiven me, especially after I have spoken to them, but the abuse was hard to take at times. I can appreciate their feelings because it must be difficult to see a Rangers player going to play for the other side. Fortunately, a lot of the fans have mellowed and it's just something that I have to live with.'

Conn signed for Celtic in March 1977 and the irony is that he won his only League championship medal with the Parkhead club that season. He further infuriated the Light Blue Legions by helping Celtic to victory in the Scottish Cup final that year, becoming the first man to win medals with both sides of the Old Firm.

Four years earlier Alfie had starred for Rangers against Celtic in the Centenary final, which finished 3–2 in the Light Blues' favour, and it is a memory he cherishes. He said, 'The 1973 Scottish Cup final which was one of the greatest Old Firm finals – if not the best. The Rangers supporters were unbelievable that day. I have never seen as many Rangers fans at one game. They were actually spilling into the Celtic end as well.

'It was a fantastic game and a lot of people remember it for Tam Forsyth's winner, but I was fortunate enough to score in the game too. I didn't realise I had that much pace at the time but it was Billy McNeill who was chasing me so I knew I had a chance of getting there first. I did and slipped the ball under Ally Hunter.

'It was funny, before the game we all had short studs in our boots and Big Tam said, "I'm putting two big ones in the back". And it was just as well he did! If he had had the short studs he might have missed it.'

Of course, the previous year, when just 20, Conn and Rangers lifted the European Cup-Winners' Cup after beating Moscow Dynamo. He said, 'I can still remember the game clearly, but the thing was I had no idea I was playing until the last minute.

'It was announced before the game that Andy Penman was going to be playing so it looked as though I would be on the bench. I didn't find out until the pre-match meal when the team was read out that I was in the starting line-up.

'I then couldn't eat because I was in the toilet being sick! It was such a shock to me. I had spoken to my father the night before and he had been told that Andy Penman was in. Then Willie Waddell dropped the bombshell! Actually, it turned out to be the best way to prepare – other than throwing up in the toilet! – because I had no time to be nervous really.

'It was quite a young team at the time. Derek Johnstone was only 18 and the elder statesman was John Greig who was only 29. However, the strange thing was that the team that won that night never really played together again. Within a year, Colin Stein and Willie Johnston had gone, Willie Henderson had left just prior to the final and I was off the following year. I would say that the Cup-Winners' Cup team – in a one-off game – was the best Rangers team I played in and could have competed with anybody in Europe.'

Peter McCloy (1970–1986)

BORN: 16 November 1946, Girvan, Ayrshire

APPEARANCES: 533
GOALS: 0

HONOURS WON WITH RANGERS
League titles (2) – 1975/76, 1977/78
Scottish Cups (4) – 1972/73, 1975/76, 1977/78, 1978/79
League Cups (4) – 1970/71, 1978/79, 1983/84, 1984/85
European Cup Winners' Cup (1) – 1971/72
CAPS: 4 (Scotland)

MOST GOOD goalkeepers are renowned for shot-stopping, reflexes or the ability to hold cross balls, but the man known as the 'Girvan Lighthouse' can boast two other major attributes – longevity and fantastic kicking. A Peter McCloy clearance was something to behold. He seemed to launch the ball into the atmosphere and when it came down it invariably caused havoc in the opposition defence. This skill was never more apparent than in the European Cup-Winners' Cup final of 1972 when McCloy's huge kick was controlled by Willie Johnston and promptly fired into the net to put Rangers 3–0 up against Moscow Dynamo.

Route one football it might have been, but it was thoroughly successful and with players Derek Johnstone and Derek Parlane in the Rangers front line in the 1970s, a McCloy clearance was a regular ploy. The Light Blues were losing the 1976 Scottish Cup semi-final to Motherwell when, with ten minutes to go, McCloy launched the ball forward and, after one bounce, Johnstone headed it into the net for an equaliser before netting a winner two minutes from time.

However, there was much more to the 6ft 4in Ayrshireman who spent 16 years at Ibrox and made more appearances than any other goalkeeper in the club's history, achieving 214 shut-outs in 533 games. His height – hence the nickname – meant that he was highly adept at dealing with cross balls or corners but he was a good shot-stopper too.

It was Willie Waddell who signed him from Motherwell in March 1970, with Bobby Watson and Brian Heron going in the other direction. Peter had spent six years at Fir Park and he relished the transition. He said, 'I was actually playing in the reserves when Willie Waddell signed me so he must have seen something he liked before then . . . I had no idea I would play for Rangers for so long. When you are a player you just take one season at a time and when you come from a smaller club it's not just about ability it's about adjusting mentally as well.'

Rangers, of course, were struggling domestically when McCloy joined but he helped them win their first silverware in over four years when, in only his second Old Firm game, they beat Celtic 1–0 in the 1970/71 League Cup final made famous by 16-year-old Derek Johnstone's winning goal.

A common perception of Jock Wallace is that he was a growling disciplinarian who favoured fitness over finesse, but McCloy benefited more than most from the man who was coach at the time he joined but became the hugely successful manager of the 1970s. Wallace had been a goalkeeper as a player and took a special interest in the giant Girvan man. McCloy said, 'It was not quite like goalkeeping coaching of today, but it was the first time I had specialist work. Of course, I still had to do all of the hard training but it was good to work specifically on technique and situations. John Greig was also a big influence on me when I joined because he was a great captain and he had a wealth of experience. But I was also lucky that I had some good defenders in front of me like Ronnie McKinnon and Davie Smith initially and then Colin Jackson.'

Like all ten other Barcelona Bears, there is no doubt that 24 May 1972 constitutes the greatest moment of McCloy's career. He said, 'There is no doubt the European run was the biggest highlight. We took some great scalps on the road and then to win it in Barcelona was fantastic.

'One of the secrets to winning it was the way we played away from home. We secured great results by defending from the front. The biggest achievement was knocking out Bayern because of their quality but obviously the final will live with us forever. The Russians were a bit of an unknown quantity to us but they'd taken a lot of good scalps on the way there.

'Our season had finished two or three weeks earlier, so match-sharpness was a bit of a worry. I'm sure that had an effect in the latter stages of the game when we allowed them back into it after looking like cruising when we were 3–0 up. We took our foot off the pedal because we saw the finishing line coming and at the end we were hanging on a bit.

'People didn't realise the achievement, you know. They say it is only the Cup-Winners' Cup but back then it was a major tournament, filled with top teams. I know the Lisbon Lions are revered by the Celtic supporters, and rightly so. Maybe we didn't always get that recognition but you won't find us complaining because we know how hard it was to win that trophy.'

Rangers won the Scottish Cup the following season, beating

Celtic 3–2 in a classic final, but McCloy still cannot understand why they didn't make it a League and Cup Double. Rangers won 17 and drew one of their last 18 matches but still lost out on the title by one point. McCloy said, 'The 1973 final was a great memory too. We had played really well that season and I think we were unbeaten from November but just missed out in the League, so to beat Celtic to win the cup was great.

'It wasn't until 1975 that we finally won the title and stopped Celtic's run and we went on to win another two League titles in the next three years.'

In the summer of 1973 Jock Wallace signed a new keeper, Stewart Kennedy from Stenhousemuir, and the two men battled for the gloves for the next five years. Kennedy got the nod for the 1974/75 campaign – the season Rangers finally ended Celtic's stranglehold of the title – and was also between the sticks in the League Cup final triumphs of 1975/76 and 1977/78. However, the resilient McCloy fought back to win League and Scottish Cup medals in each of those two seasons. Indeed, there is a marvellous photograph of McCloy swinging on the Hampden crossbar after Steve Ritchie had scored a rather freakish late goal in the 1978 Scottish Cup final, but they all count as a second Treble in three years went to Ibrox.

Again McCloy's resolve was tested when John Greig signed Middlesbrough keeper Jim Stewart in March 1981 but he fought back again and played in the League Cup-winning teams of 1983/84 and 1984/85. He said, 'A club like Rangers always has to have a few good goalkeepers and in those days if you lost your place you just had to fight your way back in. You can lose form but you never lose ability. I had a few offers to move away and there was more money in England, but I was happy at Rangers.'

Come the Souness Revolution in 1986 McCloy became the

club's goalkeeping coach, working with Chris Woods, and then moved on to do freelance work, at Hearts and Dundee among other clubs. You will find him back at Ibrox these days working for the hospitality department on match days.

Derek Johnstone (1970–1983, 1985–1986)

BORN: 4 November 1953, Dundee

APPEARANCES: 546

GOALS: 210

HONOURS WON WITH RANGERS
League titles (3) – 1974/75, 1975/76, 1977/78
Scottish Cups (5) – 1972/73, 1975/76, 1977/78, 1978/79, 1980/81
League Cups (5) – 1970/71, 1975/76, 1977/78, 1978/79, 1981/82
European Cup-Winners' Cup (1) – 1971/72
CAPS: 14 (Scotland)

IN ONE instant during the afternoon of 24 October 1970 Derek Johnstone became an Ibrox icon. Willie Johnston's cross came over from the right and the strapping teenager leapt between Billy McNeill and Jim Craig to head the ball into the Celtic net in front of 106,263 to win the League Cup for Rangers. It was the club's first major honour in four years.

For the next ten years and more he thrilled the Rangers supporters with his goals and especially his headers, invariably from Tommy McLean crosses. Only Ally McCoist has scored more than Johnstone's 132 League goals in the post-war era and the overall total of 210 is all the more remarkable given that he played a large percentage of his 546 games at centre back or in midfield.

He was 16 years and 355 days old when he was picked by manager Willie Waddell to play in the League Cup final against Celtic that day in 1970. He had made his debut just a month before, scoring twice in a 5–0 League victory over Cowdenbeath. His only other first-team appearance had been as a substitute against Motherwell two weeks later.

Waddell's coach, Jock Wallace, told Johnstone to get a good night's sleep on the eve of the big game – but the excitement was too much for a teenage kid and he tossed and turned all night. However, when his moment came he took it with relish. He said, 'The game was a bit of a blur for me, to be honest. It all happened so quickly and I have told many people since that if you get to a cup final try to savour every minute . . . I didn't really realise how important it was at that time to win that trophy and I suppose it was the same a couple of years later when we won in Barcelona.'

He was just 18 when Rangers travelled to Barcelona to face Moscow Dynamo in the European Cup-Winners' Cup final in May 1972. He recalled, 'I wasn't actually playing until the day of the game. Colin [Jackson] had been carrying an injury for a few weeks and had been limping quite a bit. I thought he would have made it and I think if he had had another couple of days he would have played. But on the morning of the game he had a fitness test and it was clear to everybody that he was unfit. That's when I was told I was playing, just a matter of hours before kick-off. I had played at the back before but doing so in a major European final was something else.

'It was all a bit difficult to comprehend because I was so young, but I was glad to go in beside Davie Smith in defence because he was the biggest influence on me when I was asked to play that position. He was one of those players who spoke to you constantly during the game. He told me to go for everything as it didn't matter if I missed something because he would be at my back. That was a big comfort for me. I was worried about making a mistake and a forward cashing in on it and getting a goal.'

Johnstone played like a veteran in the heart of the Light Blues defence as Rangers won 3–2 and cherishes the memory of the greatest night in the club's long and distinguished history.

Before he was 20 years old he had claimed a Scottish Cup winner's medal in the epic 1973 final when Celtic were beaten 3–2. The Hampden woodwork denied him the chance of scoring a cup final winner for the second time when his header hit one post, ran along the line and hit the other post before Tom Forsyth famously forced the ball over the line. Johnstone said, 'I didn't mind that much because Tom was such a nice guy he deserved his moment.'

Johnstone won his first championship medal in 1974/75 when Rangers finally ended Celtic's dominance of the League, a triumph to which he contributed 14 goals, his best return so far. But as Rangers' form soared, so did his goalscoring. In 1975/76 he scored 31 goals and in 1977/78 he blasted 38 as Rangers swept the board on each occasion.

The 1975/76 season started with a bang as Johnstone scored a fantastic goal from the edge of the box in a 2–1 win over Celtic on the first day of the first ever Premier Division. In March he single-handedly defeated Motherwell in the Scottish Cup semi-final, earning a penalty and then scoring twice as Rangers won 3–2. In April he scored a goal after 22 seconds against home town club Dundee United to clinch the title for Rangers as his brothers watched from the terraces. In May he scored after 42 seconds in the final against Hearts, a goal actually recorded as coming at 2.59 p.m., before the scheduled kick-off time, as referee Bobby Davidson had started the game early. Johnstone scored a second goal nine minutes from the end as Rangers romped to a 3–1 win.

However, season 1977/78 was even better. His 25 League goals helped Rangers secure the title and he scored in the Scottish Cup final, again from a McLean cross, as Aberdeen were beaten 2–1. Johnstone was on fire all season and was voted Scotland's Player of the Year. He scored for the national team in the 1–1 draws with Wales and Northern Ireland, the former being a sensational 16-yard header from Archie Gemmill's driven cross.

He went to Argentina for the World Cup finals but he never saw eye-to-eye with manager Ally MacLeod and, even when things were going wrong for the team, the manager did not use him. It was a miserable end to what should have been the best season of his life and the turmoil was not over as Jock Wallace resigned as manger at Ibrox during the summer of 1978.

One of new boss John Greig's first moves was to install Johnstone as skipper. Despite having to switch between centre back and centre forward all season Rangers nearly won the Treble that year. They beat Aberdeen 2–1 in the League Cup final, then disposed of Hibs in the Scottish Cup final replay thanks to two goals from captain Johnstone. However, they were pipped for the flag by Celtic, and that was as close as Johnstone ever got again.

The team began to lack consistency, but he enjoyed a fantastic 4–1 Scottish Cup final replay win over Dundee United in 1981 and won his last Rangers medal the following season in the League Cup against the same opponents.

In 1983, he was transferred to Chelsea for £30,000, but by January 1985 he was back at Ibrox for a second stint. He played

19 League games over two seasons, but he was coming to the end of his career and retired from playing in 1986. He tried his hand at managment, briefly in the hot seat at Partick Thistle, but has subsequently carved out a successful career in the Scottish media, most notably as a pundit and host on Radio Clyde.

Tommy McLean (1971–1982)
BORN: 2 June 1947, Larkhall,
Lanarkshire

APPEARANCES: 452
GOALS: 57

HONOURS WON WITH RANGERS
League titles (3) – 1974/75,
1975/76, 1977/78
Scottish Cups (4) – 1972/73,
1975/76, 1977/78, 1978/79
League Cups (3) – 1975/76,
1977/78, 1978/79
European Cup-Winners' Cup (1) –
1971/72
CAPS: 1 (of 5 with Scotland)

FEW PLAYERS can claim to have had more of an impact on Rangers for a concerted period in the modern game than Tommy McLean, who was at the hub of the 1970s glories. Although small in stature, his influence was massive because he was such a clever player. It hardly seems right to describe him as a winger, because there was so much more to his play.

He was not a dribbler or a speed merchant, although he could certainly go past defenders. His real craft was in passing, crossing and set pieces. His delivery was superb and the strikers of the period gorged on his services, most notably Derek Johnstone who invariably gave a McLean cross or free kick the justice it deserved by heading it into the net.

There are numerous examples of this, but the opening goal

in the 1976 Scottish Cup final against Hearts exemplified the point. McLean had hatched the plan with Johnstone before kick-off. Johnstone said, 'Wee Tam told me that if we got a free kick I was to walk to the back post then run to the front post and he would find me.'

Find him he did with a perfectly flighted ball with less than a minute played and Johnstone's header nestled in the corner of the Hearts net as the procession to the Treble began.

Tommy said, 'We had a good understanding and it worked well. There were two aspects to it. He would either get on the end of my crosses or, if he didn't, he would make sure the defender didn't get it and that would leave space for others.'

McLean had been a bit of a child prodigy, breaking into the Kilmarnock team at 16 and helping them win the championship in 1965 under Willie Waddell. He already had experience of international and European football when Waddell signed him for Rangers in the summer of 1971. Indeed the deal was concluded in Copenhagen the night before Scotland beat Denmark 1–0 in a European Championships qualifier. Curiously, it turned out to be the last of McLean's five Scotland appearances but Rangers most certainly benefited from his skills.

He had the chance to sign for Rangers as a young teenager but was worried he would find it impossible to dislodge players like Alex Scott and Willie Henderson. McLean was then offered the chance to join Chelsea in 1967 where he could have linked up with the likes of Peter Osgood, Charlie Cooke and David Webb but he felt he was too young to move to London.

Of course, it was Henderson, the favourite of so many Rangers fans, who made way for McLean when Waddell made the move in 1971. Henderson cut his own throat. He walked out on Rangers in January 1972 after a row with Waddell due to his lack of involvement and when he came back he only played two more matches before being freed 22 days before McLean and Rangers were crowned kings of Europe.

Not surprisingly, winning the Cup-Winners' Cup in his first season as a Rangers player ranks as McLean's greatest moment. He said, 'Celtic were the dominant force at that time so for us to go and win in Europe was a magnificent achievement. I think what we did in 1972 was overlooked a bit when you consider the quality of the teams that we eliminated on the road – especially Bayern Munich.

'They featured half of the German team that won the European Championships that year and then the World Cup two years later with players like Beckenbauer, Müller, Breitner and Maier. To be honest, we were given a hammering over in Germany in the first leg of the semi-final but we came out of the game with a 1–1 draw and that was a sign of the character of the team.'

Of course, while victory in Europe was so sweet Rangers craved local success and McLean was a pivotal figure in ending the 11-year wait for championship success. He only missed one match in the 1974/75 season – the last of the old 18-team First Division – and he scored a remarkable 15 goals in 33 games including a hat-trick against Dumbarton. His total also included the second goal in the 3–0 New Year defeat of Celtic with a great run and well-placed, left-foot shot on a muddy surface at which most modern players would gawp in disbelief.

Similarly, McLean only sat out one League match and one League Cup match the following season as Rangers really clicked into gear and swept to a glorious Treble, beating Celtic 1–0 in the League Cup final, clinching the first Premier Division title at Tannadice and then that 3–1 win over Hearts in the Scottish Cup final on 1 May 1976.

With Davie Cooper, Gordon Smith and Bobby Russell added to the ranks in 1977/78, Rangers achieved a clean sweep again and McLean was a key man once more. It was a fantastic time for Rangers and their supporters, something that was not lost on McLean who knew what it meant to so many. He said, 'I was fortunate to win a lot of medals in that period and the key was that much of the team stayed together for a five- or six-year period and that meant that the spirit was fantastic. We all played for each other and we got on well off the park too. We had stopped Celtic's dominance and we knew how important that was to the supporters.'

McLean won both the League Cup and the Scottish Cup again in the 1978/79 season when only a 4–2 defeat at Celtic Park stopped them from winning a third Treble in four years. The team was breaking up, however. Tommy was on the bench for the 1981 Scottish Cup final replay win over Dundee United and missed the League Cup final against the same opponents the following year.

He retired at the end of that season at the age of 33 but became John Greig's assistant as the legendary captain tried to revive the fortunes of an ailing giant. The stress became too much for Greig, who quit on 28 October 1983, and Tommy was in temporary charge for four matches. He was not a roaring success: losing 3–0 at St Mirren, 2–1 at home to Celtic and going out of Europe by losing to Porto on the away-goals rule. His only success was a 3–0 League Cup win over Clydebank.

However, the seeds of his interest in management had been sown. He became Morton manager initially but quickly moved to Motherwell where he did a great job, winning the Scottish Cup in 1991, beating his brother Jim's Dundee United side 4–3 in the final.

McLean returned to Rangers to work in the youth

department in 2001 and helped with the development of the likes of Alan Hutton, Charlie Adam, Ross McCormack and Chris Burke, before leaving the club in 2004 to pursue other interests.

Tom Forsyth (1972–1982)
BORN: 23 January 1949, Glasgow

APPEARANCES: 326

GOALS: 6

HONOURS WON WITH RANGERS
League titles (3) – 1974/75,
1975/76, 1977/78
Scottish Cups (4) – 1972/73,
1975/76, 1977/78, 1980/81
League Cups (2) – 1975/76,
1977/78
CAPS: 21 (of 22 with Scotland)

IT IS the ultimate dream of any football player to score the winner in a cup final, but to do it in an Old Firm game on the 100th anniversary of both the tournament and your club takes some beating. Tom Forsyth is the man who lived that dream, famously scuffing the ball into the net with his studs from six inches to clinch victory in one of the greatest ever Hampden showpieces.

Forsyth went on to become a terrific central defender for Rangers and Scotland but in those days he was a tough tackling midfielder who had joined the club from Motherwell less than a year earlier. He was certainly not known for his goals. Indeed, in a ten-year Rangers career he only scored six. However, as someone once said, it's quality not quantity and Forsyth's match-winner in 1973 in front of 122,714 fans is one of the most famous cup final clinchers of all time.

Rangers were drawing 2–2 with their Glasgow rivals when a

Derek Johnstone header hit the post, trickled along the goal-line, hit the other post and fell nicely for Tom to bundle the ball home with his studs.

The tough-tackling defender recalls that great day in front of a bumper crowd at Hampden, 'To play in your first Scottish Cup final and score the winning goal was just a dream come true. As a boy you dream about those things and it was unbelievable really . . . I just followed it in, but I honestly thought Derek's header was going in. They all say I nearly missed it but I tapped it in and they can't take it away from me. Derek did all the hard work by heading it off both posts, but I got the goal and the credit, which was unusual.'

There was certainly a bite to his tackling and his no-nonsense style earned him a nickname from a massive box office movie of the time. He said, 'A reporter, Allan Herron, made up the name "Jaws" for me. I didn't really like it but it seemed to stick.

'If I had caught him I would have killed him! I think the nickname came from the way I played. I was an uncompromising kind of player and I think the name arose from that. The film was not long out and so the reporter made the comparison between me and the killer shark!'

Of course, it was preventing goals that was his forte and he formed a terrific partnership in central defence with Colin Jackson as Rangers stormed to the Treble twice in three seasons under Jock Wallace in 1975/76 and 1977/78. Tom recalled, 'I struck up a great partnership with Colin at the back. We covered for each other really well and we got on well off the park also.

'When you are friends away from football it makes it easier when you're playing together as well. It got to the stage where we had an instinctive partnership. I knew when he was going to attack the ball and when he was going to hang back and let me go forward . . . We were quite similar players but he was much better at heading the ball than me. I was more of a ball-winner who would win tackles and then give it to someone who could use it.'

Perhaps Forsyth's most famous tackle was at Hampden Park on 15 May 1976 when the curtain came down on an incredible season of Scottish football. Rangers had already swept the board. Forsyth marked Kenny Dalglish out of the game as Rangers beat Celtic 1–0 in the League Cup final and the 24 goals conceded – 18 better than Celtic – en route to the inaugural Premier Division title was indicative of Forsyth's influence at the back. The Scottish Cup completed the Treble – the first since 1964 – when Hearts were comfortably defeated 3–1, but Forsyth's season was far from finished.

He and Jackson were the backline for Scotland in the Home Internationals and both Wales and Northern Ireland were defeated, 3–1 and 3–0 respectively, setting up a finale with England, who had humiliated the Scots 5–1 the previous year at Wembley.

Southampton's Mick Channon was the main danger and he had put England one up, but a header from Don Masson and then a mis-hit from Dalglish that famously trickled though Ray Clemence's legs, gave the Scots the lead. Suddenly, Channon seemed to be in the clear and an equaliser looked inevitable but Forsyth saved the day with a magnificently timed tackle and Scotland held on to win.

Forsyth was an integral part of the Scotland team during this period. He had captained Scotland earlier that season when they beat Switzerland 1–0 in a friendly; and he was also in the side that famously won 2–1 at Wembley in 1977 when the Tartan Army took over the home of English football, ripped down the goal frames and most of the turf. He recalled, 'That was a fantastic occasion. I've never experienced anything like that in my life. Before the game the team bus could hardly get down Wembley Way as there were so many Scotland supporters there.

'I remember walking on to the park and the hairs were standing up on the back of my neck. It was a day I will never forget. There were so many Scots there it was almost like a home tie and the fact we won made it even more special.'

He also played in the famous 2–0 win over Wales at Anfield in 1977, which sent the national team to the World Cup finals in Argentina the following summer. But it was an ill-fated campaign, as all Scotland fans remember. Forsyth appeared in all three group games and his final match for Scotland was the 3–2 victory over Holland in Mendoza, forever famous for Archie Gemmill's wonderful solo goal.

Tom had arrived in Argentina on the back of yet another clean sweep of the domestic honours with Rangers. The Light Blues beat Celtic 2–1 after extra time in the League Cup final but it was Aberdeen who were their closest rivals in the championship. Indeed, Rangers had to win their final match against Motherwell to edge the Dons by two points. They also defeated the Pittodrie men 2–1 in the Scottish Cup final on 6 May to claim the Treble for the second time in three years. However, at the end of the campaign Jock Wallace resigned as manager in a row over money and John Greig was invited to take over.

Sadly for Forsyth, injuries began to strike the powerhouse defender which put him out of action for long spells in each of the next three seasons. It was maybe no coincidence that Rangers struggled to emulate the success of the previous years. His final honour came in the 1981 Scottish Cup final replay when Rangers beat Dundee United 4–1 and he announced his retirement on medical grounds on 13 March the following year.

He started a new career in management with Dunfermline, but with no success. However, in 1985 he became close friend and former teammate Tommy McLean's assistant at Motherwell and the two of them were highly successful, most notably winning the Scottish Cup in 1991.

His life at Rangers began when he moved from Fir Park to Ibrox in October 1972 and his relationship with the Light Blues continues today through his work in the hospitality suites on match days. He said, 'I always wanted to play for a top club and when I got the chance to play for Rangers it was a fantastic moment . . . People watching games probably wonder what it's like, but words can't describe it. I think you have to experience it to be able to know what it's all about and, of course, not too many get the chance.'

Davie Cooper (1977–1988)
BORN: 25 February 1956, Hamilton

APPEARANCES: 540
GOALS: 75

HONOURS WON WITH RANGERS
League titles (3) – 1977/78,
1986/87, 1988/89
Scottish Cups (3) – 1977/78,
1978/79, 1980/81
League Cups (7) – 1977/78,
1978/79, 1981/82, 1983/84,
1984/85, 1986/87, 1987/88
CAPS: 20 (of 24 for Scotland)

FEW PLAYERS have lit up the Scottish game quite like Davie Cooper and, given the dearth of natural wide players in the 21st century, it may be a long time before we see his like again. He had a magical left foot, his dribbling skills would mesmerise opponents and he packed a ferocious shot that could turn a game in seconds. He would run at defenders, show them a glimpse of the ball, pull it back, feint and then with a shimmy he would be gone, leaving a bemused opponent in his wake.

His shooting power was never more evident than in the 1987/88 League Cup final, when his fierce free-kick was rebounding from the back of the net before Jim Leighton in the Aberdeen goal had even moved. However, his finest goal came in the Drybrough Cup final against Celtic on 4 August 1979. He received the ball on his chest with his back to goal on the edge of the box and, seemingly with nowhere to go, flicked it in the air four times with his left foot to ease past four Celtic defenders and then slipped the ball into the net. It was a majestic strike of outlandish flair and imagination and was voted by fans in a worldwide poll in 1999 as the 'Greatest Ever Rangers goal'.

It also summed up the essence of Cooper. He was a man who played off-the-cuff and was able to create something tangible out of nothing. He signed for Clydebank from local amateur side Hamilton Avondale for £300 – the previous night's taking from the social club – and inspired them to the Second Division title in 1975/76.

The big clubs began to take notice. Arsenal, Aston Villa and Coventry all tried to entice him, but Cooper was waiting for Rangers to make a move. He got his chance to impress when Clydebank were drawn against Rangers in the quarter-final of the League Cup in September 1976. Cooper said at the time, 'The press built the game up because there was a lot of talk about me moving to Ibrox and I always was a Rangers supporter so it was a big test for me.

'I remember arriving at Ibrox and I was in awe of the size of the place, it was incredible. Next thing I was standing on the halfway line waiting for the game to start and I realised I was playing against John Greig. I remember that 30 seconds into the game I picked the ball up on the wing and I knocked the ball past John who booted me in the air. I got up expecting an apology but he just said, "If I get another chance I will do it harder next time." After that I knew I was going to be in for a tough 90 minutes.'

Cooper turned it on that day, scoring the match-saving equaliser in a 3–3 draw. It took two replays for Rangers to overcome the Bankies but Cooper had done his work. He was duly signed for Rangers by Jock Wallace in June 1977 for £100,000. On his arrival at Ibrox he said, 'Right now I must be the happiest guy in the whole of Scotland. There's just not another club I would have signed for.'

He and fellow new arrivals Bobby Russell and Gordon Smith fitted the system perfectly and Rangers were sensational that season, winning their second Treble in three years. Coop scored in the 2–1 League Cup final win over Celtic and only missed two League matches all season as Aberdeen were pipped for the title and then beaten 2–1 in the Scottish Cup final.

However, Jock Wallace's decision to quit at the end of that campaign meant that John Greig took over. Greig was not as much of an admirer as Wallace had been and Cooper had to fight to make it into the starting line-up. Things went well initially, but then Greig brought back veteran Willie Johnston to take Cooper's place. However, Cooper was still capable of some sensational performances and one of the best was in the replay of the 1981 Scottish Cup final, when he inspired Rangers to a 4–1 win over Dundee United.

It seems laughable that Cooper won just 24 caps for Scotland but he did make it to the Mexico World Cup in 1986. In fact he was largely responsible for taking Scotland to the finals. He held his nerve to score the vital penalty against Wales in Cardiff which took Scotland into a play-off with Australia, although the joy was short-lived that day when manager Jock Stein collapsed and died of a heart attack.

In Mexico, he played alongside Graeme Souness, newly appointed as manager at Ibrox. There is little doubt Cooper was a rejuvenated player when he returned for the start of the next season. He scored the winning penalty in the 1986/87 League Cup final against Celtic with just minutes remaining to give Souness his first trophy, and the new manager never had any doubts. He said, 'When I saw Davie walk up and place the ball on the spot I knew, even before he had kicked it, that we had won the cup. That is how much confidence I had in him. When a player can hit the ball so well and with so much accuracy, like Davie could, the keeper had no chance.'

Fittingly, it was Cooper who delivered the cross that allowed Terry Butcher to head the goal at Pittodrie that clinched the title that year – Rangers' first in nine years. Cooper was the only survivor from the championship team of 1977/78 and the feeling was so sweet. Souness was happy to admit that Cooper 'was as responsible as anybody for the success in winning the championship'.

But, by season 1988/89, Davie was no longer an automatic choice at Ibrox and in August 1989 he went to Motherwell in search of regular first-team football. True to his talent, Cooper helped his new club win the Scottish Cup, defeating Dundee United 4–3 in the epic 1991 final. He was planning to end his career where it started, back at Clydebank, but on 22 March 1995 he collapsed while filming a soccer skills programme with Charlie Nicholas. He later died of a brain haemorrhage. He was only 39. The tragedy stunned Scottish football fans everywhere, especially at Rangers. Flowers and scarves adorned the gates at the Copland Road end of Ibrox in his memory. One of Scotland's greatest football sons had gone.

Ten years after his death Rangers and Motherwell wore specially inscribed shirts in his honour when they contested the League Cup final and the great man no doubt approved from on high as his beloved Rangers won 5–1.

Bobby Russell (1978–1987)

BORN: 11 February 1957, Glasgow

APPEARANCES: 370

GOALS: 46

HONOURS WON WITH RANGERS

League titles (1) – 1977/78

Scottish Cups (3) – 1977/78, 1978/79, 1980/81

League Cups (4) – 1978/79, 1981/82, 1983/84, 1984/85

IF YOU ask Rangers fans of a certain vintage they will tell you the best European goal they ever saw was scored by Bobby Russell in Eindhoven's Philips Stadium on 1 November 1978.

Rangers were level at 2–2 with PSV and heading through to the quarter-finals of the European Cup on the away-goals rule but were under late pressure from the Dutch side, who had never lost at home in European competition. Derek Johnstone, playing centre half that night, made yet another vital clearance. Gordon Smith took possession and clipped a quick pass to Tommy McLean on the right side just inside Rangers' half. McLean sucked in two Dutch defenders and then, seeing Russell begin to make a run, played him in superbly. Russell gracefully raced forward and curled a low shot into the Eindhoven net.

It was a classic strike, but the gifted midfielder is pragmatic these days. He said, 'A 2–2 scoreline would have taken us through and there were only seconds to go when I got the opportunity. If it had been with ten minutes to go I don't think

I would have made the run but because it was so near the end I thought I would take the gamble. The precision of Mr McLean's passing meant that the ball was played to me perfectly and I ran through and stuck it away.

'We drew 0–0 with PSV at home in the first leg and few people gave us any chance over there. They had not lost at home before in Europe but we went there and won 3–2. It was a great night.'

It was the early part of Russell's second season with Rangers and his only regret is that Rangers did not go all the way that year. They had knocked out the favourites Juventus in the first round and should have got past Cologne in the last eight but lost 2–1 on aggregate. Russell said, 'It was there for us. The remaining teams were not strong and not laden with as many international players. Unfortunately we had injuries to certain key players and we suffered accordingly.' It was Brian Clough's Nottingham Forest who went on to win that season, beating Malmo in the final.

Russell had joined up at Ibrox in the summer of 1977 when 'Anarchy in the UK' was as popular as Her Majesty's Silver Jubilee. He was the least known of three signings made by Jock Wallace – Gordon Smith from Kilmarnock and Davie Cooper from Clydebank being the others – and they all gelled brilliantly in one of the most memorable campaigns in Rangers' history.

The bulk of the team had won the Treble in 1975/76 and they did it again that year aided by the new boys. Russell recalled, 'The foundation was there, the team spirit was there and we added a little bit of guile if you like. I was not exactly the type of player that Jock Wallace liked, but he could see something in me that would add something to the team.

'I had had 14 months down at Sunderland as an apprentice but it didn't work out and I came back to play junior football with Shettleston. Laurie Cummings was the Rangers chief scout at that time and he came to watch me. He then offered me a trial and I must have done well because Rangers signed me provisionally the next day.

'I then went back to Shettleston for the rest of the season and returned for pre-season training in the summer of 1977. I was a Rangers supporter so to get the chance to sign for the club and make my way with them was great. How do you get better than that? I suppose the only way you could do it would be to win a European trophy.

'But we got off to the worst possible start. We lost our opening two matches and, although we got our first win, we then went 2–0 down to Celtic at Ibrox. However, we managed to turn things around and win that game 3–2 and we went from strength to strength.'

Russell played in midfield beside Alex MacDonald with Tommy McLean on the right, Davie Cooper on the left and Gordon Smith playing behind Derek Johnstone. It was an irresistible system ahead of a stout back line of Sandy Jardine, Colin Jackson, Tom Forsyth, John Greig and goalkeeper Peter McCloy. Russell was an elegant and intelligent footballer, who could ease past opponents before playing the perfect pass. He was ahead of his time in many ways.

He would never improve upon that incredible first season when Rangers held off Aberdeen to win the title, having already beaten Celtic in the League Cup final, and then beat the Dons 2–1 in the Scottish Cup final to claim the clean sweep. However, Rangers nearly won all three trophies again the following season when they beat Aberdeen 2–1 in the League Cup final and then needed two replays to see off Hibs 3–2 in the Scottish Cup final, but sadly lost what was effectively a title decider 4–2 at Celtic Park.

After that the team that had done so well in the 1970s began to break up, and the club began to face stiff competition from Aberdeen, who were on the brink of the best spell in their history, and Dundee United were fast becoming a force. Light Blue highlights came mainly in the cup competitions. Russell was a key protagonist in the replay of the 1981 Scottish Cup final against Dundee United. He had been left out, along with Derek Johnstone, for the initial match, which finished goalless, but they were brought back in for the replay and United were thumped 4–1 thanks to two goals from John MacDonald, and others from Cooper and Russell himself.

Russell said, 'Winning the cup that year was great and, of course, scoring a goal against United was special too. On that night David Cooper was probably at his best. I wouldn't say he single-handedly beat United because there were other players who performed very well, but he was instrumental in our win. He scored the first goal, set me up for the second and played John MacDonald in for the third.

'We had a great understanding. We joked about the fact that Coop made me a player, but it is not far off the truth. He was a great player to play with and I fed off him. He had great awareness and the uncanny ability to play balls into your path. He was a super player.'

The Souness Revolution in 1986 spelled the end for a number of Rangers players and Bobby was one of them, but he flourished in a move to Motherwell in 1987 where he was reunited with Cooper two years later. The two of them shared one final day in the sun when Motherwell sensationally won the Scottish Cup in 1991, defeating Dundee United 4–3.

A year later he left and had spells with Arbroath, Ayr United and Cowdenbeath. He even returned to the junior ranks with Cumbernauld United and he finally finished off with Albion

Rovers in 1996/97. He subsequently worked as a coach for Rangers in their Football in the Community programme.

Chapter 6
Nine-in-a-Row/
Modern Greats
(1989–2009)

Ally McCoist
Ian Durrant
Graeme Souness
Chris Woods
Terry Butcher
Richard Gough
Ray Wilkins
Ian Ferguson
John Brown
Mark Hateley
Andy Goram
Stuart McCall
Brian Laudrup
Paul Gascoigne
Jorg Albertz

RANGERS HALL OF FAME

Stefan Klos
Barry Ferguson

IT ALL began at Hamilton in August 1988 and ended in Dundee in May 1997; many feel it represents the greatest period in Rangers' history.

The incredible feat of winning nine successive championships is undoubtedly one of the most significant in the history of the club and this period produced some sensational players.

Initially under the guidance of Graeme Souness, who revolutionised Rangers and Scottish football in general, and then Walter Smith, the Light Blues enjoyed an astonishing spell of success which produced many classic moments.

The spirit of the squad was renowned and the quality of their play was exceptional. The Treble was secured in 1992/93 and they nearly did it again the following year, narrowly losing the 1994 Scottish Cup final to Dundee United.

Rangers also came tantalisingly close to reaching the 1993 Champions League final after a fabulous ten-game unbeaten run.

Dick Advocaat brought new glories when he replaced Smith with players like Albertz, Klos and Ferguson, all thriving under his tutelage.

Ally McCoist (1983–1998)
BORN: 24 September 1962,
Bellshill, Lanarkshire

APPEARANCES: 581
GOALS: 355

HONOURS WON WITH RANGERS
League titles (10) – 1986/87,
1988/89, 1989/90, 1990/91,
1991/92, 1992/93, 1993/94,
1994/95, 1995/96, 1996/97
Scottish Cups (1) – 1991/92
League Cups (9) – 1983/84,
1984/85, 1986/87, 1987/88,
1988/89, 1990/91, 1992/93,
1993/94, 1996/97
CAPS: 58 (of 61 for Scotland)

THEY SAY that timing is everything and those of us who watched Ally McCoist blast his way through every goalscoring record imaginable with that grin on his face are truly fortunate. It is almost inconceivable that there will ever be another player like him, such was his longevity at Rangers and his incredible scoring rate. The stats speak for themselves; he is Rangers' greatest goalscorer and there are few strikers in world football who can claim to be more prolific.

He was the king of the dressing room – along with close friend Ian Durrant – in arguably the best period in the club's history, but it was not always sweetness and light. He was reduced to tears after a Scottish Cup defeat on 16 February 1985 by Dundee at Ibrox after a section of the crowd chanted abuse at him. I wonder how those spiteful supporters feel now?

Rangers – well, John Greig in particular – tried to sign Ally three times before finally getting his man for £165,000 from Sunderland in the summer of 1983. McCoist had spent two years at Roker Park having started his career with St Johnstone. He scored 33 seconds into his Old Firm debut at Parkhead on 3 September 1983 and even though Celtic went on to win that game 2–1, it was a sign of things to come.

McCoist went on to inflict unbridled misery on Celtic for the next 15 years, scoring 27 times against them (only R.C. Hamilton from the turn of the 19th century scored more; 35 to be precise). He remains the last player to score a hat-trick in an Old Firm match and he picked the right occasion to do it – the 1983/84 League Cup final which Rangers won 3–2 giving Ally the first of nine winner's medals in the tournament. Actually, he scored three times in the Glasgow Cup final on 9 May 1986 in front of 40,741 at Ibrox in another 3–2 win over Celtic and, even if this game did not count as a competitive match, Ally's timing was impeccable.

After the match, Graeme Souness, who had just taken over as manager, was in his office mulling over whether to offer McCoist a new contract or not. The hat-trick hero is alleged to have burst in and said with a flashing smile, 'Have you met my accountant?'

The two had some issues further down the line, but for the first four years it was near perfection. Ally blasted 34 goals in the League campaign of 1986/87 as Rangers finally regained the championship after an agonising nine-year drought. He thrived in a good team and things only got better. He reached the same total in 1991/92 and in 1992/93 when he also won Europe's Golden Boot in successive seasons.

He was one of the few 'old school' players to survive the Souness Revolution and he developed into one of the greatest strikers of all time. Two goals in the League Cup final of 1988/89 – including a typical predatory winner – added to his already burgeoning CV as Aberdeen were beaten 3–2. The League campaign that year included 5–1 and 4–1 home victories over Celtic. He did not realise it then, but it was the beginning of an odyssey that would lead Rangers to nine successive Scottish titles.

In the summer of 1989 Souness rocked Scottish football to its foundations when he signed ex-Celtic player Mo Johnston from under his old club's noses. Of course, Johnston and McCoist hit it off immediately, finishing another championship-winning season as the club's top two goalscorers.

However, in the 1990/91 season Ally began to have problems. Souness signed another striker, Mark Hateley from Monaco, and invariably paired him with Johnston, which left Ally on the bench. In fact, he was on the bench so often that supporters began calling him 'The Judge'. There was, allegedly, a personality clash between Souness and McCoist and the manager tried to use his player as a scapegoat for two Old Firm defeats in the spring of 1991 by forcing him to make a public apology to the media for going to the Cheltenham Racing Festival when Souness had told him not to.

But within a month Souness had left for Liverpool and McCoist suddenly found himself back in favour under new manager Walter Smith. McCoist and Hateley became Rangers' new strike-force, and they began to terrorise defences all over the country. They won the League title and the Scottish Cup in 1991/92, with both Hateley and McCoist scoring in the final against Airdrie. They went one better the following season, winning the domestic Treble, and then setting off on an incredible run in the inaugural Champions League.

In the two qualifying rounds Rangers beat English champions Leeds United, home and away. McCoist scored in both legs; his goal at Elland Road a thing of beauty. Durrant sent Hateley charging down the left, he crossed to the back post and McCoist sent a diving header into the opposite corner.

Sadly, he broke his leg playing for Scotland in Portugal on 28 April 1993. At that point he was sitting on 34 League goals and 49 in all competitions. With five League games and the cup final to come there was a chance that he could have attacked Sam English's seasonal league goals record of 44 or even Jim Forrest's overall record of 57, but it was not to be. Nonetheless, Mark and Ally had scored 140 goals between them in two seasons – an incredible return by anyone's standards.

Ally's comeback the following season was another of the fairytale variety. With the League Cup final against Hibs poised at 1–1 on 24 October, McCoist was sent on and scored with an overhead kick to win the silverware. Ian Durrant, who had scored Rangers' earlier goal, said, 'I can't believe he has stolen my thunder again.'

A calf problem wrecked the 1994/95 campaign, but he still managed nine appearances in the League and received a medal for his contribution even if some historians would say he had not earned one. He was a key man again in 1995/96 and 1996/97 as the dream sequence of nine titles in a row was completed and he also played a starring role in the League Cup final of 1996/97 scoring twice in a 4–3 win against Hearts. Only three players played in all nine title-winning campaigns, Richard Gough, Ian Ferguson and Ally McCoist, testament to the longevity of three Rangers greats.

Sadly, Ally's bad luck in the Scottish Cup continued throughout his Ibrox career. At the end of the 1997/98 season, when it became clear that nine titles would not be ten, the Light Blues reached the Scottish Cup final. It was to be his last match for the club, and they lost 2–1 to Hearts despite Ally's late consolation.

That summer, many Scottish fans thought that Ally should have gone to the World Cup in France, but manager Craig Brown passed him over, selecting Scott Booth of Aberdeen instead. Ironically, he was capped later that year when he was with Kilmarnock where he played for three years after leaving Rangers.

McCoist returned to Rangers as assistant manager to Walter Smith on 10 January 2007 and there are undoubtedly more chapters to unfold in one of the greatest stories in Rangers' history.

Ian Durrant (1984–1998)
Born: 29 October 1967, Glasgow

Appearances: 347
Goals: 45

Honours Won with Rangers
League titles (4) – 1986/87,
1992/93, 1993/94, 1994/95
Scottish Cups (3) – 1991/92,
1992/93, 1995/96
League Cups (4) – 1986/87,
1987/88, 1992/93, 1993/94
Caps: 11 (of 20 for Scotland)

THERE WAS an ugly and sinister atmosphere when Rangers took to the field at Aberdeen on 8 October 1988, as there so often has been at matches between the two teams, and within eight minutes Ian Durrant had become its victim – his knee and career in tatters after a shocking challenge by Neil Simpson.

One of the most exciting talents in Scottish football had been cut down in his prime and had nearly three years taken from his career. The fact that he was able to play football again was remarkable; the fact that he went on to achieve so much is testimony to his fantastic ability.

It may seem morbid to dwell on such a negative, but that tackle changed everything. Durrant had been a prodigious talent who burst on to the scene and held his own among men very much his senior. He was only 17 when Jock Wallace handed him a debut in the Rangers first team against Morton on 20 April 1985 and he showed he had the capability to make the grade.

Three games later he made his Old Firm debut in a 1–1 draw at Parkhead and then scored in his second match against Celtic – a 3–0 win at Ibrox on 9 November 1985 – when he and fellow youngster Derek Ferguson performed superbly.

Durrant was a terrific talent. He had wonderful vision, great passing ability and the pace to get ahead of the strikers. Graeme Souness knew he had something special on his hands when he took over at the very end of the 1985/86 season, and Durrant was a mainstay in a memorable campaign in 1986/87 which brought League championship success back to Ibrox.

His clever running was never more apparent than in the first Old Firm game of that season when Davie Cooper brilliantly played him in and Durrant ran through to calmly slot a left-foot shot past Pat Bonner. The young man, born and brought up in nearby Kinning Park, then completely ignored Cooper as he raced to celebrate with Ted McMinn.

In October that year Durrant won his first Rangers medal, firing his team ahead in the League Cup final against Celtic which was settled 2–1 in Rangers' favour by Davie Cooper's cool penalty. He scored one of the great League Cup final goals a year later in a classic 3–3 draw with Aberdeen when he played a one-two with Ally McCoist, darted into the box and fired a shot past Jim Leighton. He said, 'I think I only got about two passes in 18 years of playing with him [McCoist], but one was that cup final and the other was an Old Firm game when I scored at Parkhead, so it can't be that bad!'

The match then went to penalty kicks and it was Durrant who scored the clinching one after Welsh international Peter Nicholas had hit the bar. There is a famous photograph of Durrant standing with his arms in the air with a smile as wide as the Clyde just seconds before he is mobbed by his teammates.

By this point he had forced his way into the international

team and by the autumn of 1988 he was a regular, seemingly destined to play in the World Cup finals two years later. In the event, he did go to Italia 90, but only as a spectator. His first attempted comeback from his horrific knee problems had failed and he had a dead man's tendon transplanted into his knee in California in a final attempt to save his career.

Some scars will never heal and it is unlikely Durrant will ever forgive Simpson. He went to court and was awarded £330,000 in damages but it hardly compensated for nearly three years of hell, seven operations and endless hours of heartache.

However, against the odds he came back at the end of the 1990/91 season and he played in the championship decider at the end of that season when two Mark Hateley goals beat Aberdeen to give Rangers three in a row.

The midfield star had more injury problems the following season but he still managed 13 League appearances and earned his place in the starting line-up for the 1992 Scottish Cup final when Rangers lifted the trophy for the first time in 11 years with a 2–1 win over Alex MacDonald's Airdrie.

Season 1992/93 was a joy to behold. It was the peak of Walter Smith's first era in charge as Rangers swept all before them at home by winning the Treble for the fifth time in their history. During the season the team went on a 44–game unbeaten run and Durrant was always there for the big games. He scored against Celtic in a 1–1 draw at Ibrox and netted the winner at Parkhead in a 1–0 win. Smith also gave him a slot for the League Cup final triumph over Aberdeen and he was in again when the Dons were defeated in the Scottish Cup final with Durrant setting up Mark Hateley for the second goal in a 2–1 win.

Rangers also made their mark in Europe that year and Durrant was at the heart of a fantastic ten-game unbeaten run in the Champions League. He scored a crucial away goal against the Danes of Lyngby in the first qualifier and then lapped up the Battle of Britain clashes with Leeds as Rangers made it into the group phase.

He scored a terrific goal against Bruges in a 2–1 win at Ibrox and his swerving shot to earn a draw with Olympique Marseille in the Velodrome was a classic. Sadly, Rangers missed out on making the final by just one point with the French side going on to beat Milan 1-0 with future Ranger Basile Boli scoring the winner.

Durrant thought he had secured Rangers another crack at the group phase the following season with a vital away goal in Sofia, but Nicolai Todorov's last-minute rocket crushed Rangers' hopes and they were knocked out by Bulgarian champions Levski.

The slight solace for that was another winner's medal in the League Cup when Hibs were beaten 2–1 in the final, although Durrant was upstaged by his old mate Ally McCoist. He said, 'I thought I was going to be the hero when I put us in front against Hibs, but the script was written for McCoist, who had missed much of the season after suffering a broken leg. He came on and scored with a magnificent overhead kick.'

He won a championship medal that year and again in 1994/95 but his appearances became more limited during the next two seasons. Despite that, he still managed to win his seventh cup winner's medal when Hearts were mauled 5–1 in the 1996 Scottish Cup final and he still claims the goal which looped over Stewart Kerr in the Celtic goal as Brian Laudrup bundled the ball over the line to send Rangers on their way to nine in a row.

Durrant eventually left Rangers for Kilmarnock in 1998 and, with his cultured right foot and his vision still intact, his good form earned him nine more Scotland caps under Craig Brown. Having cut his teeth in coaching at Rugby Park he was lured back to Rangers in 2005 to firstly work in the youth department and then as a first-team coach, a role he retains today. He said, 'I have supported Rangers since I was two, I was a ball boy at the stadium and then I got the chance to play for the club. I know my family are very proud and I feel exactly the same way.'

Graeme Souness (1986–1991)

BORN: 6 May 1953, Edinburgh

APPEARANCES: 73
GOALS: 5

HONOURS WON WITH RANGERS
League title (1) – 1986/87
Caps: 2 (of 54 for Scotland)

GRAEME SOUNESS was relaxing in the grandeur of his fashionable Genoa apartment in the early months of 1986 when the phone rang unexpectedly and his life changed forever. The man on the other end of the line was Rangers' chairman David Holmes and he had one intention – to convince Souness to become the next manager of the club.

Rangers Football Club was not so much a sleeping giant at the time as one that was in a coma. They had not won the title since 1978, they had not won the Scottish Cup since 1981 and they were in grave danger of failing to qualify for Europe. Holmes knew the time was right for revolution and he brought it about in the most remarkable way.

Souness was agreeable immediately. He knew the timing was right but he phoned an old friend, Kenny Dalglish – who had become Liverpool's player-manager the previous year and who was making an immediate impact – to make sure he was making the right decision. Souness got the positive sound bites that he wanted and the deal was on. Holmes then had to make financial arrangements with Sampdoria as the midfield general still had over a year to go in his contract. A fee of £350,000 was agreed and the incredible news that Souness was to succeed Jock Wallace was announced on 7 April 1986.

It was an incredible coup and the ramifications were not only massive for Rangers and Scotland but for the British game as a whole. Inevitably, he had to shake up the squad and the early signings were the key. The capture of Terry Butcher and then Chris Woods was unprecedented and groundbreaking. 'We signed some excellent players – like Terry Butcher and Chris Woods – I was still attempting to play and we were solid. England was the market I knew and that's why I went there,' he said. Existing players like Ally McCoist, Davie Cooper, Ian Durrant and Davie McPherson all responded and Souness suddenly had the beginnings of a decent team.

Souness always had that wonderful arrogant streak about him that made him one of the best midfield players in the world. He was also hard. Few opponents came out of a challenge with Souness on the winning side. And so it proved for striker George McCluskey as Souness was sent off 37 minutes into his debut on August 1986 for kicking the Hibs player, having been booked earlier in the game.

There were remarkable scenes at Easter Road that day as every outfield player – and Chris Woods – were involved in scuffles around the centre circle as Souness trooped off the field. Rangers lost the game 2–1 and the detractors had a field day. However, out of adversity came a growing belief that the team could really do something in that first season.

He said, 'I only have great memories of Rangers. We flew by the seat of our pants in the early days and we didn't get off to the best of starts with me being sent off in the very first game against Hibs at Easter Road. That's something I would like to change, but I can't.

'Having said that, there was good to come out of that first day. Of course, I was really down about what had happened but I began to realise that we had a bit of team spirit going. There was so much togetherness shown in that match that I felt we had a chance of achieving things and so it proved.'

Souness delivered the first championship in nine years that season, along with the League Cup. The revolution had begun. Celtic were defeated in the League Cup when Davie Cooper's cool penalty decided the game late on and there were amazing scenes at Pittodrie when Terry Butcher's header from Cooper's cross ensured a 1–1 draw and the title. Souness was sent off that day too, but it was incidental as the Rangers legions rejoiced.

His playing was limited in his five years at Rangers, not just due to the pressures of the job but a problematic calf injury. However, he was still capable of some special performances. In that first season he scored with a cracking left-foot shot that came off the post in a vital 2–0 win over Aberdeen, even if Jim Leighton chased the referee to the halfway line to complain the ball had not crossed the line. In the New Year Old Firm game at Ibrox he simply ruled, spraying passes and dominating a crucial 2–0 win which gave Rangers the impetus they needed.

He said, 'I didn't play that much football for Rangers because of the difficulties of trying to do both jobs – playing and managing. But I had great people around me, most notably Walter Smith, and players like Ray Wilkins, Richard Gough and Terry Butcher. There was never a lot for me to do at half-time in matches because I had so many "captains" in that dressing room. The biggest part of my job at that time was getting the players into the club.'

Celtic snatched the title back in 1987/88 as Souness continued to make changes at Ibrox and lost his captain Butcher for a long spell with a broken leg. However, they retained the

League Cup, winning on penalties after an epic 3–3 draw in the final against Aberdeen.

In November 1988 the Souness Revolution rumbled again when he persuaded David Murray to take over the club. It was the start of the most incredible era for all Rangers supporters. Top players like Richard Gough, Ray Wilkins, Mark Walters, John Brown and Ian Ferguson had already been recruited and he added Gary Stevens and Kevin Drinkell and Rangers swept to what turned out to be the first of nine successive championships.

Never a man to avoid controversy, in the summer of 1989 he pinched Maurice Johnston from under the noses of Celtic, who had already paraded him as a signing, finally ending the unwritten but well-known Rangers policy of not signing Catholic players. He was a huge success and so too was fellow summer signing Trevor Steven, whose header at Tannadice clinched the 1989/90 title.

The next campaign brought another League Cup after an epic 2–1 win over Celtic and the club was involved in a neck-and-neck race for the title with Aberdeen. But in April 1991, Souness shocked everyone when he announced he was leaving the club to take over at Liverpool. Of course, the lure of Liverpool was a huge one. Souness had captained the great side of the early 1980s to fantastic success in the championship and in Europe. He was a legend at Anfield and it is not difficult to understand why he was tempted. He was not enjoying a good relationship with Scotland's football administrators and he was also having trouble in his personal life.

However, he has subsequently admitted that it was the wrong thing to do. He said, 'When I left Rangers I had the feeling that the grass was greener on the other side but I now realise that I made a mistake. You can't go back and it's very hard for me to say I wish I never left because I'm now married again,

I'm very happy in my personal life and if I had stayed at Rangers none of that might have happened.

'In football terms there are things you would like to change, but I would like to think I did my bit and since then the club has moved forward in leaps and bounds.'

Chris Woods (1986–1991)

BORN: 14 November 1959, Boston, Lincolnshire

APPEARANCES: 230

GOALS: 0

HONOURS WON WITH RANGERS

League titles (4) – 1986/87, 1988/89, 1989/90, 1990/91

League Cups (3) – 1986/87, 1988/89, 1990/91

CAPS: 20 (of 43 for England)

IT IS perhaps unusual that an Englishman should help revive a sleeping Scottish giant but the signing of Chris Woods, coupled with the capture of fellow countryman Terry Butcher, was pivotal in launching Rangers into one of the greatest eras in its history.

It was actually a chance remark in the aftermath of the England v Scotland game at Wembley in 1986, in which Woods failed to save a Graeme Souness penalty, that set the wheels in motion. The genial goalkeeper recalls, 'I said to Graeme, "I hear you're looking for a keeper, keep me in mind" and a few months later I was on my way to Ibrox.'

The former Norwich City stopper was a revelation and spent five successful seasons at Ibrox before departing for Sheffield Wednesday in 1991. He set a terrific standard that was subsequently upheld by Andy Goram and Stefan Klos. Woods said, 'My time at Rangers was definitely the highlight of my career. Anyone I've spoken to who's ever played for Rangers agrees that once you've been there you still feel a part of the club even after you've left.

'Graeme Souness was the one who took us all up there and it was like a revolution at Ibrox. He told me Rangers was a sleeping giant and he was spot-on. I spoke to people before I moved up there and it seemed like a good career move for me at the time.

'It's a massive club and it was great to be a part of the success the club enjoyed back then. It was a tremendous privilege to play for Rangers and one I will never forget. Graeme brought some top players to the club and we had a great first season. We were something like nine points behind at the turn of the year and ended up winning the League. It all just seemed to come together at the right time.'

In his first season at Rangers, Woods set a British record for not conceding a goal when he kept a clean sheet for a total of 1,196 minutes. Sadly for the Englishman, an infamous strike by Hamilton's Adrian Sprott ended that run and also knocked Rangers out of the Scottish Cup. He recalled, 'That record was very pleasing for a goalkeeper apart from the disappointing way in which it ended.

'After about seven or eight shut-outs in a row I asked Walter Smith, who was assistant manager at that time, what the record was and he thought it was Bobby Clark at Aberdeen. We were playing Hamilton at Ibrox in the cup on the day I broke the record. The minute I finally broke it was probably the biggest cheer of the day as the rest didn't go so well . . . Dave McKellar had an amazing game in goal for Hamilton, we made one mistake at the back and Adrian Sprott scored. And that was the end of that.'

Of course, Woods will also be remembered for being subjected to criminal proceedings when he, Butcher, Frank

McAvennie and Graham Roberts were all charged by over-zealous procurator fiscal Sandy Jessop with conduct liable to cause a breach of the peace following a feisty 2–2 Old Firm draw in October 1987. McAvennie barged into Woods and slapped him on the ear, Woods grabbed him by the throat, Butcher barged in and then Roberts knocked McAvennie over. It was hardly their finest hour, but then it was hardly criminal either. Woods and Butcher were both convicted and as a result have criminal records, Roberts was not proven and McAvennie was found not guilty.

If it was a test case, the test failed because, other than Duncan Ferguson's incarceration for a head butt on Jock McStay in 1995 when he was on probation for assault, there have been no similar proceedings since in the Scottish game. Woods, though, is philosophical about it all now. He said, 'It was a strange one and when I look back I have to laugh. I still have a joke about it with Terry, Graham and Frank to this day.

'At the time it was hard because there was nothing in the incident. But the police got involved and we were charged with inciting riots. We had to sit in the court for four days and it was ludicrous that Terry and I were found guilty. But we had to put it behind us.'

The upshot from a football point of view was that Woods and Butcher missed the League Cup final against Aberdeen the following weekend as Chris was sent off in the initial incident and Butcher, booked at that point, was later sent off. Rangers won that final on penalties after a 3–3 draw but they lost out on the championship that season and suffered a humiliating Scottish Cup defeat to Dunfermline.

Woods suffered an ear problem during the 1988/89 season, which limited his appearances, but he still claimed a winner's medal in what proved to be the first season in the run of nine successive championships.

He was a terrific goalkeeper and one who inspired confidence in those in front of him. He claimed the title again in 1989/90 and he did not miss a match the following season as Rangers won the League Cup, beating Celtic in the final, and then clinched the championship on an incredible final day shoot-out with Aberdeen.

By that time Souness had gone to be replaced by Walter Smith. A new UEFA ruling allowing only 'three foreigners' to play in the side in European competition meant that Smith had to rebuild the side by buying Scottish players. Although the subsequent Bosman ruling would have negated that, Woods was sold along with other non-Scots Trevor Steven and Mark Walters to accommodate the rule. But, by the time he left, Chris Woods had played a huge part in the resurgence of the club. In 1998 he teamed up again with Walter Smith, by then manager at Everton, as the Merseyside club's goalkeeping coach, a position he still holds today.

Terry Butcher (1986–1990)
BORN: 28 December 1958,
Singapore

APPEARANCES: 176
GOALS: 11

HONOURS WON WITH RANGERS
League titles (3) – 1986/87,
1988/89, 1989/90
League Cups (2) – 1986/87,
1988/89
CAPS: 32 (of 77 for England)

DAVIE COOPER looked up, picked his spot and then delivered the perfect free kick with his exceptional left foot and Terry Butcher powered a header into the Aberdeen net to the delirium of Rangers supporters who had taken over Pittodrie. It was 2 May 1987 and it proved to be the goal that ended nine long years without championship success and signalled the return of Rangers as the major force in the land.

The supporters already adored the player, but his tangible involvement in the clinching of the crown elevated him to an icon. Butcher said, 'It was probably my best moment. The fans went berserk and when I scored all I could see was Rangers fans jumping up in the home end. They were all over the ground because they wanted to be there and I'll never forget winning that title because I know it meant so much to everyone connected with Rangers.'

There is little doubt that Graeme Souness's coup of signing Butcher – along with Chris Woods – was the catalyst for the phenomenal success that the Light Blues went on to enjoy during the next decade and beyond. If the truth be told, the giant England defender was waiting for Manchester United to come for him. But it was Rangers who did the business, signing the player from Ipswich Town for a fee of £725,000.

It was a stunning purchase. Butcher was the captain of England when Bryan Robson could not play; he stood 6ft 4in and was in the prime of his football life. No one batted an eyelid when Souness made him captain of Rangers and Butcher led by example in a roller-coaster first campaign, punctuated with Souness's red cards, great performances and the general reawakening of the sleeping giant.

He skippered Rangers to the League Cup on 25 October 1986 when Celtic captain Roy Aitken pulled him down in the box with the Old Firm final tied at 1–1 and Cooper slotted the penalty. It was a vital victory as it gave the Souness Revolution the momentum it needed to go on and claim that highly craved title.

Butcher recalls, however, that the players had failed to negotiate a bonus for winning the championship. He said, 'We spoke to the chairman David Holmes and he agreed to give us a split of the gate money for the final game with St Mirren. There were nearly 44,000 there and we got £10,000 each which was a lot of money then.'

The contrast the following year could hardly have been greater. Butcher broke his leg in November in an accidental clash with Aberdeen's Alex McLeish and wrecked his season. He nearly left Rangers after becoming a convicted criminal in the wake of the scandalous prosecution of Woods, Butcher, Graham Roberts and Frank McAvennie following their scuffle in the Old Firm game on 17 October. Butcher was in plaster at the time of the trial and was forced to miss the European

Championships finals in the summer of 1988. It was a huge loss for England and Rangers suffered considerably too as Celtic won the title back and the Scottish Cup to boot in their Centenary year.

But he came back even stronger the following season, 1988/89, and was magnificent beside Richard Gough as more silverware came to Ibrox. Butcher got his hands on the League Cup again, when Rangers defeated Aberdeen 3–2 in a fantastic match. But the greatest satisfaction came in wrestling the title back from the Parkhead men, thrashing them 5–1 and 4–1 during the campaign and finishing six points clear of their great rivals.

Only a slip by Gary Stevens that gifted Joe Miller a goal in the Scottish Cup final stopped Rangers from winning the Treble that season. Butcher had a goal disallowed in the game for an alleged foul by Davie Cooper on the Celtic keeper Pat Bonner. Butcher said, 'I still dispute that and it should have been a Rangers throw in the move that led to Celtic's goal, but we seemed to be a tired team in that final and Celtic were desperate to stop us from winning the Treble.'

The powerful defender gained revenge of sorts in the opening weeks of the following season. Rangers had made an inauspicious start to the campaign having lost their opening league fixtures to St Mirren and Hibs when they went to Celtic Park. Butcher scored with a looping header at the Celtic end of the ground and ran past the Jungle clenching his fist in celebration. The match finished 1–1.

Later on in the season Rangers lost 1–0 in the Scottish Cup to Celtic at Parkhead and Butcher booted a door in sheer frustration as Celtic manager Billy McNeill was being interviewed live on BBC. Terry had previous convictions for this type of action. He left a hole in the referee's changing room door at Pittodrie on 8 October 1988 – the day when Ian Durrant's knee was nearly destroyed in a challenge with Neil Simpson – and he was fined £500 by the SFA for his actions. The irony was he was staying with Aberdeen captain Willie Miller that night as the two families had become friendly on a Florida holiday! But it was just this kind of commitment that endeared the big defender to Rangers supporters.

Butcher suffered his first defeat in the League Cup in three years on 22 October 1989 when the Gers lost 2–1 to Aberdeen. But there was compensation as the club celebrated its third championship success in four seasons, thanks to a Trevor Steven header that secured a 1–0 win at Tannadice.

Little did he know it was going to be part of a remarkable nine-in-a-row sequence; little did he know it was to be his last success with Rangers. Butcher had been bothered by knee problems and after the 1990 World Cup, in which he had captained England to the semi-finals, he announced his retirement from international football.

Surgery was required but Butcher was back in the Rangers side by late August. However, he scored a spectacular own goal at Tannadice on 22 September and Dundee United went on to win 2–1. He never played for Rangers again. Souness dropped him for the League Cup semi-final with Aberdeen and then Butcher refused to play in the final against Celtic because he felt the manager was forcing him out. It was over and Butcher was sent to Coventry, quite literally, as their new player-manager.

It was a sad end to his time at Rangers but he and Souness buried the hatchet within a short space of time. Butcher, of course, has been back in Scotland for most of his life since 2001 when he went to Motherwell as assistant manager, taking charge of the team until 2006. Remarkably, for a former England captain, he became Scotland assistant manager to George

Burley, his old Ipswich teammate, in February 2008 and then took the Inverness Caledonian Thistle job in January 2009.

For many, though, he is still revered as a giant in Rangers' recent history.

Richard Gough (1987–1997, 1997–1998)

BORN: 5 April 1962, Stockholm

APPEARANCES: 427
GOALS: 34

HONOURS WON WITH RANGERS
League titles (9) – 1988/89, 1989/90, 1990/91, 1991/92, 1992/93, 1993/94, 1994/95, 1995/96, 1996/97
Scottish Cups (3) – 1991/92, 1992/93, 1995/96
League Cups (6) – 1987/88, 1988/89, 1990/91, 1992/93, 1993/94, 1996/97
CAPS: 28 (of 61 for Scotland)

MANY PLAYERS made an impact at Rangers during the success-filled 1980s and 1990s, but if there was one man who epitomised the effort, drive and skill needed to achieve such triumphs it was the nine-in-a-row skipper Richard Gough. Club captain and a great leader of men, Gough was one of only three players to appear in all nine campaigns, but he alone received winner's medals for all nine championships.

It was a unique distinction for an accomplished player. While he could time a tackle to perfection, he also had a fine touch and ensured that once possession was won the ball was distributed to those who could do most damage. His dominant presence on the ground was matched in the air, where Gough was commanding. But it was his calm authority under pressure, a refusal to panic and a confidence that transmitted itself to the rest of the team that made him not only a hugely successful captain but also one of the greatest in the history of a great club.

Everyone respected Gough, an articulate man who understood the fans' passion and conducted himself with great dignity. Gough was born in Stockholm on 5 April 1962 and brought up in South Africa. His mother was Swedish and his father, a Scot, had played for Charlton Athletic in the 1960s, so he had football in his blood.

Rangers actually let Gough slip through their fingers when, as an 18-year-old, he came to Ibrox for a trial but failed to impress. He was taken on by Dundee United, where he played in the reserves alongside his future Rangers boss, Walter Smith.

He was a major player in Dundee United's incredible championship win in 1982/83. When Graeme Souness became Rangers manager in 1986 he tried to sign him, but United boss Jim McLean would not sell. Instead, he moved to Tottenham and captained Spurs in the FA Cup final of 1987, in which the Londoners lost to Coventry City. Souness finally got his man, however, in October that year, when Gough became Rangers' first million-pound signing.

He made his league debut at right back against Dundee United on 8 August, and became an instant hit in his second game when he scored in the 2–2 draw with Celtic, more famously known for the penalty box altercation involving Butcher, Chris Woods, Graham Roberts and Celtic's Frank McAvennie, which resulted in all four being taken to court.

Throughout the famous nine-in-a-row charge, Gough was a constant source of inspiration and leadership, especially after replacing Terry Butcher as captain at the start of the 1990/91 season. Indeed, within weeks of his appointment he showed that he had all the credentials to be a terrific captain. The Old Firm League Cup final in October had gone into extra time after Mark Walters had cancelled out Paul Elliott's goal for Celtic, and the fans held their breath as both sides missed chances to win. Then Gough took the game by the scruff of the neck when he surged forward to get on the end of a long ball into the box, he forced a shot past Pat Bonner to win the game and claim his first major honour as skipper.

He was a rock at the back beside such varied partners as John Brown, Dave McPherson, Basile Boli, Alan McLaren, Gordan Petric and Joachim Bjorklund as the titles rolled in for Rangers. The 1992/93 season was probably the zenith of the nine-in-a-row era as Rangers completed a magnificent Treble and went ten games unbeaten in the inaugural Champions League, defeating Leeds United home and away, and missing out on the final by a whisker. Gough was at the heart of it all and his appetite for success never dissipated.

Unfortunately, a row with Andy Roxburgh ended his international career the following season and looking back now it seems remarkable that he was overlooked in the ensuing years by Craig Brown.

With eight League winner's medals under his belt Gough let it be known that the 1996/97 season would be his last in a Rangers shirt as he planned a move to America to play for Kansas City Wizards. As the crescendo began to build, he scored in the 2–0 victory over Celtic at Ibrox in September and the momentum was maintained with Gough's sixth League Cup final victory, this time a 4–3 win over Hearts.

The season reached its climax at Tannadice in the spring, Gough was missing through injury as Brian Laudrup scored the goal that gave Rangers the incredible nine-in-a-row. Gough was clearly overcome with emotion as he went on to the pitch to receive the trophy in what he believed would be his last act as a Rangers player.

But by October 1997 he was back, and he played in 24 League games in his final season. It was no wonder that throughout those glory years Walter Smith referred to Gough as 'my cornerstone'. A dedicated professional and role model for all that is best in the game; Gough was truly a captain colossus.

He returned to America to play for San Jose Clash in 1998, but in March 1999 agreed to join English Premier League strugglers Nottingham Forest in their fight against relegation. And to prove that age really can play second fiddle to skill and leadership, he still had time for one more move, to Everton, where he played until he was almost 40 under his old boss Smith.

He had a spell as Livingston manager in 2004 in which he managed to maintain their SPL status but has not been involved in the game since. It seems criminal that no one is utilising considerable talents.

Ray Wilkins (1987–1989)
BORN: 14 September 1956,
Hillingdon

APPEARANCES: 96
GOALS: 3

HONOURS WON WITH RANGERS
League titles (2) – 1988/89,
1989/90
League Cup (1) – 1988/89

'ABSOLUTELY MAGNIFICENT from Ray Wilkins' – these were the words of commentator Jock Brown when the former England captain scored one of the great Old Firm goals of recent times, one that Rangers fans never tire of watching. On a gorgeous sunny day at Ibrox on 27 August 1988 with Celtic defending the championship and the score tied at 1–1, the ball dropped to Wilkins 25 yards out and he produced a stunning strike that ripped into the net almost before Celtic keeper Ian Andrews saw it.

It was a classic goal and it took the Rangers players until the halfway line before they could catch the ecstatic Englishman. The fact that Rangers went on to inflict a 5–1 mauling on their great rivals made it a day never to forget for all those of a blue persuasion who were there.

Wherever he is in the world, if he bumps into a Rangers fan they will thank him for that strike. He said, 'It's a fantastic memory on what was a fantastic day and I'm naturally pleased that the fans still talk about it. I actually think I scored a better one for England against Belgium at the European Champion-ships in 1980 – but I know I will always be remembered for that goal in Scotland.'

He only scored three times in his two years at Ibrox, which many may argue is too short a period to merit inclusion in the Hall of Fame. However, it was his exceptional ability that ensured his induction. Apart from the man who signed him for Rangers, Graeme Souness, there has scarcely been a better midfielder at Ibrox. Wilkins was a beautiful player. He performed the holding midfield role to perfection, linking the play with consummate ease. His passing was superb. He could play it simple or he could play it long and he scarcely lost possession.

However, there was so much more. His influence on teammates was priceless, a fact that was not lost on Souness. He said, 'He was as important in the dressing room as he was on the pitch – maybe more so. He was so well respected that all the players looked up to him in the same way they looked up to Terry Butcher. If there was a problem in the first half of a match, by the time I got to the dressing room from the directors' box it was usually sorted out because I had men like Ray in there.'

Souness actually signed Wilkins to replace himself. They had been old foes in English football, Souness with Liverpool and Wilkins with Chelsea and Manchester United. They had locked horns again in Italy when Souness swaggered for Sampdoria and Wilkins pulled the strings at Milan. The Rangers player-manager was troubled with a calf injury at the start of the 1987/88 season, which was limiting his involvement, and he saw Wilkins as the ideal man to hold things together in his team. It was a masterstroke.

There was a real touch of John le Carré in the way in which Rangers managed to complete the deal in November 1987 with Paris Saint-Germain, where Wilkins had spent an unhappy period after moving from the San Siro the previous summer. The contract was actually signed in a private jet over the English Channel in the early hours of the morning, and when the

Rangers party – on their way back from the PSG visit – arrived at Glasgow Airport they dressed their new player in a hat and scarf disguise to keep his signing secret. Wilkins went straight into the team the next day when Rangers defeated Hearts 3–2.

The first season was mixed in the sense that Rangers, hampered by the absence of Terry Butcher as a result of a broken leg, could not find consistency and Celtic won the title. However, on the back of that stunning 5–1 win the title came back to Ibrox in 1988/89. Wilkins also won the League Cup that year when Rangers beat Aberdeen 3–2 in a fantastic final. They were only denied the Treble when Celtic beat them 1–0 in the Scottish Cup final thanks to a Joe Miller strike.

Wilkins barely missed a match all season and the Rangers fans savoured his terrific talents. He said, 'It was probably the happiest two years of my life and I have Graeme Souness to thank for that. I think he underestimated the job he did for Rangers. When I came into the dressing room it was the happiest dressing room I had ever gone into and it had success written all over it. The foundations were there and the collectiveness of the group meant that you were never beaten.'

For a combination of family reasons and the fact that there were younger players – such as Derek Ferguson, Ian Ferguson, Ian Durrant and Trevor Steven – vying for midfield places, Wilkins decided to move back south to sign for Queens Park Rangers in December 1989. Fittingly in his final game for Rangers he produced a trademark pinpoint pass. Looking up he saw Mo Johnston on the edge of the Dunfermline box and threaded the ball perfectly to the striker's feet. Johnston was in the clear and made sure the justice was done to the pass by sweeping the ball into the net. At the end of the game Wilkins received a standing ovation from all four Ibrox stands.

Ian Ferguson (1988–2000)
BORN: 15 March 1967, Glasgow

APPEARANCES: 336
GOALS: 46

HONOURS WON WITH RANGERS
League titles (10) – 1988/89,
1989/90, 1990/91, 1991/92,
1992/93, 1993/94, 1994/95,
1995/96, 1996/97, 1998/99
Scottish Cups (3) – 1993/94,
1995/96, 1998/99
League Cups (5) – 1988/89,
1990/91, 1992/93, 1993/94,
1998/99
CAPS: 9 (Scotland)

ONE OF the significant attributes of the all-conquering nine-in-a-row squad of the 1990s was the unstinting desire to win and the willingness to do anything for the cause. There were men in that dressing room who would happily spill blood for the team in the quest for success, and few were more committed than Ian Ferguson.

A lifelong fan who marvelled at the Treble wins in the 1970s as a starry-eyed kid – ironically brought up in the shadow of Parkhead – he lived the dream in a quite incredible trophy-laden Rangers career that spanned more than 12 years. He played in all of the nine-in-a-row campaigns from 1987/88 to 1996/97 and managed to claim a tenth League winners' medal in

1998/99 as one of the few survivors in the wake of Dick Advocaat's revolution.

The fans loved his combative style because they knew he was one of them. If he had not been out on the Ibrox pitch giving his all, he would have been beside them in the stands roaring the team on. Diehard hardly begins to describe Ferguson, who had more in his locker than tough tackling and strength. He packed a ferocious shot, which he used to great effect on a number of occasions, most notably in the 1988/89 League Cup final when Aberdeen were defeated 3–2 and in a 4–1 thumping of Celtic that same season. He also had terrific energy to get from box to box and could thread passes with some style. Injury and illness affected him at times, limiting his appearances in 1990/91 and 1991/92 particularly, but his near 13-year Rangers career is one of the longest in the modern era.

Ferguson first showed his potential while playing for Clyde in the mid-1980s. His youthful enthusiasm caught the eye of St Mirren boss Alex Smith and the player signed at Love Street for £60,000 in 1986. He stamped his name in the Saints' history books when he scored a memorable winning goal in the 1–0 victory over Dundee United in the Scottish Cup final in 1987.

With several clubs chasing his signature, the youngster got wind that Graeme Souness was interested in taking him to Ibrox and he signed for his boyhood heroes in February 1988 for £850,000. Ferguson had all the attributes Souness looked for in a player. He was a tough competitor who had an intelligent football brain and could also chip in with his fair share of goals for the team.

He relished the Old Firm games with a passion. It was uncanny how he would be missing for a few weeks and then come back in for the derby when, invariably, he prevailed. Some thought they were hard enough to have a go at him, but few, if any, carried it through – the prime example being Celtic's Italian playmaker Paolo di Canio.

In the wake of a crucial Rangers win at Parkhead in March 1997, di Canio motioned with his hands that he would snap Ferguson in two after they had been involved in some confrontations. Ferguson asked if he would care to further discuss the matter after the game and not surprisingly there was no sign of di Canio. He laughed, 'I remember that, all right. We were in the players' lounge after the game and most of the Celtic players came in – apart from one.

'I would probably rate that game as one of my best because it effectively clinched nine-in-a-row. Brian Laudrup scored the only goal of the game and the atmosphere that day was incredible as everyone knew that winning that game put us on course to win the title. What some people forget is that we had lost 2–0 to Celtic in the Scottish Cup ten days earlier and we were battered by injuries. We were patched-up, we had loan players and emergency signings but we showed our true colours to win that game.

'It is very hard for me to say what my favourite moments are from my time at Rangers as I was lucky enough to have had so many. My favourite season would have to be 1992/93 when we went 44 games unbeaten in all competitions and also won the Treble. We were so close to getting to the European Cup final too but, unfortunately, it wasn't to be. We had a great team and to go so many games without defeat was a great achievement.

'I remember when we were going to play Leeds in our attempt to get into the group phase of the Champions League and the English press gave us no chance. Archie Knox did a great job. He got all the press cuttings from down south and put them all up on the wall. We were all written off as no-hopers and our English players were also slated for moving north to play in a so-called easy league. That worked in our favour. It fired everyone up and we played so well in the two legs.'

Ferguson had two seasons with Dunfermline after leaving Rangers in 2000 but he has been in Australia since 2002 and has been manager of the newly formed North Queensland Fury since the spring of 2009. Clearly Ferguson had nothing to do with the choosing of the 'franchise' colours because they are green and white. He said, 'Moving to Australia has been great for both me and my family and we have all settled in really well. We are really enjoying being out here and it has been a great experience.

'There is definitely a difference between the standard of football that is played in Australia and that played in Scotland but the football down-under is improving all the time. In Scotland, football is far more professional but there are some great young players coming through in Australia.'

Ferguson made the journey from one side of the world to the other with relish in 2008 to receive his induction into the Hall of Fame and he cites it as one of the greatest moments in his life. He said, 'You think back to the players that played at Rangers and the players that I used to go and watch like John Greig, Sandy Jardine and Derek Johnstone and to be thought of in the same category as them is unbelievable.

'It was a boyhood dream. If I didn't play for Rangers I would have been on the terracing supporting the team. It was a fantastic experience and I enjoyed every minute of it.'

John Brown (1988–1997)

BORN: 26 January 1962, Stirling

APPEARANCES: 278
GOALS: 18

HONOURS WON WITH RANGERS
League titles (6) – 1988/89,
1989/90, 1990/91, 1991/92,
1992/93, 1993/94
Scottish Cups (3) – 1991/92,
1992/93, 1995/96
League Cups (3) – 1988/89,
1990/91, 1992/93

FOR THE uninitiated the clue was in the title of his biography. Blue Grit maybe a well-used pun but it rather succinctly describes the incredible zest John Brown had – and still has – for Rangers. Brown genuinely loved being a Rangers player and that was glaringly apparent in his pre-match routine – especially for Celtic matches. He would be fully kitted out and marching up and down the dressing room a good 90 minutes before kick-off but that wasn't the half of it.

He recalled, 'At 6.30 a.m. when the papers came in to the hotel where we were staying before an Old Firm game I was up and ready. I just couldn't wait for the kick-off. Maybe it was a bit weird but that was the way I used to prepare and it worked for me. The coaching staff thought I would tire myself out but I was always ready to play. The thing was I had supported the club all of my years and I knew exactly how much it meant to so many and I wanted to enjoy every minute of it.

'I never thought I would get the opportunity of playing for Rangers. There was talk that Jock Wallace was interested when he was in his second spell at Ibrox and I was at Hamilton but nothing happened at that time. However, Graeme Souness came for me in 1988 and it totally transformed my life.'

'Bomber', as he was known, had been a decent midfield player and defender first at Hamilton and then Dundee. He was a resolute competitor and had a good left foot. Indeed on 23 November 1985 he scored a hat-trick for Dundee against Rangers in a 3–2 win at Dens Park. Nine months earlier he had dumped Rangers out of the Scottish Cup at Ibrox with the only goal of the game.

Brown enjoyed nine glittering years at Ibrox but he may never have earned his dream move had he completed a transfer to Hearts in 1986. Following a medical, Tynecastle's hands-on chairman Wallace Mercer chose not to sign him – and John still counts his blessings. He said, 'Failing that medical was the best thing that happened to me. So I need to say thanks to Wallace Mercer for turning me down.

'If I had gone to Hearts my dream move to Rangers would probably never have happened. So I need to thank them for all medals and trophies that I picked up when I went to Ibrox two years later!

'Being turned down by Hearts served as a massive motivator for me as I wanted to prove the doubters wrong and two years later I earned my dream move to Ibrox. The day I signed was a very proud day for me as well as my friends and family who all supported Rangers.'

The Souness Revolution was in full flow when Brown signed up, although the championship went to Celtic in 1987/88. It was a minor blip as Rangers embarked on arguably the greatest period in their history, winning nine consecutive League titles, the Scottish Cup three times and the League Cup five times, with Brown at the heart of most of those triumphs.

He thrived in central defence beside Richard Gough, beating off the competition for places as the club brought Dave McPherson back from Hearts and then signed Basile Boli, Alan McLaren and Gordan Petric among others. He said, 'It was a great team and the thing was the "three foreigner" rule was applicable at that time so the nucleus of the side was British. I am not decrying the foreigners because I think everyone knew what it meant to play for a British team . . . We had a special bond and we achieved a lot together.'

An undoubted highlight for Brown was the New Year's Day game at Celtic Park in the 1991/92 season. Rangers were leading 2–1 when he came on as substitute for Stuart McCall to shore things up in the final minute. The cameo he produced was legendary. He took possession just inside Celtic's half, charged forward and thundered a left-foot shot that struck the inside of the right post and flew into the net. With both arms above his head he raced past the Celtic goal, vaulted the advertising hoardings and celebrated with the Rangers fans. He subsequently said of the moment that 'the new Colin Jackson was born'. Many thought he was referring to the former Rangers player of that name who was also known as 'Bomber' but he actually meant the Welsh hurdler.

The great European run of 1992/93 was another highlight when Rangers came within an ace of winning the Champions League. The Light Blues qualified for the group stage by beating Lyngby of Denmark and Leeds United, champions of England. In the group stage of the inaugural tournament they met Club Brugge, Belgium and CSKA Moscow. Despite completing their matches unbeaten, they missed out on the final by one point, as Marseille went on to win the trophy, beating AC Milan 1–0.

Brown said, 'That was a special time and my only regret is that we didn't make it to the final because I think that team deserved it. We were unfortunate that Hateley and McCoist didn't play together in either of the Marseille games and I think that cost us over the piece.

'I think there was an 18-month spell when we felt that if the opposition scored then we would be able to come back and score more than them and I think they felt that too. We ended up going on a run of 44 games unbeaten and it was a fantastic time to be at the club.

'Ironically enough, the run started after a defeat at Dundee where Simon Stainrod was the manager and some of his comments after the game just seemed to spark us off. We then went on the run, which included the ten European Cup games, and eventually ended with a defeat at Parkhead.'

That season was very special as Rangers secured a Treble for the fifth time in their history with their closest rivals Aberdeen defeated in both Scottish and League Cup finals by a 2–1 scoreline.

Brown's appearances became less frequent from 1994 but he had a glorious swansong when he played in the 1996 Scottish Cup final when Brian Laudrup dazzled and Gordon Durie scored a hat-trick as Hearts were hammered 5–1. You might imagine how John enjoyed that, given the snub he had received from the Tynecastle club ten years earlier. In 1997, he moved into coaching with Rangers, firstly with the youth side and then with the reserves. He is currently manager of Clyde.

Mark Hateley (1990–1995, 1997)

BORN: 7 November 1961, Wallasey, Liverpool

APPEARANCES: 222

GOALS: 115

HONOURS WON WITH RANGERS

League titles (5) – 1990/91, 1991/92, 1992/93, 1993/94, 1994/95

Scottish Cups (2) – 1991/92, 1992/93

League Cups (3) – 1990/91, 1992/93, 1993/94

CAPS: 1 (of 32 for England)

IT WAS 11 May 1991, a day that will live on in the memory of Rangers supporters. Aberdeen were the visitors to Ibrox and needed a draw to become champions, Rangers needed to win to claim the League title. The tension was palpable as Mark Walters took possession on the left wing, sent a hanging cross into the Aberdeen penalty area where Mark Hateley rose superbly and bulleted a header into the net to put Rangers one up five minutes before half time. The stadium, under reconstruction at that time, went berserk and Rangers, under-strength and under enormous pressure, went on to win the match 2–0, with Hateley also scoring the second, to claim the championship for a third successive season.

It was an incredible end to Hateley's first campaign and he recalls the occasion as if it was yesterday. He said, 'The squad was down to the bare bones after injuries to Ally McCoist, Richard Gough, Trevor Steven and Oleg Kuznetsov and

Graeme Souness had left to join Liverpool just a month before.

'We were still favourites to pick up the League title when we faced Motherwell in our second to last match but we were awful and ended up losing 3–0. Mark Walters even missed a penalty. So it went down to the last game and we had to beat Aberdeen to lift the title – we did like to keep things exciting!

'We only had 12 fit players for the match and it got worse when Tom Cowan went off on a stretcher having broken his leg. John Brown had taken an injection just to make the match in the first place and towards the end of the game Terry Hurlock had to play left back as we were so short.

'We stamped our authority early on and, although they missed a few early chances, as soon as we scored there was only going to be one winner. I was delighted to score the opening goal as it was so important to take the lead. I have spoken to Alex McLeish about the goal and he insists he had a shout from the keeper and that was why he didn't jump. The second goal was a tap-in but I think Michael Watt spilled the ball because of an earlier challenge when I hammered him. That goal finished the match as a contest and it was great to end the season on such a high. The atmosphere after the game was incredible and it was a day that I am sure every Rangers fan will never forget.'

Souness had twice tried to sign Hateley before finally getting his man in the summer of 1990. He had craved a big target man and had tried a few, like Colin West and Mark Falco, without much success. Hateley, who had started his career with Coventry and then Portsmouth, had spent three years with AC Milan where he played with Ray Wilkins when Souness was also in Italy at Sampdoria. He then had three years with Monaco working for Arsène Wenger although he was dogged by an ankle injury for half of that period.

He was fit and fresh when he came to Rangers, but he

walked into a storm. In order to accommodate his new signing to partner Mo Johnston up front, Souness dropped Ally McCoist, and some Rangers fans were not happy. However, Hateley's power, pace, brilliant ability in the air and good left foot won over those dissenters and he went on to become one of the greatest strikers in the club's history.

With Johnston gone at the beginning of the following season, Hateley and McCoist went on to form an incredible striking partnership. They smashed a fantastic total of 140 goals between them in two seasons as Rangers charged to a League and Cup Double in 1991/92 and then a magnificent Treble the following year.

Both players were on target in the 1992 Scottish Cup final against Airdrie when Rangers ended a painful 11-year wait to get their hands on the old trophy, winning 2–1 against Alex MacDonald's side. The following season witnessed the club's 44-game unbeaten run. Rangers defeated Aberdeen 2–1 in both cup finals, with Hateley on target in the Scottish Cup final, and clinched the title at the Dons' expense five games from the end of the League campaign when Gary McSwegan's goal beat Airdrie 1–0 at Broomfield.

Rangers also enjoyed an incredible run in Europe that season, missing out on the Champions League final by a whisker and Hateley has mixed emotions about it. He was a massive figure in the qualifying games with Leeds United – especially at Elland Road where he scored with a speculative long-range strike and then brilliantly set up McCoist with a pinpoint cross for the second goal which gave Rangers a stunning victory. Hateley also headed a vital equaliser in a 2–2 draw against Olympique Marseille at Ibrox, but was then controversially sent off against Bruges at Ibrox in an amazing group game that Rangers won 2–1. He was then banned for the two remaining group matches, most crucially the away game in Marseille. Rangers drew in the Velodrome 1–1 and then played out a goalless draw in their final game with CSKA Moscow. They finished the group stage one point behind the French side, who went on to defeat Mark's old club AC Milan in the final.

In the wake of that result there emerged accusations of dirty tricks. The CSKA coach said some of his players were offered bribes before playing Marseille in a match they lost 6–1, but he later changed his story. However, it was later revealed that Marseille had bribed Valenciennes players in their final League game of that season. They were stripped of their Ligue 1 title and banned from defending the European Cup the following year. However, their triumph in the European Cup remained. Hateley said, 'We put so much effort into that campaign and the whole Marseille thing still leaves a sour taste in the mouth.'

With McCoist sidelined for much of the 1993/94 season, Hateley picked up the mantle on his own and was magnificent as Rangers won the title again. He became the first non-Scot to win the Scottish Football Writers' Association Player of the Year award. He was equally effective in 1994/95, finishing top scorer for the second year running and playing a huge part in what was a seventh successive crown.

He left Rangers that summer for Queens Park Rangers where his old friend Wilkins was manager but he was dramatically brought back by Rangers in the chase for nine-in-a-row, specifically for the final League clash with Celtic. Amazingly, he was sent off in that game but his mere presence was important as Rangers won 1–0 to set them on their way to the remarkable achievement.

Hateley is still very much involved with Rangers these days in an ambassadorial role and continues to be revered by Rangers supporters.

Andy Goram (1991–1998)
BORN: 13 April 1964, Bury

APPEARANCES: 260
GOALS: 0

HONOURS WON WITH RANGERS
League titles (5) – 1991/92,
1992/93, 1994/95, 1995/96,
1996/97
Scottish Cups (3) – 1991/92,
1992/93, 1995/96
League Cups (2) – 1992/93,
1996/97
CAPS: 28 (of 43 for Scotland)

LARGER THAN life, ferociously passionate about Rangers and quite simply the best goalkeeper in Ibrox history – that's Andy Goram. He remains a hero of the Rangers supporters despite leaving the club in 1998, since when he has become one of them, regularly attending matches at home and abroad.

He was a special player with tremendous ability and perhaps his make-up was encapsulated on a November night in 1996 when Scottish football was intensely gripped with Rangers' attempt to win the club's ninth successive championship and Celtic's mission to prevent it. Rangers were leading 1–0 at Celtic Park after Brian Laudrup had capitalised on a Brian O'Neil slip to drive a low shot into the net early in the game.

In the frantic action that followed, Paul Gascoigne, uncharacteristically, had a penalty saved, and Peter van Vossen then managed to scoop the ball over the bar from eight yards out with an empty net gaping in front of him and the fans out of their seats in anticipation.

With only minutes remaining, Rangers supporters were stunned when the referee ruled that Richard Gough had tripped Simon Donnelly inside the box and awarded the home side a penalty. It looked like Rangers would be robbed of victory right at the death. Goram takes up the story as Pierre van Hooijdonk prepared to take the spot kick, 'Gazza had missed a penalty and Peter van Vossen had missed a chance that I am sure he will have nightmares about for the rest of his life. However, just when it seemed that we were going to hold on to the lead we lost a penalty with eight minutes remaining and it seemed that all the hard work we put in to the match would count for nothing.

'I had been involved in a few clashes with van Hooijdonk earlier in the game and was unhappy with his performance to say the least. I had made a few good saves and I was gutted at the prospect of us losing points when we had done so well in the game.

'I had watched him taking penalties before but really in these situations you just pick a side and take a chance. He hit it low and to my right. I dived and turned it around the post. I was elated and I think I showed that in my reaction! It's every schoolboy's dream to play in big football matches and I could not believe that I had managed to save a penalty at the end of such an important game.'

As the Rangers players mobbed their goalie, Celtic heads dropped – they knew there was no way back. He said, 'I loved playing in matches against Celtic but this has to be one of my personal favourites.' Goram was a constant thorn in the side of Celtic, seemingly reserving his best performances for Old Firm encounters.

He had few rivals when it came to shutting out the

opposition. His record of 107 clean sheets, spread across the last six of the nine-in-a-row years, saw him voted the best goalkeeper of all time in a poll among Rangers fans in 1999. During the 1992/93 season, Rangers enjoyed a remarkable run of 44 games without defeat in both Scottish and European competition, a sequence lasting seven months. Nothing was more crucial to this achievement than Goram's heroics in goal, playing in every one of those games and conceding just 30 goals.

He wasn't the tallest of keepers, standing 5ft 11in, but he had superb anticipation, fast reflexes and courage in abundance. He was one of the earliest British advocates for the Continental preference of punching away crosses and corners rather than coming off his line to catch them. Technically he was one of the most completely equipped keepers in British football.

But, above all, he had a great sense of positional play that made him quick to confront danger. He would close down angles to reduce a striker's options before the attacker even had a chance to consider them. Left one-on-one with an advancing attacker he would impose himself on his opponent, either standing up tall to beat off the shot, or advancing bravely to dive at his feet. And of course, like most great keepers, he had an amazing shot-stopping ability. He was the rock that gave the Rangers defence confidence to know that even when their lines had been breached, there was always a chance they'd be saved by another improbable Goram stop.

He joined Oldham Athletic in 1980 as a teenager and stayed there seven years, a spell that saw him earn the first of his 43 caps for Scotland. He joined Hibernian in October 1987, playing 138 League games in four seasons for the Edinburgh club. During that period he joined a rare group of sportsmen, becoming a double international when he also represented Scotland at cricket.

Then in June 1991 Walter Smith spent £1 million to take him to Rangers, one of Smith's first transfer deals since taking over the managerial reins, to succeed England's Chris Woods who was moved on as a result of a new UEFA rule allowing only three non-foreign players in European competition.

He played in all 55 of Rangers' competitive matches during his first season, in the process winning the League title and Scottish Cup. He knew nothing but success in his time at Ibrox, though ironically in 1997/98, his final campaign, Rangers finished empty handed for the first time in 12 years. It was a real watershed at Rangers as manager Walter Smith, Goram and most of the nine-in-a-row heroes left that summer.

Goram went on to play for Motherwell and had spells with Notts County, Sheffield United and even Manchester United, when Alex Ferguson signed him as cover for Fabien Barthez in the spring of 2001. He had further spells with Queen of the South, Oldham again and finally Elgin City before retiring.

Constantly vying with Jim Leighton for the Scotland gloves, Goram played all three games at the 1996 European Championships but walked out on the squad ahead of the 1998 World Cup in France for personal reasons. It seemed his stunning ability in matches was contrasted with the odd scrape off the field. When asked once what his highlight at Rangers had been, teammate Brian Laudrup replied, 'My nights out with the goalie!'

Stuart McCall (1991–1998)
BORN: 10 June 1964, Leeds

APPEARANCES: 264
GOALS: 20

HONOURS WON WITH RANGERS
League titles (5) – 1991/92,
1992/93, 1993/94, 1994/95,
1995/96
Scottish Cups (3) – 1991/92,
1992/93, 1995/96
League Cups (2) – 1992/93,
1993/94
CAPS: 29 (of 40 for Scotland)

MORNING HAD broken in Manchester on 5 November 1992 after Rangers' marvellous 2–1 defeat of Leeds United at Elland Road the night before and Walter Smith arrived in the hotel foyer to prepare for the flight back to Glasgow. Rangers had slain the English champions both home and away to qualify for the inaugural Champions League and Smith had allowed his players some 'leisure time' as a reward.

He was, however, horrified to see Stuart McCall and his coach Davie Dodds sitting with full pints of beer and cigars at a time when most guests were contemplating breakfast. When he inquired what they were up to McCall responded, 'Don't worry gaffer, it's only Celtic on Saturday.' A little over two days later Celtic were beaten 1–0 at Parkhead with Ian Durrant scoring the goal.

The 1992/93 season was undoubtedly the zenith of the

Walter Smith team of the era – a team in which McCall was an integral figure. Rangers were winning so freely that such indiscretions as that Manchester hotel episode could be overlooked.

Perhaps curiously for a man born of a Scots father in the city of Leeds, the 'Battle of Britain' matches with Howard Wilkinson's side are not the favourite matches of the flame-haired midfielder. Make no mistake, he revelled in the two victories but it was an Old Firm game eight months earlier that ranks as the greatest.

He said, 'The best match that I ever played in was against Celtic at Hampden in March 1992 when we won 1–0 in the Scottish Cup semi-final. The rain was pouring down and to make matters worse David Robertson got sent off for a tackle on Joe Miller after six minutes. Ally McCoist managed to score and I personally believe that this was the night that Walter Smith's side came together.

'We had been beaten by Sparta Prague in the European Cup and also by Hibs in the League Cup so it was a massive match. We also had some new signings including myself, Andy Goram and David Robertson, so to win this game having played almost the entire 90 minutes with ten men was phenomenal.'

McCall had joined Rangers in the summer of 1991 – only just beating the European signing deadline – when Smith began to mould his own side having taken over from Graeme Souness in the dramatic climax to the previous season when the League was won with a final-day win over Aberdeen. Despite the broad Yorkshire brogue, McCall was undoubtedly a Scot and one of the reasons for his capture was his nationality as the 'three foreigners' rule had just been introduced into European football. He had played at the 1990 World Cup – and scored against Sweden – and had been an accomplished player with Everton for three years before joining Rangers for £1.2 million, having begun his career with Bradford City.

McCall was easily one of Smith's best signings. His drive and endeavour in midfield was impressively apparent but there was much more to his game than steel. His passing was accurate and he was good in possession, scarcely letting an opponent win the ball from him. While players like Laudrup, Gascoigne, Mikhailichenko or Albertz would win plaudits for their creativity, McCall was the heartbeat of the Rangers team of the time.

He won five titles in his time, though his one personal disappointment was missing out on most of the 1996/97 season through injury as Rangers completed the journey to nine successive championships. However, this was arguably the greatest period in Rangers' history and the Light Blues' success over Celtic at the time served to delight the fans even further. Walter Smith's side had the uncanny ability to travel across the city to the home of their greatest rivals and, more often than not, get a victory. During McCall's time at the club Rangers played Celtic at Parkhead 15 times in domestic competitions, winning nine, drawing three and losing three.

McCall believes he was fortunate to be in a side that had fantastic team spirit both on and off the park and that the manager had players who were able to rise to the occasion. He said, 'I think our team had great character but we were also fortunate to have great players. We had Hateley, McCoist, Albertz, Laudrup and Gazza. These players could always get a goal against Celtic and then we had guys like Goram and Gough at the back. We were a very difficult team to beat and I think mentally we had the upper hand over Celtic as we always thought we could win.

'The proudest I've felt probably was the Scottish Cup semi-final against Celtic in 1996 when Richard Gough was injured and I was captain for the day. I managed to win the Man of the Match award as well and the team won 2–1, so it was a great day for me.

'My most memorable match at Parkhead was in fact the first time I played there in August 1991. We won 2–0 and Mark Hateley scored both goals. I managed to put big Mark through for the first, which was a great feeling. At that time, there were 15,000 Rangers fans standing behind the goal and I remember the noise they were making at the end of the match after we had won. You never forget moments like that.'

As a Rangers player McCall played at Euro 92 and Euro 96 on his way to 40 Scotland caps but it might have been all so different. He was selected by England's under-21 team for a game against Turkey and was due to go on as a substitute in the final minute. But he realised at that moment that he should really be playing for Scotland and so avoided the 'cap' by pretending to tie his boot laces. It meant he was later free to pull on the Scotland shirt and he was an excellent player for both Andy Roxburgh and Craig Brown.

Like many of his teammates, he left Rangers in 1998 but Rangers never left him and his career was far from over. A subscriber to the *Rangers News* magazine, McCall tries to see Rangers when he can and he was in the crowd at Easter Road when Alex McLeish's side won the championship on that incredible final day in 2005.

After leaving Ibrox, he played four seasons back at Bradford where he was captain and then spent another three at Sheffield United before finally retiring just short of his 41st birthday. He played an amazing 763 League matches during his career – nearly reaching 1,000 games in all competitions – a record which puts him in 12th place in the all-time list in British football.

It had been his dream to become manager of his first club Bradford City one day and he realised it in 2007. Life is not easy in League Two, but McCall goes about his business with the same determination and drive that delighted the Rangers fans in the 1990s.

Brian Laudrup (1994–1998)
BORN: 22 February 1969, Vienna

APPEARANCES: 151
GOALS: 45

HONOURS WON WITH RANGERS
League titles (3) – 1994/95,
1995/96, 1996/97
Scottish Cups (1) – 1995/96
League Cups (1) – 1996/97
CAPS: 27 (of 75 for Denmark)

FEW PLAYERS have given Rangers supporters more pleasure than the Great Dane, Brian Laudrup. Most Rangers fans feel privileged that he spent the best years of his career at Ibrox and many of them will tell you that there has never been a more exciting and talented player to have pulled on a Light Blue shirt. It is difficult to argue with them. Laudrup was utterly exceptional. His sublime skills, electric pace and shooting power took Rangers to a new level.

The Dane was utterly devastating during his four years with Rangers, single-handedly destroying teams on numerous occasions with his fantastic close control, electrifying pace and uncanny ability to deliver the killer pass or cross. His close control was extraordinary – the ball just obeyed his wishes. His exceptional acceleration saw him tearing through midfield and releasing a pass, while leaving himself time to be in for the kill as he reached an entirely different area of the pitch. He was the complete master, terrifying defences any time he was anywhere near the ball. Premier League opponents had no answer to his skills.

Laudrup, though Danish, was born in Vienna on 22 February 1969, and seemed destined to become a footballer. His father Finn was a Danish international and his elder brother, Michael, was also a world-class player, starring for Juventus, Barcelona and Real Madrid among others. By the time he arrived at Ibrox, Brian had already been an important member of the Danish team that caused such an upset by winning the 1992 European Championships.

His professional career began at Brondby where he played in the same team as Peter Schmeichel. He played there three years before being transferred to Uerdingen in Germany for £650,000. After one season, Bayern Munich paid £2 million for his signature and his reputation continued to grow, prompting Fiorentina to equal that fee to take him to Italy in 1992. Laudrup, however, was not happy in Florence and when Fiorentina were relegated in 1993, he was loaned out to Italian giants AC Milan.

In July 1994 Rangers, already with six League titles in a row, tabled a bid of £2.3 million for him. The price turned out to be a snip. From his first game, against Motherwell on 13 August, it was clear that the Danish star was a sensational capture. First he supplied the inch-perfect cross for Mark Hateley to score with a header. Then, in an audacious move, he collected a clearance from a corner on the edge of his own box and ran diagonally through midfield before releasing a pass for Duncan Ferguson to notch the second.

One thing that is guaranteed to endear a player to the Rangers fans is to star in matches against Celtic. Laudrup, involved in some of the most important Old Firm games in living memory, not only starred in them, he often destroyed the opponents. He played in 17 Old Firm games in total, winning nine, drawing four and losing four, one of which was an unimportant end of season League clash as the title had already been secured.

Laudrup was a loser on his Old Firm debut but he soon made up for it. In his second game against Celtic he was sensational and the abiding memory is the Danish star racing away to score the third goal in a 3–1 win. He said, 'That game was at Hampden and it was one to remember. I had lost my Old Firm debut, which was disappointing, but I was delighted to do well in the second one.

'For any foreign player coming to play in Glasgow the first thing you hear about is the Old Firm game and it is undoubtedly one of the greatest derbies in the world. I loved playing in these games because the atmosphere was always electric and the stakes were so high.'

Laudrup was also a scorer in the classic 3–3 draw with Tommy Burns' Celtic side in November 1995 when he netted the first goal. However, it was the strike in the Scottish Cup semi-final the following April which was probably his finest. He flicked the ball to Gordon Durie on the right wing, raced forward, took the return pass on his chest then lifted the ball over the advancing Gordon Marshall to score Rangers' second and clinching goal in a game which finished 2–1.

In the final he reached even greater heights. Laudrup scored twice and set up all three goals for a Durie hat-trick, the first scored by a Ranger in the Scottish Cup final, in the 5–1 demolition of Hearts. It was one of the most breathtaking individual performances ever seen at the national stadium and has certainly never been bettered since.

He also scored two crucial goals against Celtic in the 1996/97 season – on his way to becoming the club's top scorer that year – as Rangers battled to achieve the club's ninth championship in a row. The first came at Parkhead in November when he capitalised on Brian O'Neil's slip to crack home a 25-yarder for the only goal of the game. But there was more to come. He recalled, 'We went to Parkhead again in March 1997 and we knew that if we won that day then it would be a massive step towards the title.

'Durranty flicked the ball over Stewart Kerr and I'm still not quite sure if it was in before I touched it, but the main thing was we won that game and that was so crucial.'

However, it was at Tannadice against Dundee United on 7 May 1997 that Laudrup scored the sweetest goal of all. There were those who said that he couldn't head the ball, but that day he ran into the box, flew through the air to meet Charlie Miller's cross, and the ball hit the net like a bullet. It was the goal that won the nine-in-a-row title, and there could have been no more fitting player to score it. He said, 'It was a magical moment and one of so many during my time with Rangers.'

He received any number of accolades that spring, and was voted the Scottish Football Writers' Player of the Year for the second time in three years, having become the first foreign player to be awarded the honour in 1995.

Ajax wanted to sign him that summer but he was persuaded to stay as Rangers attempted to clinch an unprecedented tenth successive title but it was an anti-climax. The Light Blues stumbled in the final matches and Celtic stopped the championship run on the final day of the season. Laudrup left in the summer of 1998 for Chelsea, before moving on to Copenhagen, and finally Ajax, where he was forced to quit football through injury in 2000 at the age of 31.

There is no doubt he was one of the most gifted and talented entertainers in the club's history and few players have brought so much joy to Rangers supporters in such a short period of time.

Paul Gascoigne (1995–1998)

BORN: 27 May 1967, Gateshead

APPEARANCES: 104

GOALS: 39

HONOURS WON WITH RANGERS

League titles (2) – 1995/96, 1996/97

Scottish Cup (1) – 1995/96

League Cup (1) – 1996/97

CAPS: 22 (of 57 for England)

SIMPLY MENTION the name Paul Gascoigne and a broad smile will form on the face of any Rangers supporter who will immediately recall the joy and genius he brought to Rangers for a short but hugely enjoyable period. Gazza was the ultimate maverick, at times a sensation, at others a hindrance. Few British sportsmen have carried such media attention in their careers, but then few footballers can compare to Gascoigne.

Some questioned Walter Smith's wisdom in paying £4.3 million to Lazio for his services, given that he had broken his leg in Italy and suffered serious knee ligament damage in 1991 playing for Tottenham. However, it was one of those buys that the manager justified purely on football terms and buying Gascoigne could have been justified, at any time in his career, on pure entertainment value alone.

Smith said, 'For two and a half years Paul played to an exceptional level and helped the club to a great deal of success so from that aspect he deserves the recognition. People looked upon his signing as a bit of a gamble because of his injuries, but in terms of ability there was no gamble.'

He was the most talented England player of his generation, and while his problems off the field were well documented – and still are – Gazza in full flow on the football pitch was peerless. His close control was simply awesome – there was almost nothing Gascoigne could not do with a football. His passing was pinpoint, his finishing was fantastic, and his ability to glide past opponents was a joy to watch. A player of great vision and anticipation, he was invariably too quick for his opponents.

And then there was his shooting. He had a high strike rate for a modern-day midfield player – 39 goals in 104 games for Rangers. But it was in the variety that he was special. Power shots, curved free kicks, gentle placements – they all came alike to Gazza. Yet despite being a genuine world-class player, he will always leave his admirers wondering why, with such an abundance of talent, he did not achieve more than he did in his career.

Like any of the top strikers he could simply pass the ball into the net and Rangers fans lapped it up, especially when the sufferers of such skill and verve happened to be Celtic. His strike in a 2–0 win at the partially refurbished Parkhead in September 1995 – just four games into his Rangers career – was typical of his sublime skills and made him an instant hero.

The move began with a long clearance out of defence. The ball was picked up in midfield by Oleg Salenko and worked out to Ally McCoist on the right. At the time McCoist received the ball, Gascoigne was inside his own half. But somehow he ran to the edge of the Celtic box in time to pick up McCoist's pass and slip it past the keeper.

It was a magnificent example of what Gazza could do. But his most important contribution in his first season came, inevitably, when the chips were down. It was 28 April 1996 and

Rangers were facing Aberdeen. Victory would give them their eighth successive League title, but they were 1–0 down and looking far from comfortable when Gascoigne took the game by the scruff of the neck.

First, he collected the ball from a corner on the left side of the Aberdeen penalty area. He went past two defenders and from the narrowest of angles chipped the keeper for goal number one. Next he got possession inside his own half, and then ran more than 50 yards straight at the Aberdeen defence. His strength and determination saw off the challenges and with his left foot he placed the ball into the far corner for goal number two. He sealed his hat-trick and the championship with a penalty. It was a one-man show; the stuff dreams are made of. But it took a Gascoigne to make them come true. It was a fitting climax to what had been a magnificent season for him. It was one of the most breathtaking individual performances Rangers fans had witnessed in many years. Not surprisingly he ran away with the Scottish Football Writers' Player of the Year award.

He mirrored that Aberdeen performance with two stunning goals in the following season's League Cup final to defeat Hearts 4–3 after – allegedly – downing a couple of whiskies in a hospitality suite at half time. If the story is true it surely encapsulates the extraordinary character he was. He was the original prankster. He once hid rotten fish in Gordon Durie's car and it took months to get rid of the smell – if it ever went.

With Gazza and Brian Laudrup in the line-up at the same time, the opposition were invariably powerless to prevent Rangers from beating them. Gazza could charge off on a 40-yard run when nothing appeared to be on, and dribble his way through a maze of defenders before setting up the strikers with apparent ease.

However, during his career he was frequently in trouble with the officials, and at Rangers it was no different. In his first season he collected yellow cards like confetti, and in Europe in the 1996/97 campaign he let Rangers down when he was sent off for stupidly kicking Ajax's Winston Bogarde.

But it was a controversial red card against Celtic in November 1997 that led to his eventual downfall, although no one knew it at the time. He was sent off for using his elbow, when it appeared he was only trying to escape the clutches of his opponent. It resulted in a five-match ban and by the time he came back, the cutting edge seemed to have gone from his game.

Despite chasing a record-breaking tenth consecutive title, chairman Sir David Murray felt that Gazza's indiscipline had gone too far and decided to cash in on him by selling him to Middlesbrough in March 1998 for nearly £3.5 million. It was, perhaps, inevitable that his departure would be controversial, and many fans were dismayed when he left, but there is little doubt that Paul Gascoigne remains one of the most talented and exciting players in the history of Rangers Football Club.

Jorg Albertz (1996–2001)
BORN: 29 January 1971,
Möenchengladbach

APPEARANCES: 182
GOALS: 82

HONOURS WON WITH RANGERS
League titles (3) – 1996/97,
1998/99, 1999/2000
Scottish Cups (2) – 1998/99,
1999/2000
League Cups (2) – 1996/97,
1998/99
CAPS: 1 (of 3 for Germany)

STEWART KERR lined up his defensive wall and positioned himself with just nine minutes gone in the New Year Old Firm derby in 1997, but he need not have made the effort as a thunderbolt free-kick ripped past him and nearly tore a hole in the net. It was measured at nearly 80 miles per hour and it had come from the left boot of a genial German who instantly achieved iconic status.

Jorg Albertz was known as 'The Hammer' and, if anyone wondered why, the evidence was glaring in that Celtic game, which Rangers went on to win 3–1 thanks to two late goals by Erik Bo Andersen. It was a huge result at a crucial time in the quest for nine successive League titles and it is little wonder that the former Hamburg midfielder rates it as his best. He said, 'I never really practised hitting the ball hard, it just seemed to come naturally. I used to kick the ball in the back garden when

I was young and it seemed I had a hard shot. That's just the way it was.'

Albertz had served notice that he was going to be a major Old Firm player when he set up both goals in Rangers' 2–0 win over Celtic on 26 September 1996. His outswinging corner from the left was powered into the net by Richard Gough and then his precision cross was headed home by Paul Gascoigne as Celtic were caught on the break in the final moments.

Few had heard of Albertz when Walter Smith announced he had paid £4 million to Hamburg for his services in the summer of 1996. But few players have had such an impact on the supporters. Albertz might have been a foreigner but, like people such as Brian Laudrup and Paul Gascoigne, he was regarded as one of the boys in the dressing room by dyed-in-the-wool fans and seasoned campaigners such as Ian Ferguson, Ally McCoist and Ian Durrant.

He had to play a large part of his first season in a left wing back role due to David Robertson's injury but it was in midfield that he really flourished. There was so much more to his game than power shooting. He was far from the quickest, but he had fantastic feet for a big man and seemed to ease past opponents. His ability to split open defences was exceptional and he was superb in possession, scarcely ever giving the ball away.

He collected two honours in his debut season by winning the League Cup in an epic 4–3 victory over Hearts, and then helping Rangers to their ninth successive championship. It should have been ten in a row the following season, but Rangers agonisingly fell two points short when they lost two of their final four matches – 1–0 away to Aberdeen and 1–0 at home to Kilmarnock. Albertz had certainly played his part, finishing third top scorer behind one-season wonder Marco Negri and Ally McCoist, but there was more despair for him on the final day of the League season.

He secured Rangers' 2–1 victory over Dundee United with a penalty but was then sent off and suspended for the Scottish Cup final the following week. Celtic, meanwhile, won their final fixture against St Johnstone and therefore prevented a tenth successive title.

It was torture for The Hammer as he then watched his team lose 2–1 to Hearts in the Hampden final. He recalled, 'It was a terrible time. To get a red card on the day the League was lost was a nightmare and then to miss the cup final was so disappointing. I remember sitting in the stand watching teammates playing their last game for Rangers and I wanted to be out there helping them. It was a terrible situation.'

That summer Dick Advocaat arrived in place of Walter Smith and began building a new team with 14 players coming in and 15 leaving in his first season. Albertz, however, was one of the 'old guard' who flourished in what was a sensational campaign as the Dutch coach swept the board. Jorg scored the winning goal in the League Cup final against St Johnstone at Celtic Park. And then the German star kept his cool when many around him were losing theirs to score a crucial penalty at the same venue as Rangers famously won the championship on 2 May 1999.

Referee Hugh Dallas needed treatment when his head was cut by a coin thrown by a Celtic supporter after the referee had correctly awarded a penalty for Vidar Riseth's trip on Tony Vidmar. Stewards had to restrain other Celtic supporters and all the while Albertz waited to take his kick. It was perfection as he sent Kerr the wrong way and Rangers were on their way to a famous victory. He said, 'I would have to pick my free-kick against Celtic in my first season at Rangers as my best goal but that penalty I scored at Parkhead in 1999 was very special because it helped us win the title on the ground of our biggest rivals, which was a huge thing.'

At the end of the month he played his part as Rod Wallace's goal settled the Old Firm Scottish Cup final and Rangers were Treble winners for the sixth time in their history.

In his five years at Ibrox Albertz scored eight times against Celtic and he was equally prolific on the European stage where he netted 11 times, scoring memorable goals against PSV Eindhoven, Bayern Munich and Kaiserslautern among others.

Season 1999/2000 was also successful as Rangers won the League and Cup Double, romping to the title by 21 points, hitting four goals against Celtic twice, and then thumping Aberdeen 4–0 in the Scottish Cup final with Albertz netting the final goal.

However, he never really saw eye-to-eye with Advocaat and their relationship soured further during the 2000/01 season when Albertz felt the Dutch contingent in the Rangers squad were getting preferential treatment. It was a tempestuous season as Celtic, resurgent under Martin O'Neill, swept to the Treble and Rangers were strangely inconsistent although they were not helped by injuries to key men like Giovanni van Bronckhorst, Ronald de Boer and Claudio Reyna. Even though he only started 30 matches, Albertz finished the season as top scorer. However, it was to be his last in a Rangers shirt.

Suitably, he scored in his final match – a 4–0 win over Hibs – and he was reduced to tears as the Rangers fans showed their appreciation during a lap of honour. He was sold back to Hamburg and subsequently played in China and then back in Germany with Greuther Fürth and Fortuna Düsseldorf before former Rangers player John Brown convinced him to play for Clyde at the end of the 2007/08 season.

The Hammer remains one of Rangers' best-loved players of recent times.

Stefan Klos (1998–2007)
BORN: 16 August 1971, Dortmund

APPEARANCES: 298

GOALS: 0

HONOURS WON WITH RANGERS
League titles (4) – 1998/99,
1999/2000, 2002/03, 2004/05
Scottish Cups (4) – 1998/99,
1999/2000, 2001/02, 2002/03
League Cups (2) – 2001/02,
2002/03

IT IS a measure of his huge contribution to Rangers that Stefan Klos became only the third non-Briton to be chosen for the Hall of Fame, following fellow countryman Jorg Albertz and the Great Dane Brian Laudrup.

The German goalkeeper, retired since 2007 and living in Switzerland, won ten major honours with the club but his career rather fizzled out on the back of a training ground knee injury in January 2005. However, for six years he was a top player for Rangers and still revels in his time at Ibrox. He said, 'It was a great experience for me in Scotland with Rangers. It was a big decision for me and my family to go there but I'm so happy that I did. I had some great moments there – and also some difficult ones – but overall it was the right move for me.'

The great thing about Klos was that he was so reliable his expert displays barely merited a mention. Excellence was simply expected of him. The Rangers fans thought they might never replace Andy Goram, but 'Der Goalie' was an inspirational signing – and it is the chairman who should take the credit. Klos revealed, 'It was David Murray who signed me before Dick Advocaat was appointed manager. I made an agreement with him to join but after that I had problems with my contract in Dortmund. It should have finished in the summer of 1998. But they had a clause in my contract where they could offer me another year, because of the Bosman ruling, which had just come in.

'I had some problems, but Rangers were so loyal to me at that time and I was loyal to them and eventually, six months later, I was able to join. The thing was I had to go to court to sort the problem out. It wasn't a nice time because I loved playing for Dortmund as well and I didn't want to leave the club in such a way, but I was determined to fight my case. I had no problems with the team or manager but it was the chairman who was causing me the trouble. I won in the end and I'm obviously happy that things worked out.

'It was a great time for me in Dortmund when I look back because I had won the Bundesliga title and, of course, the Champions League in 1997. It was a tough decision to leave the club but I think it was the right thing to do.'

Two days after joining Rangers, Klos went straight into the Boxing Day game at Ibrox against St Johnstone and kept a clean sheet as Rangers won 1–0. He was on the winning side again four days later as Rangers won 2–1 at Tannadice. And then on 3 January 1999 he played in his first Old Firm derby, a 2–2 draw when Gaby Amato and Rod Wallace scored the Rangers goals.

He said, 'My first Old Firm game was great. It was a quite amazing atmosphere. The noise was different from Germany. We had great support and a great stadium in Dortmund but the Old Firm game is much noisier. It was a 2–2 draw but that was OK because we were ahead of them at that time. It allowed us to go into the winter break in good shape.'

Klos, though, was concerned that he faced a major fight for the No. 1 jersey as there were two good keepers already on the books at Ibrox. He said, 'When I came Antti Niemi was here and Lionel Charbonnier had also signed. Andy Goram had moved on the previous summer and I knew how well he was liked by the Rangers fans. I had to challenge the keepers who were here. I had to fight for the jersey and you have to remember that Antti was already a Finnish international at that time while Lionel was part of France's World Cup squad. However, I managed to get into the side and at first when I came everything was great. The team was ahead of Celtic and then it was the perfect finish when we won the Scottish Cup against Celtic at Hampden.

'The following season we won the Double, which was also great, but the disappointing thing was the Champions League. We had invested to make progress and we did quite well but we were pipped from going forward in the final game in Munich.

'The following year some things did not go our way and it was a really bad season. But that is what can happen in football. However, the bad things made the successes after that all the sweeter. Alex McLeish came in and got things going again and the championship win in 2002/03 was really fantastic – perhaps the best of them all for me.'

Rangers lost key players for the following season – most notably Lorenzo Amoruso, Arthur Numan, Barry Ferguson, Neil McCann and Claudio Caniggia. It made for a tough campaign in which the club won nothing, but things picked up for the 2004/05 campaign with the arrival of Dado Prso, Nacho Novo, Alex Rae and Jean-Alain Boumsong. Klos was made captain of the team and he was doing a good job when he was struck down with the knee problem in January of 2005. He missed out on the League Cup triumph over Motherwell and the stunning last-day title victory at Hibernian, otherwise known as 'Helicopter Sunday'.

When he recovered from his injury he could not get back into the side, with Alex McLeish opting to keep faith with Ronald Waterreus, the man who had been brought in to replace him. A mountain bike injury in the summer of 2006 meant that Paul Le Guen swapped between Lionel Letizi and Allan McGregor and with Stefan's contract expiring in the summer of 2007 it looked as though he had played his last game for Rangers. However, he featured twice for Walter Smith – both games coming in the 2006/07 UEFA Cup against Hapoel Tel Aviv and Osasuna. He made a final bow to the fans at the end of that season.

Barry Ferguson (1996–2003, 2005–2009)

BORN: 2 February 1978, Glasgow

APPEARANCES: 431

GOALS: 61

HONOURS WON WITH RANGERS

League titles (5) – 1998/99, 1999/2000, 2002/03, 2004/05, 2008/09

Scottish Cups (5) – 1999/2000, 2001/02, 2002/03, 2007/08, 2008/09

League Cups (5) – 1998/99, 2001/02, 2002/03, 2004/05, 2007/08

CAPS: 35 (of 45 for Scotland)

BARRY FERGUSON'S debut as a Rangers player on 10 May 1997 was virtually hidden amid the wild celebrations of a record-equalling nine successive Scottish League titles. Few supporters paid much attention to the youthful midfielder who wore the No. 7 jersey as Rangers unimportantly lost 3–1 to Hearts at Tynecastle having seized the crown at Tannadice in their previous match.

However, during the next ten years Ferguson went on to become a fantastic Rangers player – for many the best of his generation. Reared on Rangers from an early age, he was the kid who became the king. The spoils included an incredible haul of 15 major honours; he became club captain – leading the side to nine domestic honours – was twice voted Scotland's Player of the Year and awarded an MBE for his services to charity and football.

It is sad, therefore, that his time as a Rangers player was tinged by his indiscipline while on international duty in March 2009, in an incident that led to a Scotland ban and heavy club sanctions, and which ultimately led to him leaving the club. Ferguson was involved in a drinking session – along with Allan McGregor and others – at the Cameron House Hotel. Having returned from a World Cup qualifier against Holland in Amsterdam the players started drinking in the hotel bar and the session dragged on until nearly lunchtime the following day. He was instantly kicked out of the squad though he was subsequently named as a substitute for the next match against Iceland on 1 April. Sitting on the bench during that game he and McGregor made childish, rude gestures to press photographers.

These actions – and a subsequent lack of contrition – forced Walter Smith to act and Ferguson was fined and suspended by the club for two weeks. The SFA followed up by announcing they would not select Ferguson or McGregor for Scotland again. It was a very public demise for a man who had captained Scotland in 28 of his 45 appearances.

Many continue to throw stones at Ferguson, but his influence on Rangers and Scottish football as a whole cannot be denied. It is somewhat ironic that it was Smith who set the wheels in motion for Ferguson's rise to prominence. The young man was frustrated at his lack of involvement under Smith but most people at the club agreed that easing him into the first team was the best policy. It meant that when Dick Advocaat replaced Smith in 1998, Ferguson was more than ready to become a top-team player on a regular basis.

The new manager wasted no time in tying the young man

down with a five-year contract and he got his reward with mature performances in midfield that belied Ferguson's age. The UEFA Cup matches against Bayer Leverkusen in particular were pivotal in establishing Ferguson as the top emerging talent in the country. What was more remarkable was that a young Scot could hold his own in Advocaat's multi-national force that had been assembled at a considerable cost.

Sadly, injury prevented him from being involved in the run-in to the 1998/99 Treble and he had to watch from the main stand at Hampden as the clean sweep was achieved in the sweetest way possible – a Scottish Cup final win over Celtic.

Ferguson was so influential the following season that he was named Scotland's Player of the Year, albeit in a close contest with Giovanni van Bronckhorst. That is undoubtedly one of the reasons why Advocaat named Ferguson as his new captain in the autumn of 2000 when the Dutchman decided that Lorenzo Amoruso should relinquish the armband. But there is also little doubt that there was a large amount of PR behind Advocaat's decision. He hoped the appointment would take the heat out of the predicament Rangers found themselves in at the time when a run of poor form saw them firmly behind Celtic in the League and out of the Champions League at the group stage.

Though many supporters felt that Advocaat was wrong to burden Barry with the captaincy at that moment, he went on to prove – albeit under the tutelage of the Dutchman's replacement Alex McLeish – that he was an exceptional leader on the field. Yes, there was the silly sending off in a humiliating 6–2 defeat at Parkhead in August 2000 and the petulant throwing of an ice bag in a 2–0 reverse against Celtic at Ibrox in September 2001. There were some troubles off the field too with stories of his misdemeanours appearing regularly in the newspapers.

However, you only have to examine the drive and determination displayed by the combative midfielder to recognise his worth. In McLeish's first season, 2001/02, the Light Blues completed a domestic cup double. Having already won the League Cup, Rangers met Celtic in the Scottish Cup final. Trailing 2–1 but playing the better football, Ferguson rallied the troops. Rangers won a free kick just to the right of centre 25 yards out from the Celtic goal. Displaying sensational technique in such trying circumstances, Ferguson hit the ball over the wall and curled it away from Rab Douglas to the left corner of the net. It was one of the great Hampden goals. Ferguson ripped off his shirt and raced to the Rangers support behind the goal in utter joy, which became greater in the final moments when Peter Lovenkrands headed Neil McCann's cross into the net to seal a 3–2 victory.

The following season, 2002/03, it got even better as Ferguson provided the purpose and inspiration on numerous occasions during a remarkable campaign that produced a seventh Treble for Rangers. He scored 18 goals in the League, won in an incredible final day shoot-out with Rangers defeating Dunfermline 6–1 to finish one goal ahead of Celtic, who won 4–0 at Kilmarnock.

Supporters were shocked, however, when Ferguson left Rangers in autumn 2003 to take possession of the captain's armband at Blackburn Rovers. Though it was clear that he wanted to sample Premiership football, Rangers fans found it hard to understand why their captain would make such a move.

However, he came back to Ibrox in January 2005 and played a key role as Rangers returned to the winners' enclosure with the League Cup and then went on to claim the League title on a dramatic final day. Rangers beat Hibs 1–0 at Easter Road and Celtic crashed 2–1 at Fir Park, forcing the helicopter holding the SPL trophy to famously change direction.

The 2005/06 season was traumatic in many ways. The club achieved little other than qualification to the last 16 of the Champions League. Ferguson played on with an ankle problem when he should have rested and when he arrived back for preseason Paul Le Guen had taken over from Alex McLeish. His relationship with the Frenchman was poor and became untenable by the end of the year when Le Guen stripped him of the captaincy and dropped him. However, Le Guen's tenure was short-lived and he left Ibrox in January 2007 saying that he was being 'undermined' by personnel at the club. Walter Smith soon returned and Ferguson was restored to the team and the captaincy.

Season 2007/08 threatened to be the greatest in Rangers' history as they won both domestic cups, reached the UEFA Cup final and had the SPL title in their grasp. Sadly, the sheer volume of 17 matches in 51 days at the business end of the season meant that Rangers fell short in Manchester, losing 2–0 to Zenit St Petersburg – ironically managed by Dick Advocaat – and lost out on the League on the final day.

More ankle problems ruled Ferguson out for the first four months of the 2008/09 season but he came back only to be embroiled in the drinking incident while on international duty. It seemed likely he would never play for Rangers again. But fate was kind to him as he was involved in the fantastic last-day title triumph at Tannadice when Rangers claimed the League crown with a 3–0 win over Dundee United. And he went out at the top, playing in the Scottish Cup final on 30 May when Rangers defeated Falkirk 1–0 to win the Double for the 18th time in the club's history.

He was reunited with Alex McLeish when he signed for Birmingham City for £1.25 million in July 2009.

His time at Ibrox was turbulent, but there is no doubt that Ferguson remains one of the greatest modern Rangers.

Inductees arranged in alphabetical order by surname, with page reference.